Galloglas

From the Western Isles to Ireland

Dave Swift
Maximilian Bunk
Hagen Seehase

Translation by Jan Eschbach

The merciless Macdonwald
(Worthy to be a rebel, for to that
The multiplying villainies of nature
Do swarm upon him) from the western isles
Of kernes and galloglasses is supplied.

William Shakespeare, The Tragedy of Macbeth, I, 2, 9-13

Author:	Dave Swift
	Maximilian Bunk
	Hagen Seehase
Translated by:	Dr Jan Eschbach
Editing (German edition):	Michael Danhardt
Artwork:	Sascha Lunyakov
Maps:	Bernhard Glänzer
Layout:	Stefan Müller
Publisher:	Zeughaus Verlag GmbH
	Knesebeckstr. 88
	10623 Berlin, Germany
	Telephone: +49 (0)30/315 700 30
	Email: info@zeughausverlag.de
	Website: www.zeughausverlag.de

All rights reserved.
Reproduction, translation, and photographic reproduction (including extracts) are prohibited. Storage and distribution including transfer onto electronic media such as CD-ROM etc. as well as storage on electronic media such as the internet etc. are not permissible without the express written permission of the publishers and are punishable. All violation is liable to legal prosecution.

Bibliographic information from the Deutsche Bibliothek. The Deutsche Bibliothek lists this publication in the German National Bibliography; detailed bibliographic information is available at http://dnb.ddb.de

Printed in the European Union
Originally published in German as *Die Galloglas – Irlands Fremde Krieger*
in the Heere & Waffen series number 44
(Berlin: Zeughaus Verlag, 2023)

© 2024 Zeughaus Verlag GmbH, Berlin, Germany
ISBN: 978-3-96360-063-0

Frontispiece:
A galloglass guards a large Tower House in County Munster
(© Claíomh – Dave Swift 2010).

CONTENT

Acknowledgements	8
Introduction	9
Authors' Foreword	11
Ireland in the Middle Ages	13
The Norse-Gaelic Kingdom of the Isles	19
The Norman Conquest, and the first galloglas	23
The exiled clans	29
The Scottish Invasion	37
The 14th and 15th centuries	45
The Battle of Knockdoe in 1504	53
Under Tudor rule – the fall of the House of FitzGerald	61
Queen Elizabeth I and the Lords of the North	74
Galloglas face galloglas in Connacht	81
The Nine Years War	87
The galloglas' last stand – the Battle of the Curlews in 1599	93
Twilight of the galloglas	99
Enter Mulmurry MacSweeney	102
Galloglas – a warriors' tradition	103
Organisation, command, and logistics	105
Overview of the principal elements of Galloglas arms & armour	109
Armour	109
Offensive Weaponry	124
The Redshanks	139
Bibliography	150

ACKNOWLEDGEMENTS

We would like to thank our publisher Stefan Müller and his team at Zeughaus Verlag in Berlin. Our thanks also go to Dr. Tammo Luther for contributing the introduction to this book.

We are deeply indebted to Marko Tjemmens for his marvellous photographs of Irish castles. Thank you also to Ralf Bergendahl for his pictures of Castle Sween in Scotland, and to Jessica Greenwood for her photographs of the English reenactors.

We are also grateful to Marc Grunert for his highly atmospheric illustration of a galloglas and his retainer contemplating a mist-shrouded Irish valley.

Our special thanks go to those long serving comrades who have worked with Claíomh Living History & Mobile Museum and who have long committed to trudging the galloglass path with Dave Swift over the last couple of decades: Will O'Shea, Michael Selby-Bennetts and Dave Senior.

This list would be incomplete without our mentioning of those enthusiasts and craftsfolk who have provided invaluable support over the years – some of whom appear in the reconstruction photographs herein: Ian Lynch, Alan Eagle, Marcus Seóighe, Boyd Rankin, Lynne Williams, Alistair James, Iain Bowden, Paul Binns, Seán Ó Brógáin, Nathan Barber, Dave Hewitt, Tomasz Samula, Shay Buckley, Ashley O'Rourke, David O'Reilly, Mark ‚Smiley' Flynn, Keith O'Dwyer, John Fay, Darragh O'Laoghaire, Tony Whyte, John Heathwood, Andrew Ó Donnghaile, Derek Gallagher and Jacek Robotka.

All of this was photographed and documented by Rob Hunt, Niamh Niamh O'Rourke, Shirley Lougheed, Jimmy Doyle, Judith Schoen, John Nicholl, Katherine Bond, Katharina Temirati, Arthur Boyton, and Ruby Gallagher. This book would not be what it is without their invaluable contributions. Many thanks to you all for your support.

INTRODUCTION

They are an all but forgotten part of Ireland's past – the galloglas, Ireland's formidable warriors. But then their history, which spans the greater part of 350 years, is full of dramatic and often very surprising events.

This work with its many photographs and illustrations seeks to bring back to life the spectacular yet widely unknown history of this peculiar medieval tradition of war, soldiering and mercenary service, and it is truly worth the while to do so.

In the turmoil of medieval Scottish, English and Irish armed conflicts evolved a true warrior caste of awe-inspiring reputation and grim ritual, which deserves the special attention of the contemporary historic enthusiast. For centuries, the galloglas mercenary clans served both Gaelic-Irish and Anglo-Irish provincial kings. They were originally recruited from the warlike populations of the West Highlands and the Hebrides, and provided numerous warriors that were dispatched to Ireland in several waves. Among these contingents were entire clans forced to leave their Scottish homelands as a consequence of domestic strife. The son of a galloglass followed in his father's footsteps as warrior traditions were passed down the generations from fathers to sons. Contemporary chroniclers almost unanimously describe these men as extraordinarily strong and well-built.

The reader will learn from this work that it was common for a galloglas clan to faithfully serve a specific Irish noble family for generations. Chapters in this book will be specially devoted to aspects such as galloglass equipment, clothing and weapons. The large amount of detail ought to make reading this book rewarding even for the expert.

These fearsome élite fighters were masters of their trade. They were clad in mail armour worn over a padded aketon, and protected their heads with an assortment of different helmets. Their preferred weapon was a distinctive long-hafted war-axe, which contributed to their fierce reputation as fearless warriors. Galloglas also employed two-handed swords, spears and knives as well as the bow, as contemporary sources show. A separate chapter will focus on the equipment of the galloglass in all its variety. Descriptions of the skirmishes and battles in which the galloglas carved out their reputation as tough and fearless warriors conclude this highly informative and inspiring work. Legend has it (or was it in fact the case?) that the galloglas were the first to appear on the field of battle and the last to leave it, having secured their own side's victory or retreat – if they lived to see it.

The authors invite you on a journey back in time to witness the making and rise of the mysterious galloglas from the 13th to the 16th centuries, and to discover the eventful and fascinating history of these Celtic warriors.

Credit goes to the authors for embarking on this interesting chapter of Irish military history and preventing the men who wrote it from falling into oblivion. I therefore hope that this book will find a wide circle of interested and enthusiastic readers beyond the medieval historian and the military reenactor.

I wish the reader joy and plenty of new insights with this exciting book.

Dr. Tammo Luther

AUTHORS' FOREWORD

The events discussed in this book took place in a region in which either Gaelic or English were spoken, or both. The names of English persons will be spelled in the common English manner, while for Irish names, be they persons or places, the anglicized versions have mostly been adopted in order to facilitate both comprehension and individual further reading. For example, Professor Hayes-McCoy, whose standard reference work *Irish Battles* has provided valuable information in the creation of this work, also uses the English forms of persons' and place names. His approach has been adopted as a guideline for this book, although we occasionally choose to ignore this whenever there is the risk of confusion. Gaelic names as far as they can be reconstructed will be given once. Hugh O'Neill, 2nd Earl of Tyrone, will be referred to by his English name instead of the Gaelic *Aodh Mór Ó Néill*. The English name Hugh corresponds with both the Gaelic forms of *Aodh* and *Aedh*. The Scottish and Irish variants of the Gaelic tongue began to diverge from the 12th century onwards. Numerous important sources were composed in an earlier form of Irish Gaelic, namely Early Modern Irish. The *Annals of the Four Masters,* for instance, were written in this language, although occasionally interspersed with Latin. Many Gaelic names used in reference works are in fact retranslations from an anglicized variant. Anglicization itself is an age-old phenomenon, although it was not always consistently applied. The Irish Gaelic *Muircheartach* and the Scottish Gaelic *Muireadach* can be traced back to a common root, although the former was usually anglicized as *Murtogh*, while the latter appeared as *Murdoch*.

The sources render different spellings of both family and individual names. The present authors have attempted to provide a certain consistency; however, *FitzMaurice*, for example, ought on some occasions not to be confused with *Fitzmaurice*. Here again we choose to follow the approach taken by Hayes-McCoy.

Irish clan leaders will be referred to as chiefs in this book, the leaders of a clan's various family lines as chieftains. In this we follow the Scottish nomenclature variant, while many works use both words synonymously when referring to Irish history. During the time of English rule, clan chiefs and regional rulers were called Lords, and we adopt this practice. Of course, these persons mostly thought of themselves as kings, as their ancestors had indeed been. However, they only actually adopted their royal title when rebelling against their English overlords. The chroniclers gave different names to these Irish Lords depending on their political importance. When in doubt, the title of *magnate* has been adopted.

The protagonists' name has been spelled *galloglas* (singular: *galloglass*). Other works occasionally favour *gallowglas (gallowglass,* or *gallowglasses)*. All of these variants are anglicizations derived from the Irish Gaelic *gallóglach* (sing.) and *gallóglaich* (plural).

This illustration shows a galloglass and his retainer in a typical Irish setting.
(Illustration: Marc Grunert)

The weapon commonly known in Europe as the Danish axe exercised strong influence on both the galloglas and Irish warfare as a whole.
(© Claíomh – Dave Swift 2017)

IRELAND IN THE MIDDLE AGES

The warrior rose from the undergrowth where he had concealed himself ever since his own side had been defeated by the enemy. He had been forced to witness the slaughtering of his warriors one by one, and one allied contingent after the other taking to its heels. However, he had also watched the scieldburg *of picked household warriors who had protected the enemy's royal leader gradually crumble away, as the warriors chose to join their victorious comrades in the looting of the enemy slain. The warrior summoned his courage, and gripping his war-axe tightly approached his man at a run in true* berserkr *manner. Catching the astonished enemy ranks off their guard, he found his foe at prayer, and slew him. Yet the enemy recovered swiftly from their surprise and felled the attacker.*

This is just one – though not entirely convincing – variant of a number of traditions which found entry into countless Icelandic sagas. It can nevertheless be safely said that both protagonists met their end on the day of battle. On Good Friday of the year 1014 (23rd April), the political careers of both Brian Boru, High King (*Ard Ri*) of Erin, and Brodir, Nordic kinglet from the Isle of Man, ended on the field of Clontarf.[1]

According to some Irish annals, Brian Boru (or rather Brian Boruma) had by the time of the Battle of Clontarf entered his 87th year. This is highly improbable however. Boru was probably born around the year 940 AD, which would have made him around 74 years at the time of his death.

Brian Boru hailed from the Province of Munster, where he had assumed leadership of the Dal Cais clan following the death of his brother Mathgamain. In decades of fighting he proceeded to bring the whole of Munster under his control. In his campaigns Brian Boru made skilful use of small boat squadrons, operating on the Shannon and its tributaries. This way he also managed to capture the Viking settlement of Limerick in 977, personally slaying the local *jarl* Ivar in single combat, if Irish chroniclers are to be believed. It would nevertheless be wrong to consider the war a one-dimensional conflict between indigenous (or "mere", i. e. pure [cf. lat. *merus*]) Irish against Norse invaders (let alone Christians battling heathens), as many later depictions are wont to make us believe. At the time of Brian Boru's death, it was a certain Osli who served as the king's *mormaer* (chief advisor). This most important office at the High King's court was thus held by the dead *jarl* Ivar's grandson. Clontarf itself was by no means a battle between Irish and Norsemen. The contingent of the Irish Province of Leinster stood in the ranks of an army led by the Norse king of Dublin, Sigtrygg Silkenbeard. On the other hand, countless Vikings served in Boru's army. Annals report of ten ships' crews from the Isle of Man led by Ospak, brother of the afore-mentioned Brodir.[2]

In the year 980, at the time when Brian Boru was extending his power over south-western Ireland, the Norse kinglet of Dublin, Amlaib Cuaran, challenged the supremacy of Irish king Máel Sechnaill (often latinized as Malachias). Máel Sechnaill was King of Mide (or Meath) based at the ancient holy place of Tara, and chief of the southern Uí Néill clan. He claimed for himself the royal title of *ard ri*, High King. This political concept had originally been contrived by the Irish clergy, only to be exploited by the ruling dynasty of the southern Uí Néill[3]. The title itself constituted more of a pretension than a reality since even the northern Uí Néill (who dominated Ulster) refused to back it. Amlaib Cuaran likewise did not show the slightest inclination to submit to Máel Sechnaill, at least not indefinitely. He attacked Tara in 980, but the campaign ended in disaster. Màel Sachnaill in his turn besieged Dublin and forced it to surrender. Cuaran fled into exile, where he died in the following year. It is impossible to ascertain whether his widow, the Irish princess Gormlaith (whom Irish chroniclers unanimously describe as a very attractive woman), actually married Máel Sechnaill, only to go her own way shortly after. A few years later she did however marry Brian Boru, and their marriage proved dynastically sound since Gormlaith gave birth to Brian's son Donnchad.

In 997 Máel Sechnaill and Brian Boru divided the Emerald Isle between them. While Máel Sechnaill was given the North including Connacht, Mide, and Ulster, Boru took the South comprising Munster and Leinster. Dublin became part of Brian Boru's sphere of influence, whereas the title of High King remained with Máel Sechnaill. In 999 the Dubliners led by their *jarl* Sigtrygg Silkenbeard (son of Cuaran and Gormlaith) rebelled against Brian Boru.[4] With the support of Máel Sechnaill, Boru defeated the Norsemen at Glenn Máma and captured the town. He accepted his stepson Sigtrygg's submission and reinstated him as a vassal kinglet, even giving him one of his daughters in marriage. Now that he had all the wealth and ships of Dublin at his disposal, Boru could finally set about realizing his own claim to the title of High King of Erin.[5] Máell Sechnaill meanwhile had failed to make any further progress in persuading his northern brethren of the Uí Néill clan to accept his own claim to suzerainty. In 1002 the

---

1 Ó Corráin, Donnchadh: „Ireland, Wales, Man, and the Hebrides", in Sawyer, Peter (ed.): *The Oxford Illustrated History of the Vikings*, Oxford 1997, pp. 83-109 (p. 101).

2 According to tradition Ospak accepted baptism, apparently because he was unwilling to fight against a king as good as Brian Boru. Newman, Roger Chatterton: *Brian Boru, King of Ireland*, Cork 2011, p. 124.

3 The clan's name was later anglicized as O'Neill.

4 Anders, Sabine and Seehase, Hagen: „Die Schlacht bei Clontarf. Geburt einer Nation", in: *Geschichte* 7/2015, p. 36f. (p. 37).

5 Nicolle, David: *Mediaeval Warfare Source Book. Warfare in Western Christendom*, London 1995, p. 216.

At the beginning of the 11th century, Norse influence on Irish military affairs was considerable. Arms and armour of Norse jarls and Irish nobles resembled each other closely.
(© Claíomh – Dave Swift 2014)

title of High King finally fell to Brian Boru without a fight. With the help of the Dublin fleet he proceeded to mop up what resistance was left among the clans of Ulster.

Trouble was also brewing in Leinster, where the local king Mael Mórda, one of Gormlaith's brothers, rose against Brian Boru, who had meanwhile divorced Gormlaith. The Dublin Vikings under Sigtrygg Silkenbeard allied themselves with numerous Norse kinglets, among them *jarl* Sigurd of the Orkneys, the Vikings of the Hebrides, and even several ships' crews from as far as Iceland. The brothers Ospak and Brodir from the Isle of Man also joined swords with Silkenbeard. The conflict gained momentum as both rebellions merged into one. This was hardly surprising given the fact that Gormlaith was both Sigtrygg's mother and Mael Mórda's sister. Whether Sigtrygg indeed betrothed his mother to Brodir as some sagas claim, is impossible to ascertain. In Irish tradition Brodir not only features as Brian Boru's antagonist but is also portrayed as an evil caricature of the High King himself. Supposedly an apostate Christian, Brodir comes across as an altogether highly unpleasant and malicious character. He also seems to have conspired against his brother, which prompted Ospak and his part of the 30-ship fleet from Man to alter their course.

Ospak sailed around Ireland, joined Brian Boru and consented to adopting Christianity. Newly baptized, he and his warriors marched on Dublin in the ranks of the High King's forces. Further support came from the troops of Máel Sechnall. For unknown reasons however, the latter did not take an active part in the fighting. They remained poised in the wake of Brian Boru's Irish-Norse army when it took up position at the River Tolka and locked shields in preparation for the coming battle.[6]

Sigtrygg's Norse-Irish troops also formed a shield wall. Both armies were similarly armed and organized, with the Norse warriors mostly more heavily armoured than their Irish comrades-in-arms. As for the numbers involved, information is vague. The contingents of Boru's army were probably commanded by close relatives of the High King, for example his son Murdach, and his grandson, Toirdelbach. In the opposing ranks stood Sigurd Hlodvirsson, *jarl* of Orkney, whose Orcadians probably formed the centre of Silkenbeard's army. For a long time, both armies hacked away at each other's shield wall with no particular tactical refinement, neither side gaining an advantage. Tradition celebrates heroic duels, Brodir apparently felling one opponent after the other until confronted by Ulf the Quarrelsome (*Ulf Hreda*, probably identical with Brian Boru's brother Cuiduligh), who struck him down. Brodir picked himself up and fled, hiding in the Forest of Tomar. Murdach wielded a sword in each hand, killing fifty enemy warriors with each weapon, *jarl* Sigurd among them. He and his son Toirdelbach were eventually

---

6   McCullough, David Wills: *Wars of the Irish Kings. A Thousand Years of Struggle from the Age of Myth Through the Reign of Queen Elizabeth I*, New York 2002, p. 111.

Despite the defeat of the Norsemen at Clontarf, Scandinavian cultural, economic and military influence remained as strong as ever following permanent Norse settlement on the Hebrides.
(© Claíomh – Dave Swift 2017)

slain, but towards nightfall Sigtrygg's shieldwall finally gave way, and his men took to their heels. The victors proceeded to plunder the enemy fallen, thereby probably offering Brodir the opportunity to kill Brian Boru.[7]

Brodir himself came to a gruesome end – furious at their king's death and thirsty for revenge, Boru's men led by Ulf the Quarrelsome cut Brodir open, tied his entrails to a tree and forced him to circle the tree until disembowelled. This according to the annals concluded the great Battle of Clontarf (which literally translates as "Bull's meadow").

According to legend, Brian Boru's body was interred in the northern wall of St Patrick's Cathedral. Be that as it may, his death marked the end of the Irish High Kingship. Although the title continued to be borne, no king would forthwith be able to claim to have ruled Ireland in its entirety. Donnchad, one of Boru's surviving sons, managed to retain the crown of Munster. He was nevertheless forced to constantly wage war against the kings of Leinster and Connacht to defend it, and even at home his position did not go unchallenged. Donnchad was deposed in 1063, and died in the following year while on a pilgrimage to Rome. The O'Brien clan, so named after Brian Boru, was able to hold on to the petty kingship of Munster in the 11th and 12th centuries, their rule occasionally interrupted by the MacCarthys.

After the Battle of Clontarf, Brian Boru's army failed to take Dublin, and Sigtrygg remained in power until 1036. Unassisted by other Norse contingents, he even succeeded in defeating three Irish kinglets in a battle fought along the lower reaches of the Boyne in 1032.[8]

Contrary to modern perception, ancient Irish society was not particularly warlike. Although the annals report seemingly incessant campaigning, these events were hardly ever more than individual heroics in the comparatively harmless context of cattle rustling or squabbles over inheritances.[9]

The idea of centralized power was alien to the peoples of Celtic Ireland; political power rested with a handful of provincial kingdoms[10] and innumerable petty kingdoms, which often amounted to no more than mere village communities ruled by local chieftains. There were neither permanent royal household troops, nor was there compulsory military service, with serfs excluded altogether from carrying arms. The numerous clerics, physicians and bards were not required to serve in their lords' levies, but many joined the ranks anyway. Irish castles were mostly

---

7 Logan, Donald F.: *The Vikings in History*, New York and London 1983, p. 38.

8 Hudson, Benjamin: *Viking Pirates and Christian Princes: Dynasty, Religion, and Empires in the North Atlantic*, Oxford 2005, p. 110.

9 Hayes-McCoy, Gerard Antony: *Irish Battles. A Military History of Ireland*, Belfast 1969, p. 41.

10 Leinster, Ulster, Munster, Connacht, and Mide (*Meath*).

A traveller of the later Viking age armed with a light spear. At this time, Ireland was a more densely wooded country than today.
(© Claíomh – Dave Swift 2017)

Leacanabuaile Cashel, built in County Kerry at the time of the Norse invasions, is situated only a short distance from the coast.
(Photograph: Peter Moore (Moorso); Creative Commons Attribution Share Alike 3.0. Unported Licence)

refuge fortifications and thus of defensive character. Compared to the arms of the Norse people, Irish weapons were mostly considered inferior in quality.

The significance of the hunting and warrior societies which originated in Leinster, the so-called *Fianna*, has been exaggerated, especially so since they played a large role in the legend surrounding the Irish hero Finn MacCumaill. The military success of the Vikings was based on their nautical superiority and military prowess, yet they were unable to conquer Ireland completely. As shown above, the result was a gradual intermingling of indigenous Irish and Norse invaders. The Battle of Clontarf was thus anything but the often celebrated "national liberation". Neither did the battle terminate Norse presence in Ireland, with Dublin remaining the most important settlement.[11] Ireland never formed the prime focus of the Viking expansion led by the royal power evolving in the various Scandinavian kingdoms. The Norman (or rather, Cambro-Norman) conquest of Ireland would prove to be of a completely different quality.

Born at Tonbridge in southern England in 1130, Richard FitzGilbert de Clare is usually credited with being the first Norman to set his foot on Irish soil and thus beginning the Norman conquest. In fact, he was not. Nevertheless, he did play an essential part in the events to come.

The de Clares' original estates were situated in Wales and western England. In 1148 Richard (nicknamed "Strongbow") inherited these lands and the offices and titles from his father Gilbert de Clare, First Earl of Pembroke. However, in the civil war between Stephen de Blois and Henry Plantagenet, Strongbow unwisely nailed his colours to the former's mast, and probably saw himself stripped of his Earl's title when the latter mounted the throne as Henry II in 1154. King Henry was to keep a suspicious eye on Richard de Clare for as long as he lived. Dermot Mac Murrough (*Diarmait Mac Murchada* in Old Irish) King of Leinster had lost his kingdom when an army allied to High King Rory O'Connor (Gaelic: *Tairrdelbach mac Ruadri Ua Conchobair*) and Tiernan O'Rourke King of Breifne had conquered Leinster. Meeting the English king in Aquitaine, Diarmait appealed to Henry II for assistance. Although Diarmait became Henry's vassal, the king did not bestir himself in the matter. Diarmait attempted to raise an army in Wales, but without success. Only with Strongbow's help did he finally manage to raise an invasion force, promising Strongbow his daughter Aoife in marriage and proclaiming him his heir. In view of his somewhat strained relationship with Henry, Strongbow decided to ask the king's expressive permission before accepting Diarmait's offer.

---

11 Graham-Campbell, James (ed.): *Die Wikinger*, Munich 1994, p. 221.

Richard de Clare, 2nd Earl of Pembroke, as depicted in Gerald de Barri's *Expugnatio Hibernica*.

King Henry bided his time, and so Strongbow was forced to entrust Barons Robert FitzStephen and Raymond FitzGerald with the command of the first two expeditions, before himself finally embarking for Ireland in 1170. Strongbow conducted a lightning campaign which was crowned by a ruse winning him the Hiberno-Scandinavian city of Dublin. In August 1170 he was married to Aoife. Diarmait died in the following May, and Strongbow succeeded his father-in-law as the new King of Leinster. This however constituted a violation of ancient Irish customary law. Both the Irish and the Norse population of Dublin rose against him. King Henry flatly refused to come to Strongbow's aid, but with a combination of archery and cavalry tactics the new King of Leinster managed to defeat the High King's forces in a pitched battle outside the gates of Dublin. He was however forced to cede his entire newly-won Irish estates to King Henry as a fiefdom. The English King presently visited Ireland with a large entourage of knights. Until his death on 20th April 1176 Strongbow, now holding the titles of Lord of Leinster and Justiciar of Ireland, fought in the King's name against Gaelic and Hiberno-Scandinavian Irish. He was able to hold only Leinster and Dublin (later to be called "The Pale") with its immediate surroundings.

King Henry had acknowledged Richard FitzGilbert de Clare's position as King of Leinster, and invested Hugh de Lacy with Meath. In 1177, the Norman baron John de Courcy conquered eastern Ulster, having invaded the northern Irish kingdom of Ulaid with a small army and defeating the northern Irish Kings.[12] The entire eastern Irish coast was now firmly in the hands of the Norman barons – *not* the English crown.

Gaelic Ireland saw itself confronted with a colonization of profoundly different dimensions to that of the Norsemen. The Normans were interested primarily in large estates, which formed the basis of their political power. In contrast to the Norman Conquest of England in 1066, King Henry had no legal title to claim as his due.[13] When in Ireland, Henry in person acted as king, but oddly enough not specifically as a representative of the English crown. Only making a brief appearance, he soon returned to England.

The Norman barons were glad to see him go. Unimpeded by royal authority, they gleefully set about conquering the island and dividing it among themselves. By the end of the 13th century, they had managed to bring much of the entire island under the Norman yoke until confronted with a new type of warrior, of which more anon.

---

12 Beckett, James C.: *Geschichte Irlands*, Stuttgart 1977, p. 14.
13 King Henry had appealed to the Pope for help for his Irish campaign. The Pope had welcomed the Norman conquest of Ireland since he hoped to bring the Irish clergy to heel. The Pope presented the English King a ring as a token of his infeftment, reminding him that according to the Donation of Constantine, all isles were subject to Papal rule (Kluxen, Kurt: *Geschichte Englands. Von den Anfängen bis zur Gegenwart*. Stuttgart 1985, p. 59).

THE NORSE-GAELIC KINGDOM OF THE ISLES

The brutal Viking raid on Lindisfarne Priory, itself a plantation of the Scottish abbey of Iona, in the year 793 was only the beginning. A short while later, the sinister longships appeared before Iona itself, and then everywhere on the western and northern coasts of Scotland. In 797, the Norsemen attacked the Isle of Man. After several waves of pillage and plunder, the Vikings eventually came to stay, founding settlements in the Orkneys and the Shetland Isles, later also in the Hebrides and in Caithness on the western Scottish coast. Archaeological finds on the Hebridean island of Uist point to a series of bloody conflicts between the Celtic population and the Scandinavian invaders. Nearly all the names of local Hebridean bays and coastal villages are of Nordic origin, while the names of settlements further inland mostly possess a Celtic etymology.[14]

The Vikings also settled in Ireland, Galloway, and the Isle of Man. While Scotland was the preferred destination of settlers from Norway (called *Fiongall* by the Irish chroniclers), the Danes (*Dubhgall*) mostly chose England as their new home.

Scandinavian settlers and indigenous Celts eventually began to mingle and intermarry. The Norse-Germanic heritage was more pronounced in the Orkneys and Shetland Islands, while in the Hebrides and Galloway Celtic culture prevailed (hence *Gallgael*, "Celtic Strangers"[15]). Soon the newly-arrived Hebridean Vikings remembered their former calling and began to plunder their old Norwegian homesteads. King Harald Fairhair (or Finehair), the unifier of Norway, was not a man to be trifled with however, and promptly conquered the islands along with their troublesome inhabitants. The islands proved difficult to control, and so the local Vikings enjoyed a comparatively large amount of political freedom, which was only occasionally curtailed by headstrong and powerful rulers such as Olav Tryggvasson or Canute the Great.

The Nordic islanders were different from their mainland countrymen in more than one respect. One local idiosyncrasy for example was the simultaneous worshipping of both Odin and Christ (various sagas confirm this religious practice), and anyone rejecting this theological compromise was considered quite godless – after all, the Icelandic name of *Godlaus* stems from the Hebrides.

The Hebrides were ruled by several *jarls*, and there existed a certain cultural homogeneity, but this did not extend to politics. A king who managed to briefly unite the Hebrides under one rule (albeit with questionable methods) was *Eiric ri na n-Innsi*: Eric, King of the Isles. This man was none other than Eric Bloodaxe, a descendant of Harald Fairhair of Norway. Banished from his motherland, he had briefly ruled in York (Jorvik). In 954 he was driven from the city and subsequently succeeded in establishing himself as ruler of the Hebrides for several years.

Godred Haraldson was the first King of Man. Godred was descended from the dynasty of the Viking rulers of Dublin. One of his descendants, Godred Sigtrygsson, made the fatal mistake of receiving into his household a distant relative by the name of Godred Crovan. Crovan was the son of a Viking chieftain from Islay and had fought as a mercenary for King Harald Hardrada of Norway, narrowly escaping from the battle of Stamford Bridge in 1066. His two attempts to conquer the Isle of Man in 1075 ended in failure. In 1076 Godred Crovan defeated his enemies in the Battle of Skyhill, severing the political ties with Dublin and establishing the Kingdom of Man and the Isles. This also comprised the Hebrides, Kintyre, Bute, and Arran.

A diocese was established in Man. In 1152 it was placed under the authority of the archbishopric of Nidaros (the later Trondheim). Soon Godred Crovan's sons began to quarrel among themselves over their father's legacy. Lagman, the elder, defeated his younger brother Harald and had him hideously disfigured. In 1093 the Norwegian King Magnus Bareleg briefly succeeded in bringing the wild Viking chieftains of the Irish Sea under control, appointing as governor one of his trusted retainers, a man named Ingemund. Ingemund swiftly became so unpopular however that the chieftains attacked his headquarters on the Isle of Lewis and burned the hapless Ingermund's house to the ground with its owner inside.[16] Shortly afterwards war broke out on the Isle of Man between its Norse inhabitants under a certain *jarl* Otta, and the Celtic population led by a man named Macmaras. In 1098, King Magnus Bareleg restored Norwegian supremacy in the region by subduing the Irish Sea region with fire and sword. In this respect at least Man proved a disappointment, since its quarrelsome inhabitants had themselves hardly left anything still worth destroying. Parts of the island had become completely depopulated. King Magnus planned to make Man the center of a kingdom, but died during an unwise invasion of Ireland in 1103. His campaign had completely disrupted the political balance of

---

14 Simek, Rudolf, *Die Wikinger*, Munich 1998, p. 54.

15 The Gallgael, also referred to as Gall-Gaedhill, had already become so powerful in the 9th century that they drove the Vikings of Dublin to sign an alliance with the Leinster Irish. This was one of the first Irish-Norse treaties. In 856, High King Maelsachnaill (of the O'Neill clan) hired the leader of the Gallgael, Caithill Finn ("White Ketil") to fight for him against the Dublin Vikings. The Gallgael were also ordered to subdue the unruly people of Leinster. This led to the afore-mentioned Irish-Norse alliance in 858. The Gallgael were so completely defeated that henceforth they were no longer mentioned in the Irish chronicles. They appear to have been of mixed ethnic origin, a feature common enough during the migration period during and after the fall of the Western Roman Empire. They were probably of Norwegian stock mixed with Strathclyde Britons and Gaelic-speaking Vikings from the Hebrides, with a sprinkling of adventurers hailing from various homelands for good measure. They finally settled down in Galloway, which bears their name to this day.

16 Bugge, Alexander: *Die Wikinger*, Halle 1906, p. 153 f.

These ruins situated on an island in Loch Finlaggan on Islay are all that is left of the court of the Lords of the Isles.
(Photograph: MSeses, wikimedia, CC BY-SA 4.0)

power in Man itself. Gilladomnan, a petty king married to a Norwegian noblewoman, lost his power base in the southern Hebrides.

In the time of the Kingdom of the Isles the Hebrides were known as the Southern Isles (*Sudreyar*). Assemblies were held at Tynwald on the Isle of Man. Man sent sixteen deputies, Lewis, Islay, Skye and Mull each sent four (including the neighbouring smaller islets). The appearance of a particularly warlike chieftain was to change the political situation significantly however.

Gillebride MacGille Adomnan[17] was a Gallgael chieftain who had been driven from his estates. He fled to Ireland, where he persuaded a small clan to support him. With a force of between 400 and 500 warriors he returned to Scotland, and was defeated. His son Somerled was forced to live the secluded life of a hunter until he eventually began to assemble followers around him.

In 1156 Godred II, a descendant of Godred Crovan of the house of Ynglingar, lost a sea battle off Colonsay. His opponent was the ruler of Argyll, a formidable warrior of Norse-Celtic descent: the now famous Somerled, founder of the MacDonald, MacDougall, MacRuaridh and MacAllister clans.

The name of Somerled (or *Sumarlidi*) is Norse in origin, meaning "summer seafarer" or "summer Viking".[18] Sailing from Ireland, he raided the Scottish coast as his father had done. He was able to win a number of engagements against Viking forces on the Ardamurchan peninsula, a fact still commemorated in local place names. The name of Glenborrowdale for example is derived from Borodil, a Norse warrior defeated by Somerled in single combat. Eventually Somerled conquered all of Morvern, Lochaber, and northern Argyll.

In 1135 King David I of Scotland campaigned against the Kingdom of the Isles, taking Bute and Arran, which he gave to Somerled as a fiefdom. In 1140 Somerled married Ragnhild, the daughter of King Olaf the Red of Man. The couple had three sons, Dugall, Reginald, and Angus. When Somerled married Ragnhild he already had a son by the name of Gillecallum.

Before long, Somerled felt strong enough to rebel against the Scottish king, but he was not successful. He once again turned his attention to the Isles. His brother-in-law Godred II had with his overbearing manner kindled strong political opposition, which had found a leader in Thorfinn, a crafty local chieftain. Thorfinn allied himself with Somerled, and Somerled's son Dugall was chosen to replace his uncle on the throne. Together with Dugall, Thorfinn visited the Isles in order to convince the local chieftain of the righteousness of their cause and to secure hostages. However, the *jarl* of Skye refused to comply and sent word to Godred II.

Somerled attacked his brother-in-law with eight ships. The naval engagement off Colonsay in 1156 ended in a draw, but Godred was forced to acknowledge Somerled's superiority, and ceded to him all of the land south of Ardnamurchan, a peninsula on the western Scottish coast.

---

17   Son of the above-mentioned Gilladomnan.
18   Seehase, Hagen and Oprotkowitz, Axel: *Die Highlander. Die Geschichte der Schottischen Clans*, Greiz 1999, p. 14.

Two years later Somerled mustered fifty ships and invaded Man. Godred was forced to flee and sought refuge at the Norwegian court. Somerled had now reached the height of his power and proclaimed himself *Rex Insularum*.

Somerled now joined an aristocratic clique which intended to depose King Malcolm IV of Scotland and put in his place the "Boy of Egremont", a nobleman of the FitzDuncan clan. The King himself had long since grown tired of Somerled's virtual independence in the west of the realm, and wanted to make a vassal of him. Naturally, Somerled was not amused when he received the news, and promptly moved against the King. In 1164 he allegedly landed his 163 ships at Renfrew on the River Clyde. The royal army sent against him was commanded by High Steward Walter Fitzalan. In the ensuing battle, Somerled was defeated and died together with his son Gillecallum. Godred took advantage of the situation and returned to Man to resume power. In 1221, Gillecallum's son Somerled the Younger rose against Scottish King Alexander II, and was killed in battle.

The three sons from Somerled the Elder's second marriage divided his estates among themselves. Dugall took Coll, Tiree, Mull, and Jura, while Reginald (or Ranald) received Islay and Kintyre. Angus took Bute for himself, while Arran was divided between Ranald and Angus. Angus and his three sons were killed by the Islemen of Skye in 1210.

Ranald likewise had three sons, who each founded powerful clans: Roderick, founder of the MacRuaridhs, Donald, founder of the Macdonalds, and Dugall, ancestor of the MacDougalls. Donald was the foster father of Donnell Óg O'Donnell of Tyrconnell.[19]

Caught between the two political spheres of influence, Ranald and his descendants managed to maintain the precarious balance between Alexander III King of Scots, and King Hákon of Norway. Alexander III encouraged the Earl of Ross to attack and plunder Skye. The resulting devastation caused nearly all of the chiefs of the West Highlands to side with Norway. Hákon prepared to attack with his powerful fleet, but the elderly king made the fateful mistake of dividing his force when he attacked western Scotland across the Irish Sea. On 30th September 1263 a gale severed the anchor line of Hákon's greatest warship with himself on board and swept it out to sea, while ten smaller craft were beached at Largs in Ayrshire. Scottish archers attacked the Norwegians, who returned fire furiously from the cover of their ships. The exchange of missiles finally subsided at nightfall. In the night, Hákon's sailors succeeded in once more bringing his flagship under control, and the King of Norway decided to sail to the rescue of his beleaguered men. The Norwegians landed in force and were met by a half-hearted Scottish cavalry charge which failed to break their shield wall. The Norwegians took heart and counterattacked, winning the necessary time to push their ships off the beach, and finally rowed out to the safety of the open sea.

One of the famous Lewis Chessmen, now on display at the British Museum. The equipment of this piece probably reflects that of contemporary Hebridean warriors.
(Photograph: Nachosa)

---

19 Donnell was the younger brother of Goffrey O'Donnell, King of Tyrconnell (Gaelic: Goffraidh Ó Domhnaill). Schlegel, Donald M.: "The MacDonalds of Tyrone and Armagh. A Genealogical Study", in: *Seanchas Ardmhacha, Journal of the Armagh Diocesan Society*, vol. 10, No. 1 (1980-1981). Armagh 1980, pp. 190-219 (p.193).

King John Lackland.
(Illustration from the Statutes of England, British Library)

THE NORMAN CONQUEST, AND THE FIRST GALLOGLAS

Only few rulers from the House of Plantagenet ever bothered to visit Ireland. King John was an exception. When he was a young man, his father Henry II had attempted to instal him as King of Ireland to counterbalance the political ambitions of Hugh de Lacy, Henry's governor.

Henry sent to Pope Alexander III for his consent to crown John, and knighted his son. In April 1185 John and his army landed at Waterford, where he was acclaimed by a number of Irish petty kings. To the west however there was rebellion (probably fomented by Hugh de Lacy). Prince John's Irish campaign ended in complete disaster – he suffered a few minor setbacks and proved unable to pay his mercenaries (having previously shown himself as a spendthrift), who promptly deserted him. Utterly humiliated, he returned to England.

In 1199 he was crowned King of England. He managed to play the various Anglo-Norman barons off against each other but was unable to prevent Ireland from becoming the focal point of baronial resistance against his rule.

In 1208 a former favourite, William de Braose, rose in revolt. He owed the king a large sum and was unable to repay the debt. John had simply confiscated the de Braoses' English estates, but this measure resulted in his debtor's rebellion. His rising quelled, de Braose escaped to Ireland. Soon, several local barons rebelled against the King's Justiciar and defeated him in battle in 1208.

The King was forced to intervene. John landed in Ireland in June 1210. In only two months he led his knights from Waterford in the south to Carrickfergus in the north, then marched west into central Ireland, and eventually on Dublin. While de Braose was able to flee to France, his wife Maud and his son William escaped to Carrick in Scotland. The local ruler Duncan MacGilbert (Gaelic *Donnchadh mac Gille Brigte*) however was not interested in putting the English king's nose out of joint and sent mother and son to Carrickfergus locked up in cages. King John had both thrown into the dungeons and there let them starve to death.

The King took the ruler of Scottish Galloway, Alan, and his younger brother Thomas, into his service. Both were cousins of Duncan MacGilbert. Their task was to conquer Donegal and other parts of Ulster beyond the reach of the English crown. Alan, who did not wish to snub William I King of Scots, remained hesitant. Thomas of Galloway however led his *Gallgael* warriors in two campaigns against Derry in Ulster in 1212 and 1214. In 1212 the number of ships at his disposal amounted to 67, two years later the fleet was only insignificantly smaller. Thomas was able to establish himself at Coleraine until finally expelled by Hugh de Lacy[20].

Despite his poor choice of personnel, King John nevertheless managed to considerably augment the reputation of the "Lordship of Ireland", whose job it was to represent the English crown's claim to souzerainty over Ireland. In fact this claim was more of theoretical nature than a political reality. Outside the Pale, the Anglo-Norman barons did as they pleased. They took great delight in feuding, and the de Courcys, the de Lacys, the de Burghs, Marshals, Butlers and Fitzgeralds enlarged their estates at the expense of the local Old Irish petty kings. When they were not actually engaged in extending their estates, they busied themselves fighting one another. To secure their territorial gains, the barons excelled at building castles, many of which nevertheless remained comparatively small.

English peasants and artisans rarely moved to Ireland, and those who did only settled in the Pale area. An Anglo-Norman baron was free in his decisions wherever the influence of the English crown did not extend, but he was nevertheless forced to come to terms with local Old Irish chieftains. The majority of the population was Irish, even in those territories firmly under Norman control. Anglo-Norman nobles took Irish wives and adopted local customs. This "going native" was carried out despite decrees from the Lordship of Ireland to the contrary. In the second half of the 13th century, the Lordship government was nevertheless able to increase its political influence in Ireland.

Towards the end of the century there were nine counties[21] and five so-called liberties with sovereign rights.[22] Both counties and liberties despatched deputies to the Irish parliament. Legislature was restricted to Norman-occupied territory, the assembly's legal claim however comprised Ireland in its entirety. In order for the Lordship of Ireland to assert its claim to political souzerainty, it was essential to secure the support of the independent (or semi-independent) Old Irish kings. Just as Anglo-Norman barons adopted Old Irish customs, the Old Irish rulers took to emulating Anglo-Norman regal practice, especially by building their own castles[23].

In 1257 Anglo-Norman forces led by Maurice FitzGerald clashed with an Irish-Gaelic army under Goffrey O'Donnell, King of Tyrconnell, at Roscede.[24] The Normans were defeated. O'Donnell and FitzGerald fought a personal duel, both men receiving wounds which proved fatal;

---

20 Hugh de Lacy the Younger, son of Hugh de Lacy, Lord of Meath. The younger Hugh was born c. 1176. Since 1205 he was the first Earl of Ulster, dying in 1243.

21 Connaught, Cork, Dublin, Kerry, Kildare, Limerick, Louth, Tipperaray, and Waterford.

22 Carlow, Kilkenny, Meath, Ulster, and Wexford.

23 One of the first castles to be built by a Gaelic chief was Harry Avery's Castle, erected in the late 14th century by a member of the O'Neill clan. If however Ballintober Castle near Roscommon was indeed built by the O'Connors, it would own pride of place, having been built around the year 1300.

24 The battle of Roscede is also referred to as the Battle of Creadran Cille.

Roscommon Abbey: relief from a tomb depicting galloglas (detail).
(Photograph: Maximilian Bunk)

they died in the following year.[25] Goffrey O'Donnell's brother and successor Donell Óg O'Donnell sailed from Scotland, where he had married a daughter of Eoin MacSween.[26]

In 1259 Hugh O'Connor (Gaelic: *Aed mac Felim Ua Conchobair*), son of King Felim O'Connor, married a daughter of Dugall MacRuaridh[27] (Gaelic: *Dubhgall mac Ruaidhri*). Dugall was a Hebridean clan chief who had fought against the Anglo-Normans in Connacht the previous year.[28] He gave his daughter a dowry of 160 household warriors commanded by his brother Allen[29] (*Ailéan*). These 160 armed men are the first historically documented galloglas[30] - according to the *Annals of Loch Cé*, Allen brought with him "eight score of óglaich"[31].

In accordance with an agreement between Hugh O'Connor, Tadhg O'Brian, son of the King of Thomond, and Brian O'Neill (Gaelic: *Brian mac Néill Ruaidh O'Neill*), the two former princes had renounced their claims to the title of High King in favour of Brian O'Neill. The fact that Hugh married his bride in Derry, and that the galloglas landed there, points to a concerted move against Anglo-Norman rule. Tadhg O'Brian died in 1259.

On 14th May 1260 the combined armies of Hugh O'Connor and Brian O'Neill faced the troops of the English Justiciar of Ireland, James de Audley, at Druim Dearg[32]. Both forces consisted mainly of Irish warriors. If the galloglas were present, they do not seem to have made much of an impression. The Irish kings' forces were beaten, and Brian O'Neill was among the slain. Following the death of his father, Hugh became King of Connacht in 1265.

In 1269 Robert D'Ufford, the new Justiciar of Ireland, began construction of a castle at Roscommon.[33]

In the following year, his deputy led an army across the River Shannon and joined forces with Walter de Burgh,

---

25 Kelly, Matthew (ed.): *Cambrensis eversus seu potius historica fides in rebus hibernicis Giraldo cambrensi abrogata*, Dublin 1848, p. 208.

26 Schlegel: "The MacDonalds of Tyrone and Armagh", p. 193.

27 Dugall was the nephew of a renowned warrior likewise named Dugall (*Dubhgall mac Ruadrhi*) identical with a certain Mac Somhairle mentioned by Irish annals, who together with Melaghlin O'Donnell fought against the Anglo-Normans under Maurice FitzGerald at a battle near Ballyshannon in Donegal in 1247, and was killed. Woolf, Alex: "A dead man at Ballyshannon", in Duffy, Seán: *The World of the Galloglass. Kings, Warlords and Warriors in Ireland and Scotland 1200-1600*, Dublin 2007, pp. 77-85 (p. 77).

28 Dugall and his fleet had sailed all the way to the coast of Connemara, seizing a merchantman. The English Sheriff of Connaught pursued the pirates but was defeated.

29 Alan, according to some sources.

30 Cannan, Fergus and Ó Brógain, Sean: *Galloglass 1250-1600. Gaelic Mercenary Warrior*, Oxford 2010, p. 10.

31 The Gaelic word *óglaich* means „young warriors". The *Annals of Loch Cé* were composed before 1590. Prendergast, Muriosa: "Scots Mercenary Forces in Sixteenth Century Ireland", in: France, John: *Mercenaries and Paid Men. The Mercenary Identity in the Middle Ages*, Leyden and Boston 2008, pp. 363-381 (p. 364).

32 Near Downpatrick in Northern Ireland.

33 McNeill, Tom E.: *Castles in Ireland. Feudal Power in a Gaelic World*, London 1997, p. 54.

Roscommon Abbey. (Photograph: Maximilian Bunk)

Roscommon Castle. (Photograph: Maximilian Bunk)

Roscommon Castle.
(Photograph: Maximilian Bunk)

1st Earl of Ulster.[34] Negotiations with Hugh O'Connor achieved no agreement. O'Connor's warriors harrassed the combined army on its retreat. When De Burgh attempted to ford the Shannon at Áth-an-Chip, Hugh's army attacked and defeated the Anglo-Norman force. Hugh followed up his success by destroying Roscommon Castle.

Walter de Burgh died in 1271, his death concluding his family's expansion in Connacht. His old adversary Hugh O'Connor died on 3rd May 1274, likewise bringing local Irish resistance against the Anglo-Normans to a close. When Hugh's brother succeeded him as King of Connacht, quarrels over his succession broke out almost immediately. The Kingdom of Connacht thus saw no less than thirteen kings between 1274 and 1315, the resulting domestic unrest once again benefiting Anglo-Norman expansion.

The 1270s were also a period in which royal power in England consolidated itself.

As a postscript to these political events, Allen MacRuaridh fought against the Scottish crown side by side with King Hákon of Norway in 1263. The Hebrides were sold to Scotland in 1266, Allen making occasional appearances at the Scottish court. His son Duncan presumably founded the MacRory galloglas clan.

In the years 1285 and 1286 Allen MacRuaridh seems to have made a name for himself as a pirate roaming the Hebridean waters, as bitter complaints about his behaviour reached the Scottish court. His daughter Christiana was to become one of the most ardent supporters of Robert the Bruce in Scotland's struggle for independence from England.

---

34   Walter de Burgh also owned large estates in Connacht.

Other mercenaries

The galloglas were not the only mercenaries serving in Ireland. Others also hailed from Ireland itself, or came from foreign shores. The MacQuillins, of Anglo-Norman origin, were based in Antrim. The first MacQuillin mentioned by the sources was Malcolm, who in 1300 signed a treaty with Edward I of England in which he agreed to attack the western coast of Scotland with his fleet. In 1307 he changed sides, ferrying a landing force of several hundred men to Scotland in 18 longboats. Among these warriors were Alexander and Thomas Bruce, brothers of Robert the Bruce. This force was defeated by Dungal MacDowall. Malcolm MacQuillim was killed in the fighting.

Johnock MacQuillin (called John Hovelin by some sources) was a leader of mercenaries in the service of Sir William Liath de Burgh. These mercenaries formed a standing force, a most unusual thing at the time. They were referred to as "Bonaghts", or "Bonnachts" (Gaelic *buannaidhe*). Before entering Sir William's service, MacQuillin had killed his former lord Aodh Breifnach O'Connor, presumably at de Burgh's prompting. Johnock did not live long enough to reap the fruits of his deceit: in 1311 he was felled with his own axe. A few years on, Richard de Burgh, Earl of Ulster, appointed a certain William MacQuillin commander of his mercenaries in Ulster. In September 1313 Stephen MacQuillin was appointed "Constable of Bonnacht" and received the remarkable sum of two hundred pounds as recompensation for his service.

The county's armed forces were normally the responsibility of the senescal. This office was hereditary and held by the de Mandeville family. Family ties may have existed between the MacQuillins and the de Mandevilles. Some sources imply that the MacQuillins were descended from a certain Hugelin de Mandeville, but firm evidence is lacking.

When the English crown took stock of the situation after the death of the 3rd Earl of Ulster in 1333, it was noted that the late Earl had permanently kept under arms a force of 345 mercenaries.

The MacQullins gradually became the MacQuillans. In 1460 the MacQuillans purchased the Twescard region (later called "the route") from the de Mandevilles. The term "route" is here derived from the word *rout*, which denotes an assembly area for mercenaries.

There was also the Irish Barrett clan, which presumably had Franco-Norman roots. The Barretts held estates in Munster and north-eastern Connacht. They are first mentioned in a military context when towards the end of the 15th century a Barrett (Gaelic: *Baróid*, or *Bairéad*) escaped from Connacht with 24 galloglas and entered the service of the Earl of Kildare.

It remains improbable that a Barrett should have fought for the later King Henry VII at Bosworth Field in 1485 and received a knighthood in return, but this cannot be entirely ruled out.

[After Simms, Katherine: "Gaelic Warfare in the Middle Ages", in: Bartlett, Thomas and Keith, Jeffrey: *A Military History of Ireland*, Cambridge 1996, pp. 99-115.]

Sween castle in Scotland. (Photograph: Ralf Bergendahl)

Sween Castle, former home to the banished MacSween clan. (Photograph: Ralf Bergendahl)

THE EXILED CLANS

For whatever reasons, Walter Bisset[35], Lord of Abonye, could simply not get over the outcome of a tournament which had taken place at Haddington in 1242. He bore a particular grudge against Patrick, the 5th Earl of Atholl. To settle matters, Sir Walter set fire to the young Earl's house, and Patrick perished in the flames.

That of course was not the end of it. The fact that King Alexander II merely banished all male members of the Anglo-Norman Bisset family may serve as evidence of the high favour in which they had heretofore been held.[36] Many Bissets went to Ireland, from whence some moved on to England to enter the king's service.

The Bissets' estates and possessions were shared among the unmarried daughters of the banished menfolk, much to the delight of their future husbands. One line of the Bissets settled in Antrim on the Ulster coast, dubbing themselves "Lords of the Glens". Walter Bisset himself served the English King, making a name for himself in the chronicles as a dangerous enemy of the Gaelic Irish. He died in 1257.

One of Walter Bisset's descendants was Hugh Bisset. Hugh proved to be a turncoat during the Scottish War of Independence, changing sides several times.[37] It is not improbable that he sheltered Robert the Bruce after he had been driven from the Scottish mainland.

The Bissets were by no means the only ones to suffer the above-mentioned fate. The members of the MacSween and the MacDougall clans who had to leave their homeland for Ireland were in fact even more numerous. In 1262 the Scottish crown gave its blessing to the Stewarts of Menteith driving the MacSweens from most of their lands. In the following year they were forced by King Hákon of Norway to support his attack on Scotland, the MacSweens of Knapdale taking the field under the leadership of Murdoch (*Murchadh*) MacSween.[38] After the defeat of Norway they were forced to leave Scotland for good. Most went to Ulster to await an opportunity to return[39].

The first MacSween to be exiled to Ireland was one Murchadh MacSween (presumably identical with the afore-mentioned Murchadh), whom the Irish sources name as *MurchadhMac Suibne* in 1267. Taken prisoner by an Irish provincial king, he was handed over to the Earl of Ulster, in whose captivity he died.

After the defeat of the Scots at Dunbar in 1296 and the deposition of King John Balliol at the hands of King Edward I of England, the MacDougalls continued to resist the English in western Scotland. Edward I returned to England, sending the Earl of Ulster[40] to deal with the pockets of Scottish resistance in the rough and inaccessible West. Invading from Ulster, de Burgh's forces fought against Alexander (or *Alasdair*) MacDougall, Lord of Lorne, causing him to eventually change sides. The Comyns, fearing the confiscation of their estates in northern Scotland, followed his example. Over time, the MacDougalls became fairly reliable allies of the English crown. Old rivals of the MacDonalds, they signed a treaty with Edward I in 1301.[41]

Ewen (also called Lame John) MacDougall promised to defend Loch Awe against his compatriots. Three castles were situated around the shores of the Loch. Through the mountain range to the northwest a pass led to Oban, where the castles of Dunollie and Dunstaffnage guarded the approach to the sea. To force this redoubt was almost impossible, especially since the MacDougalls were a seafaring clan capable of supplying the castles from the sea with their longboats. To the south the MacSweens, allies of the MacDougalls, held Sween Castle.

Eventually the Scots found a new leader in Robert the Bruce. At first his kingship was mostly symbolic however. His small force was crushed by the English at Methven. During his flight he was confronted with Lame John MacDougall of Lorne blocking the road at Dail Righ to the south of a desolate moor. In the ensuing fight, the King of Scots and his retinue were repulsed. Robert managed to send his wife Elizabeth and his daughter Marjorie north to safety along with a small number of retainers. Bruce and his handful of remaining knights then set about fighting their way through, two hundred of them eventually reaching the shore of Loch Lomond. The crossing was arduous. Robert went into hiding in western Scotland, seeking help from the MacDonalds to rebuild his forces. His longboats later appeared on Loch Linnhe, forcing the MacDougalls to sign a temporary truce. Lame John MacDougall, sick in bed at Dunstaffnage Castle, sought to explain this move to the English King by claiming that his 800 warriors stood no chance against Robert's 15,000. In August 1308 Robert the Bruce left the Grampian Mountains and marched west. His objective was the territory of the MacDougalls of Lorne. Moving on Oban, he chose the route via the Pass of Brander. The troops were forced to march through difficult terrain. Lame John MacDougall had still not quite recovered from his illness when he boarded his own longboat to lead a squadron

---

35   Spelled *Byset* in oldersources.

36   MacDonald, Micheil: *The Clans of Scotland. The History and Landscap. of the Scottish clans*, London 1991, p. 73.

37   McDonald, Russell: *The Kingdom of the Isles. Scotland's western seaboard c. 1100-1336*, East Linton 1997, p. 167.

38   Hákon did not trust the McSweens and demanded hostages to secure their good conduct. Barrow, Geoffrey Wallace, Stuart: *Kingship and Unity: Scotland 1000-1306*, London 1981, pp. 111-115.

39   Cannan and Ó Brógáin: *Gallogllass*, p. 6.

40   Interestingly enough, Richard Óg de Burgh, 2nd Earl of Ulster, was the father-in-law of Robert the Bruce. At the height of his power at the beginning of the 14th century, he had built the mighty Northburgh Castle on the Inishowen peninsula in 1305. Fry, Plantagenet Somerset: *Castles of Britain and Ireland*, London et al. 1996, p. 218.

41   Seehase, Hagen and Oprotkowitz, Axel: *Die Highlander. Die Geschichte der schottischen Clans*, vol. 2, Greiz 2012, p. 17 f.

McSwynes Castle in County Donegal, former seat of the MacSweeney Banagh. (Photograph: Maximilian Bunk)

Kinbane Castle. (Photograph: Marko Tjemmes)

of ships to cruise Loch Awe. The majority of his highlanders were concealed in ambush on the slopes of Ben Cruachan, from which they had orders to pelt Bruce's force with rocks and boulders. Robert the Bruce had been warned in advance of this ruse however, and sent James Douglas together with a small detachment to take the MacDougalls in the flank. The MacDougalls suffered heavy casualties, and Lame John was forced to retire his ships to Innischonaill Castle. Alexander MacDougall withdrew behind the walls of Dunstaffage Castle, which was taken by Robert the Bruce in September or October of the same year. Dunollie and Sween Castle also fell, prompting Alexander MacDougall to swear allegiance to Robert, while Lame John fled south.

Although the MacDougalls' fortunes of war had eventually run out, they managed to retain their homelands, albeit suffering the loss of substantial amounts of land, and of their political status.[42] The MacSweens were not so lucky. Now landless, they were exiled to Ireland. Around 1300 a Murchadh Óg MacSweeney (Gaelic: *Mac Suibne*) married a woman from the Irish MacGinley clan. He was to become the founder of the three distinct lines of the MacSweeney clan: the MacSweeney Doe[43] and the MacSweeney Fanad came to dominate northern Donegal, while the MacSweeney Banagh (Gaelic: *Boghuine*) settled in Donegal's south-western region. Several minor Irish clans allied themselves with the MacSweeneys: the MacBrides, the MacGinleys, the Friels, and the Begleys.

Alasdair Óg MacDonald was the chief of the MacDonald clan whose power base was situated on the Scottish Western Isles. His younger brother Angus Óg was later to lay the foundations to the rise of the Lordship of the Isles. Towards the end of the 13th century Alasdair Óg was killed in battle, presumably while fighting the MacDougalls. He had been father to at least six sons, who emigrated to Ireland and became renowned leaders of galloglas. Three are mentioned in contemporary Irish chronicles as leading contingents of galloglas, and were founders of famous galloglas dynasties.[44] The most prominent member was Eóin Dubh, whose violent death was documented in the year 1349. These events constituted the dawning of the MacDonnell galloglas.[45] Some families from this galloglas clan settled in Ballygawley in Ulster.

The MacAllisters of Loup, a Scottish clan, are descended either from Alasdair Óg MacDonald, or from his uncle

Doe Castle, seat of the MacSweeneys Fanad.
(Photograph: Maximilian Bunk)

Alasdair Mor MacDonald. The MacAllisters of Antrim are a collateral line of this clan, who likewise made a name for themselves as galloglas.[46]

The MacCabes were a collateral line of the MacLeods and went to Ireland at the beginning of the 14th century. They served as galloglas, fighting for the O'Rourkes, the O'Reillys and the MacMahons in the Breifne district in southwestern Ulster. MacCabe galloglas are first recorded in 1368.

Apart from the political and military pressure exercised on individuals and entire clans in Scotland, there was also the economic aspect which persuaded many Scots to emigrate to Ireland. Ireland was richer compared to the rough and barren Hebrides, which were also fairly densely populated (population in some places actually exceeded today's numbers).

How are we to imagine the warriors from the Hebrides and the western coast of Scotland who left their homes to take foreign service? According to contemporary sources

---

42 Many MacDougalls, though by no means all, emigrated to Ireland nevertheless.

43 Doe Castle (Gaelic: Caisleán na dTuath), main seat of the MacSweeneys Doe, was built at a much later date.

44 Nicholls, Kenneth: "Scottish Mercenary Kindreds in Ireland 1250-1600", in Duffy, Seán: *The World of the Galloglass. Kings, Warriors and Warlords in Ireland and Scotland 1200-1600*, Dublin 2007, pp. 86-110 (p. 97).

45 In 1377 a certain „MacDowell the Gallogglass" fighting for the Irish O'Kelly and MacWilliam Burke clans was defeated at Roscommon.

46 They were given Kinbane Castle in Antrim in the middle of the 16th century.

Aghalard Castle, home of the MacDonnells of Knocknacloy. (Photograph: Maximilian Bunk)

they were very tall, which was presumably attributable to their Scandinavian origins. The legendary ancestor of the MacSweens was a Viking named Sweyn. Regarding dress and equipment, we must turn to the tomb effigies which form part of contemporary Scottish funereal art, the latter obviously adhering to common artistic convention at least in part. Archaeological finds from this period are extremely rare, since in a land almost devoid of iron resources arms and armour were passed on and used as long as they were serviceable. There is however one central source of lasting fame, the so-called "Lewis chessmen". These more than ninety chess pieces carved from walrus ivory were found on the Hebridean island of Lewis in the 19th century. The majority of the pieces depict warriors armed with swords and spears, both mounted and on foot.[47] The most important piece of defensive equipment was a long mail coat which could reach as far down as the knees. Some of these hauberks had attached mail coifs. Heads were protected by pointed conical helmets, some of which included a nosepiece. Some of these helmets also had cheekplates and neck protectors attached, which were either of metal or boiled leather. These helmets were supplemented by an early form of kettle hat (*chapel-de-fer*). Warriors relied on shields as their prime source of protection, the round form eventually giving way to the drop-shaped kite shield. The most popular offensive weapons were spears and war-axes, the mighty long-hefted Danish axe being particularly common. Swords resembled Scandinavian models[48]. This combination of equipment proved to be extremely long-lived and was to change only very little over the centuries. Even in later years, Ireland continued to to be the preferred choice of secondary residence for Scotsmen whose presence had become too hot to handle for their clans. Some of them were widely known, one even hailing from the ruling family of the "Lords of the Isles".

John MacDonald was the ruler of the semi-autonomous MacDonald realm in western Scotland. He even stylized himself Lord of the Isles.[49] When his brother-in-law, the last chief of the MacRuaridhs died in 1346 (John was married to his sister Amy), John was the rightful heir.

In the Scottish War of Independence, John vacillated between the English and Scottish factions. At first supporting the English against David II King of Scots, he operated from the safety of Ireland. Later he shifted his loyalty to the Scottish crown. For a short while, John took up residence in Drogheda in Ireland.[50] He had a son by his second wife named Marcus (*Marcach*) MacDonald, who settled in Ulster and founded the MacDonalds of Knocknacloy. This line fought as galloglas for the MacNeills. Marcus himself along with many of his men met his end in a battle fought in Connaght in 1397.

Marcus's older brother, John Mor Tanister *(Gaelic: Eóin Mór Tánaiste Mac Dhómnaill)*, rebelled against his elder brother Donald, who had succeeded his father John as Lord of the Isles. The rebellion collapsed, and John Mor was forced to flee, reaching Ulster via Galloway. Seeking employment, he offered his service to King Richard II. In 1399 he married Marjorie Bisset, heiress of John Bisset, Lord of the Glens.[51] John Mor thus became a semi-feudal lord over a large number of Ulster's Old Irish population, yet there was no mass immigration of MacDonalds to Ireland as a consequence of John Mor's elevated rank. In 1401 official documents mention him as "Lord of the Glens of Antrim".[52]

In 1427 John Mor and a certain James Campbell met at Ard-du on Islay. Campbell killed John Mor Tanister, possibly at the instigation of the King of Scots. John Mor's son Donald Balloch MacDonald[53] (Gaelic: *Dómhnall Ballach Mac Dhómnaill*) rose to become a famous leader of galloglas.

---

[47] Contemporary weapons excavated in Scandinavia and the Baltic region corroborate the image of warriors as conveyed by the Lewis chessmen.

[48] Seehase, Hagen: *Der schottische Clan MacDonald. Aufstieg und Fall der Herren der Inseln*, Greiz 2008, p. 129.

[49] The title of *Dominus Insularum* was acknowledged by the Scottish crown in 1350.

[50] Smith, Brendan: *Crisis and survival in late medieval Ireland. The English of Louth and their neighbours 1330-1450*, Oxford 2013, p. 31.

[51] Cathcart, Alison: "James V, King of Scotland – and Ireland?", in: Duffy, Seán: *The World of the Galloglass. Kings, Warlords and Warriors in Ireland and Scotland, 1200-1600*, Dublin 2007, pp. 124-143 (p. 127).

[52] Seehase, *Der schottische Clan MacDonald*, p. 27.

[53] Also called Donald Balloch MacDonnell in various sources.

The Battle of Dysert O'Dea

The Battle of Dysert O'Dea on 10th May 1318 was not immediately related to the Scottish invasion of Ireland. Dysert O'Dea is situated between Ennis and Corofin, a region belonging to the Kingdom of Thomond ruled by the O'Brien clan. Thomond had been given as a fiefdom to Thomas de Clare by King Edward I of England, although it was not his to give since he by no means controlled it. The de Clares had erected a mighty stronghold in the form of Bunratty Castle.

Meanwhile there had occurred a bloody feud between the different lines of the O'Briens, from which Turlough O'Brien emerged as the victor. He ruled Thomond until his death in 1306. Turlough's men had succeeded in destroying Quin Castle, which had also been built by the Normans. All attempts to seize Bunratty Castle met with failure however. While Turlough's son Donough ruled the O'Brien clan after his father's death, Thomas de Clare's nephew Richard succeeded his uncle in 1308. Richard backed one Dermot O'Brien, who had begun to challenge Donough's rule. Donough in turn did not remain idle but secured the support of the Norman de Burghs of Connacht. When Donough was killed, it briefly appeared as if his enemies had reached their goals. But Dermot O'Brien died shortly afterwards, and Donough's successor Murtough O'Brien defeated the other O'Briens in a battle fought at Corcomroe Abbey. Murtough's troops included Anglo-Norman mercenaries, the Comyns and the Condons.

Murlough's men had raided Richard de Clare's cattle stock, prompting de Clare to embark on a punitive expedition from Bunratty Castle. According to a local legend, he came across a woman dressed in white washing blood-soaked linen by the river. In response to his question whose clothing she was washing, she is said to have replied "Yours", and vanished.

De Clare had a few mounted knights at his disposal, but the majority of his troops consisted of bow- and spear-armed foot soldiers. The O'Brien faction which had suffered defeat at Corcomroe contributed a number of light-armed cavalry and foot soldiers. The Condons had changed sides and declared for de Clare (*translator's note: no pun intended*). On the morning of 10th May 1318 de Clare and his force invaded O'Dea territory. De Clare split his force into three marching columns, himself taking command of the central column. His objective was the seat of the chief of the O'Dea, which he intended to destroy (O'Dea Castle, erected between 1470 an 1490 by Dermot O'Dea, marks the spot to this day).

At Logh Ballycullinan de Clare's advance guard ran into men of Connor O'Dea *(Gaelic: Conchobar Ò Deághaidh)* fording a river with a drove of cattle. De Clare's men immediately attacked, forcing the O'Deas to gradually give ground while constantly pelting their opponents with arrows, javelins, and stones. Others meanwhile attempted to save the livestock. Hotly pursued by de Clare, O'Dea made for a second ford. O'Dea was hoping for succour from other local Gaelic chiefs, e. g. O'Connor of Corcomroe and Loughlin O'Hehir. Apart from that he had concealed a number of his men in ambush nearby. As de Clare's warriors scrambled up the river bank, O'Dea's reserves attacked. While a part of these warriors attacked de Clare's advance guard, others went for de Clare's main body, which was still negotiating the river crossing. The first attack succeeded, killing de Clare, the second was repulsed however. The Anglo-Normans rallied and counter-attacked. At that moment O'Connor's warriors arrived on the scene, presently joined by the forces of the O'Hehirs and MacNamaras. O'Dea's warriors attempted to break through the Anglo-Norman force in order to reach these fresh troops. According to legend O'Connor and Richard de Clare's son faced each other in single combat, with O'Connor killing his opponent, but still the Normans were not beaten. It was left to Murtough O'Brien himself to save the day. His arrival together with a small force tipped the scales in favour of the Irish, the Normans suffering heavy casualties. The allied chiefs' troop numbers may have amounted to around 1,000 men, while de Clare may have fielded between 600 and 800, of which about 500 were killed.

When Murtough approached Bunratty, according to legend he found it in flames. Richard de Clare's widow Joan had ordered the destruction of castle and town, and escaped to Limerick by boat. In fact the castle continued for a while to be garrisoned by five knights, twelve light-armed cavalry, and 78 foot soldiers. Only in 1332 was Bunratty razed by Irishmen from Thomond.

The kingdom of the O'Briens in Thomond was now secure. Bunratty Castle was later rebuilt by Sir Thomas Rokeby. Immediately after its completion it was captured by Gaelic Irish forces, a Gaelic chief of the MacNamara clan adding the finishing touches in 1425.

It is worthwhile taking a closer look at the leading characters on the O'Brien side. They wore mail coats over padded aketons, mail coifs, and pointed conical helmets, thus resembling early galloglas. This is how they appear in the *Caithréim Thoirdhealbhaig* Chronicle, written by a member of the MacGrath clan between 1350 and 1375.

[After Hayes-McCoy, Gerard Anthony: *Irish Battles. A Military History of Ireland*, Belfast 1969]

Bunratty Castle. (Photograph: Maximilian Bunk)

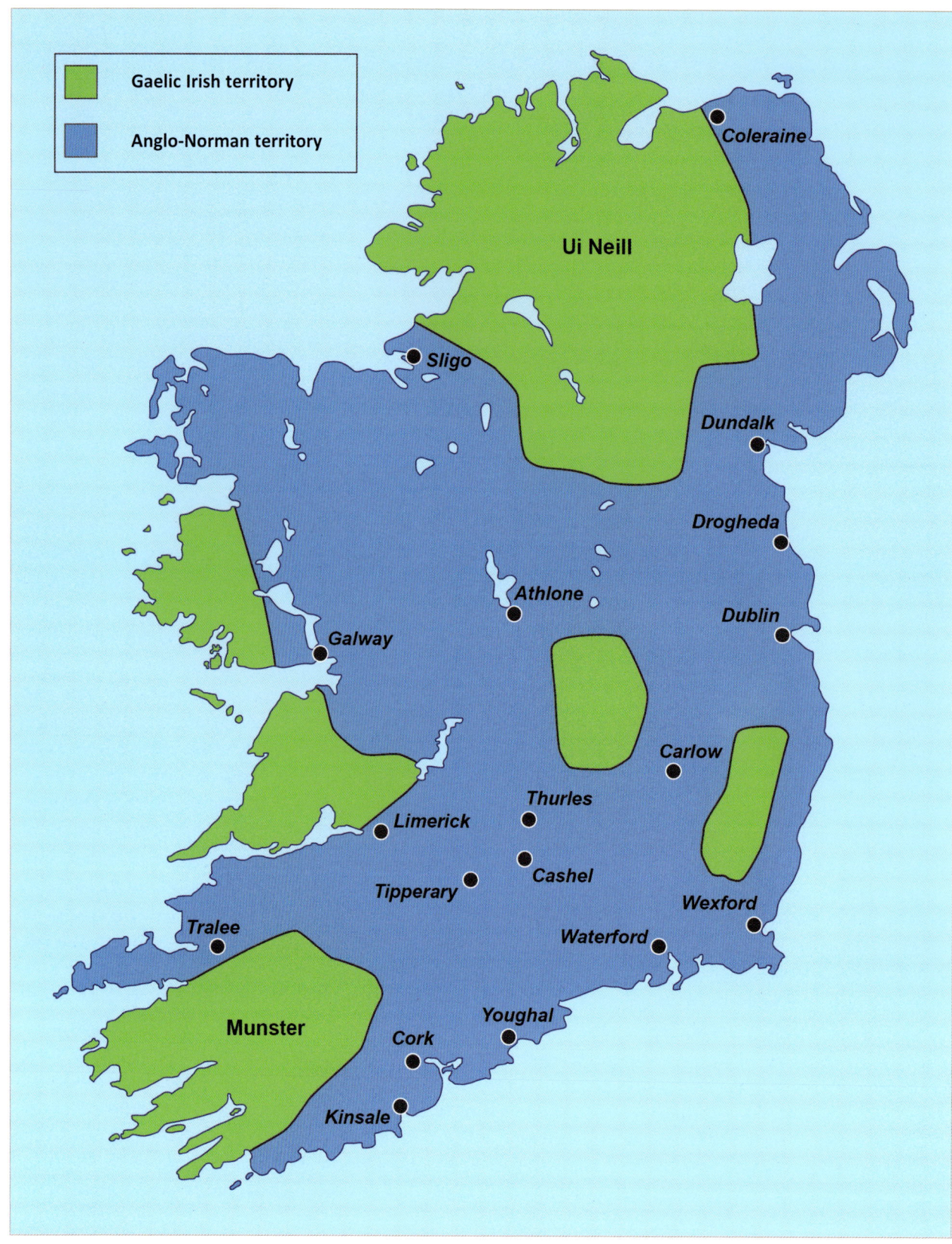

Ireland in c. 1300

THE SCOTTISH INVASION

The fleet that landed on the coast of Antrim presumably carried the largest army which Ireland had seen to date. At any rate, it was certainly the best. The battle-hardened Scots in its ranks were to have a profound influence on the military history of Ireland. The Anglo-Norman knights opposing them had already passed the zenith of their military prowess when the extent of the Norman conquest of Ireland had reached its peak.

At the end of the 13th century, the lance-armed, heavily armoured knight was no longer the unchallenged master of the battlefield. In the second half of the 13th and early 14th centuries heavily-armed contingents of foot soldiers had gained an edge over the mounted knight. In Ireland, many Norman nobles were forced to adapt to the local circumstances as Irish horses were small, stocky and austere, and lacked the size of the heavy European chargers. Cavalry charges accordingly decreased in power and impact.

Another new military evolution was that of the *hobilar*, an infantryman mounted on an Irish pony.

Taxes and Irish warriors were a valuable aid for the English crown and its incessant quarrels with the unruly Scots. After defeating a powerful English army at Bannockburn in 1314, the Scots decided to mount a full-scale campaign in Ireland with the aim of weakening or even completely destroying this stronghold of English resources.

The roots of the Scottish invasion can at least in part be traced to the Irish King of Tyrone's (Gaelic: *Tír Eógain*) appeal for help against repeated attacks by the Earls of Ulster and other Anglo-Norman barons. Together with twelve of his vassals and allies, King Donald O'Néill finally called on King Robert the Bruce for assistance.

A number of important decisions were meanwhile being taken in England: The parliament at York had appointed Lame John MacDougall of Lorne admiral of the Western Fleet. His command consisted of twelve ships, which had been financed from the coffers of the Dublin Lordship's government. MacDougall's second-in-command Duncan MacGoffrey seized the Isle of Man in mid-February 1315, capturing its Scottish garrison.[54] This lone bit of military success was enough to restore King Edward II's high spirits. He immediately ordered the recruitment of 10,000 soldiers in Ireland and the building of sixty ships to follow up this victory by landing on the western coast of Scotland. Things were to take a very different course however.

Olderfleet Castle.
(Photograph: Marko Tjemmes)

On 26th May 1315 Edward Bruce[55] landed near Olderfleet Castle[56] with an army of Scots numbering between 5,000 and 6,000 warriors. An army composed mostly of Anglo-Norman barons and their retainers (de Mandeville, de Burgh, Savage, Logan, Bisset) led by Thomas Randolph de Moray marched to meet the threat, and was defeated. Carrickfergus was taken, but Carrickfergus Castle stubbornly resisted the invaders' attempts to capture it. It was eventually taken after a prolonged siege in September 1316.

The Scottish army chiefly consisted of warriors from Carrick (Edward Bruce was the Earl of Carrick), who were armed with long spears and fought in the traditional schiltron formation. Most wore some form of armour. Other soldiers hailed from the Hebridean clans of the MacDonalds, MacRuaridhs et al.[57] Their equipment resembled that of the Lewis Chessmen.

Leaving men to garrison Carrickfergus, Bruce turned south to seize Dundalk. His Scottish veterans had no trouble in

---

54 Traquair, Peter: *Freedom's Sword. Scotland's Wars of Independence*, London 1998, p. 203.

55 Edward was a younger brother of King Robert the Bruce. With his brother away in Ireland, the King of Scots led a parallel naval campaign to subdue a number of rebellious Hebridean clans. Pennan, Michael: *The Scottish civil war. The Bruces & the Balliols & the war for control of Scotland*, Stroud 2002, p. 83.

56 The ruins on the present site are those of a subsequent structure.

57 These clans also provided most of the ships.

Roche Castle.
(Photograph: Marko Tjemmes)

Opposite page:
A Scottish warrior from the time of Robert the Bruce.
(Illustration: Sascha Lunyakov)

breaking local resistance at the Moyry Pass in June 1315.[58] Roche Castle, in the possession of the de Verdon family, was taken. The Scots then captured Dundalk. Most inhabitants, whether Irish or Anglo-Norman, were put to the sword. This brutality became the hallmark of the Scottish invasion. Any form of resistance was crushed ruthlessly.

The Scots lived off a land which had been suffering from a number of meagre harvests. The plundering of the monasteries added to the evil reputation which Edward and his Scottish army had begun to acquire. The Scottish invasion constituted a heavy blow to the English cause in Ireland. Only when King Edward sent John de Hotham to Dublin to look into affairs and who immediately requested five hundred pounds worth of subsidies did the King realize the seriousness of the situation. John de Hotham urgently needed the money to recruit soldiers to counteract the Scots, but King Edward simply lacked the means.

John Butler's Dublin government had meanwhile succeeded in raising an army, which marched to join forces with the Earl of Ulster's contingent at Louth. A rather over-optimistic Earl of Ulster persuaded Butler that he was perfectly capable of dealing with the Scots on his own. He even refused to provide the royal army with supplies from his estates. Butler was forced to disband his army, which he was now no longer able to either pay or feed.

The Earl's confidence proved premature. His Connacht allies were neutralized by a clever ruse from Edward Bruce – he promised to support King Felim O'Connor's claim to the throne of Connacht against his rivals, among them Rory MacCathal O'Connor, if he agreed to withdraw his troops in return. Edward then slyly offered the same support to Rory MacCathal, who promptly set off to Connacht to raise rebellion against Felim O'Connor.

Edward now had his hands free to deal with the Earl of Ulster. He feigned retreat and lured the Anglo-Irish force into a trap, inflicting a resounding defeat on the Earl of Ulster at Connor on 10th September 1315. He then went into winter quarters, staying with one of his friends, a Norman baron from the de Lacy family. On 26th January he defeated another English army under John de Hotham at Ardscull. On the English side William Prendergast and Hamon le Gras were among the slain, the Scots lost Fergus of Androssan and Sir Walter Moray.[59]

Edward Bruce was crowned King of Ireland on the hill of Knocknemelan near Dundalk in 1316.[60] In solemn words, Domnall O'Neill from the royal house of Ireland's High

---

58   MacDuilechain of Clanbrassil and MacArtain of Iveagh, two Irish chiefs who had paid homage to Edward at Carrickfergus, attempted to destroy the Scottish army in an ambush but were defeated.

59   Connellan, Owen (ed.): *Annals of the Four Masters*, Dublin 1846, p. 112.

60   Seehase, Hagen and Oprotkowitz, Axel: *Bannockburn. Schottlands Kampf um die Freiheit*, Greiz 1999, p. 106.

The equipment of this galloglass betrays strong Scottish influence. (© Claíomh – Dave Swift 2018)

Kings transferred his ancient rights to Edward. But possession of the Irish crown did not automatically ensure control of the country as a whole.

Several local Irish chieftains and minor Anglo-Norman nobles now joined Bruce's cause. But food had become so hard to come by in the meantime that many Anglo-Normans and Irish fought the Scots only for sheer self-preservation. So pitiful had crops become that they were simply in no position to supply both an invading army and themselves. Support for the Scots was restricted to specific areas, and a universal revolt against English rule certainly never materialized. After all, the English did not control all of Ireland, either.

Local magnates decided to take advantage of the Scottish campaign anyway. Felim O'Connor, the King of Connacht (Gaelic: *Felim mac Aedh Ua Conchobair*) seized what he thought was an opportunity to crown himself High King of Erin. He and his new ally (and former opponent) Teig O'Kelly (Gaelic *Tadhg Ó Cellaigh*), King of the provincial realm of Ui Maine on the middle reaches of the River Shannon, faced the army of the English Vice Justiciar of Ireland, Sir William Liath de Burgh, at Athenry on 10th August 1316. De Burgh's force of c. 1,100 had a number of galloglas[61] in its ranks as well as a Gaelic contingent under Murtough O'Brien, King of Thomond.[62] The Connacht and Ui Maine force (probably only 2,500 strong) was defeated, O'Connor and O'Kelly both being killed in the fighting.[63]

The Scots moved their operational base to Ulster, which was friendly to them and where the local population supported the invaders. Bruce however found that he did not have the forces at his disposal which would have been necessary to break out of the province. Thomas Randolph de Moray returned to Scotland in autumn to gather reinforcements, returning in December with fresh troops. The Scots now crossed the border of Ulster and marched south to Leinster, where they defeated the troops of Roger Mortimer at Meath and beat another English army at Skerries.[64] But the latter victory was hard-fought and brought little strategic gain. Losses were so high that Bruce was forced to withdraw to Ulster. Randolph again undertook the voyage to Scotland and in February 1317 once more managed to bring reinforcements to Ireland, along with King Robert the Bruce himself. The King of Scots reckoned Scotland safe from English invasion for the time being and took the Irish campaign into his own hands.[65]

Robert and Edward led their forces to the gates of Dublin and deep into the south of Ireland. Their objective was clear enough, namely to foment rebellion among the Gaelic Irish. In Dublin the arrival of the Scottish army caused widespread panic, but Robert made no attempt to seize the town. Instead, he turned his attention towards Munster and crossed the island from east to southwest, eventually reaching Limerick. The Scots had hoped to gain support from the local O'Brien clan, but Murtough O'Brien, who controlled the O'Brien's provincial kingdom, remained hostile. The Scots retreated to Ulster, and Robert the Bruce and Thomas Randolph returned to Scotland.

It was left to Thomas Dun, the commander of the Scottish fleet, to secure the lines of communication between Scotland and Ulster. Unfortunately, Scotland was unable to provide its forces serving in Ireland with sufficient supplies. This circumstance as well as local food shortages caused Edward's army to wither away. Many Scottish soldiers died, and the combat value of those still alive diminished steadily. Meanwhile, King Edward II had appointed Roger Mortimer Lieutenant of Ireland. With a small English force Mortimer landed in Ireland. The Scots were forced to watch helplessly, as all available reserves were employed in the fighting around Berwick. There would be no further reinforcements for Edward the Bruce.

When Edward once again attempted to cross the border from Ulster in October 1318, his force was intercepted by an English army commanded by John de Bermingham at Faughart near Dundalk. While Edward had at his disposal some 2,000 to 3,000 Scots as well as a few renegade Anglo-Norman barons and their retinues along with a large number of Irish warriors (most of them from Ulster), John de Bermingham's force numbered between 3,000 and 4,000, among them archers and a large number of mounted troops.[66]

On 14th October 1318 Edward Bruce deployed his army in three battle lines on the slopes of Faughart Hill. Unfortunately for the Scots, the distance between these lines was so great that mutual assistance was all but impossible. The Scottish schiltrons were positioned on the right with the allied Anglo-Normans and Irish from Meath holding the centre. The Ulstermen stood on the left wing. Bermingham likewise chose to deploy his force

---

[61] This was the first officially documented employment of galloglas in the service of the English crown on Irish soil. The opposing ranks probably also included a number of galloglas. A certain Duncan MacRory was killed together with 100 galloglas while serving the O'Connor clan (this incident may also have occurred slightly earlier during the conflict between Felim and Rory O'Connor). Duncan was presumably the son of Allan MacRuaridh, who had brought the first galloglas to Ireland.

[62] O'Brien took Anglo-Norman mercenaries into his service, the Condons and the Comyns. Simms, Katherine: "The Battle of Dysert O'Dea and the Gaelic Resurgence in Thomond", in: *Dal gCais* vol. 5 (1979), pp. 59-66 (p. 66).

[63] De Burgh and his second-in-command Rickard de Bermingham were both good examples of the gradual mingling of Anglo-Normans with the indigenous Gaelic populace: de Burgh was married to Finola Ni Briain, while Bermingham's mother was from the O'Kelly clan.

[64] The situation became so desperate that the English King actually considered employing 1,000 Genoese mercenaries for service in Ireland.

[65] A contingent from Breifne (presumably the O'Reillys) was defeated at Kilmore in southern Ulster in 1317. Among the slain was the galloglas commander of the MacRorys, along with 150 galloglas.

[66] Many of these mounted troops were in fact not knights but men-at-arms, who were not members of the nobility.

in three lines with his archers facing the Irish, and his own Anglo-Norman knights facing Edward's. The Scots were to be dealt with by heavily-armed foot soldiers.

The attack of the English infantry pushed the Scots back. Edward rode out and managed to rally them together with the Anglo-Normans, and then led them to renew their attack. In the meantime the English archers had hit the Irish hard, forcing them into retreat with showers of arrows. But then their ammunition gave out, and they were routed by a timely Irish counterattack.[67] At this time Edward Bruce, having engaged Sir John Maupas[68] in single combat, was cut down and killed. On hearing the news of the death of their leader, the Scots broke ranks and fled.[69] The remains of the Scottish force managed to retreat to Carrickfergus, picking up reinforcements on the way.

Most Scottish leaders had perished in the fighting. John Thomson led the Scottish army back to Carrick.[70]

The victorious Bermingham had Edward Bruce's head soaked in brine to facilitate preservation, and sent it to King Edward II. Delighted by this grisly trophy, the king made Bermingham Earl of Louth. The Scots Irish campaign was over. To many Irish chroniclers, the death of Edward Bruce came as a relief:

„Edward Bruce, destroyer of all Ireland in general, both English and Irish, was killed by the English in main battle by their valour at Dundalk (…) for there was not a better deed that redounded more to the good of the kingdom since the creation of the world."[71]

Not until 1322 would the English King be able to resume the recruitment of Irish soldiers for his Scottish campaigns. The Scottish invasion had indeed all but put an end to Ireland's effective potential as a military source for the English crown. Scottish success had however been gained mostly at the expense of the civilian population, which helps to explain the hostility towards the Scots expressed in the above-quoted chronicle.[72] The English hold on Ireland relaxed, at least for the time being: in Leinster, the heartland of Anglo-Norman rule, Gaelic chiefs elected Donal MacMurrough provincial ruler in 1327.[73]

All over Ireland, Anglo-Norman settlements and towns fell into decline. Some, among them Coleraine, Roscommon, Rindown, Athlone and Mullingar, were temporarily abandoned.[74] English rule over Ulster (which at any rate had never been complete) had been largely removed, and many local Anglo-Norman lords, having fought on both sides, lay strewn across the battlefields of the Scots campaign. Some parts of Ulster, depopulated by both famine and war, became the new home of Scots soldiers who had fought in Edward Bruce's army. Most of these Gaels, stemming from the western Scottish coasts and the Hebrides, found it fairly easy to assimilate to the culture of their new surroundings.

One of these Scots was Hector MacDonald, chieftain of the powerful MacDonald clan, cousin to Angus Òg, effective leader of the Western Scottish clansfolk. Angus Òg had married an Irish noblewoman by the name of Aine O'Cahan[75]. Hector stayed in Ireland, took an Irish wife and gave himself the epithet *Sithigh*[76]. He became the founder of the MacSheehys.

Scots mercenaries were widely sought after: already in 1316 the O'Neills had employed Scottish galloglas in Ulster.[77]

The Scots invasion combined with catastrophic harvests and the effects of the fighting between Irish petty kings and their Anglo-Norman enemies brought about the widespread collapse of Anglo-Norman rule over Ireland.[78]

---

67 Heath, Ian: *Armies of the Middle Ages*, vol. 1. Worthing 1982, p. 57.
68 Sir John Maupas was also killed. His surname is also spelled „Malpas".
69 Joyce, Patrick Weston: *A concise history of Ireland*, New York 1903, p. 160.
70 Paterson, James: *History of the County Ayr*, vol. 1. Ayr 1847, p. 39.
71 *Annala Rioghachta Eireann: Annals of the Kingdom of Ireland, by the Four Masters, from the earliest period to the year 1616, translated by O'Donovan, John (2nd ed.), 1856*, 7 volumes, Royal Irish Academy (Edt.), here: volume 3, page 520:
72 Schreiber, Hermann: *Irland. Seine Geschichte – Seine Menschen*, Augsburg 1997, p. 210.
73 Newark, Tim and McBride, Angus: *Warlords*, London 1996, p. 252.
74 Bradley, John: „Anglo-Norman Towns", in: Ryan, Michael (ed.): *The Illustrated Archaeology of Ireland*, Dublin 1991, pp. 177-183 (p. 178).
75 Aine's dowry allegedly included 140 warriors from Ulster, who settled in the West Highlands. Their descendants supposedly became the Munro clan. MacDonald of Castleton, Donald J.: *Clan Donald*, Gretna 2008, p. 61.
76 A certain *Uilliam macSithigh*, obviously son of Hector Sithigh MacDonald, was killed in battle at Belta Strand in 1367 along with other galloglas. The conflict concerned revolved around the realm of Connacht (by now largely of symbolic significance), to which several factions from the O'Connor clan had laid claim, each side in turn supported by various contesting group. of Burkes. The MacDonald galloglas, who eventually lost the battle, faced the galloglas of the MacSweeneys. Nicholls, *Scottish Mercenary Kindreds in Ireland*, p. 93 f.
77 Simms, Katharine: *From Kings to Warlords. The changing political structure of Gaelic Ireland in the later Middle Ages*, Woodbridge 2000, p. 122.
78 In 1327/8 Edward Bruce helped to instal William de Burgh, his wife's under-age nephew, as the new Earl of Ulster. Penman, Michael A.: "The MacDonald Lordship and the Bruce Dynasty", in: Oran, Richard D.: *The Lordship of the Isles*, Leyden and Boston 2014, pp. 62-87 (p. 72).

**Irish light cavalryman
(researched and recreated by David O'Reilly of the Irish Chariot Project).**
(© Claíomh – Dave Swift 2021)

The de Burgh Civil War

William Donn de Burgh, the future 3rd Earl of Ulster and 4th Baron of Connaught, was only thirteen years old when his grandfather Richard Óg de Burgh, 2nd Earl of Ulster, passed away on 29th July 1326. William Donn was the only son of Richard de Burgh, who had died in battle in 1313. Having spent his childhood in England and returning to Ireland on the news of his grandfather's death, he now inherited the province of Ulster. Though still a minor, he became Earl of Ulster in 1327. On 10th December 1327, "Baron Burgh" became a Member of Parliament by Writ of Summons. He was knighted in the following year. In the year 1328 he was also given Carrickfergus Castle by the English crown, Athlone Castle following in 1330. From 1330 to 1331, William Donn was Lord Lieutenant of Ireland. In 1327 he had married Maud of Lancaster, who later gave birth to a daughter, Elizabeth.

Paradoxically William Donn (also called "The Brown Earl"), found himself supported both by the new English King Edward III and (until his death) by King Robert the Bruce, who was married to Willam's aunt Elizabeth de Burgh.

Earl William soon suspected another powerful local magnate, Maurice FitzGerald, 1st Earl of Desmond, of conspiring against him together with Walter Liath de Burgh (son of Walter Liath de Burgh the Elder, who had won the battle of Athenry in 1316), and Henry de Mandeville, Senescal of Ulster.

In 1330 William attacked Sir Walter Liath de Burgh and Henry de Mandeville in both Ulster and Connacht. Henry de Mandeville escaped to Dublin, where he was taken prisoner, while Walter Liath de Burgh and his two brothers were captured by William in November 1331. They were taken to Northburgh Castle on the Inishowen peninsula, thrown into the dungeons, and slowly left to starve. According to local legend, one of Earl William's sisters took pity on Sir Walter, and while bringing him food fell to her death from the battlements of the castle. Walter Liath de Burgh died in February 1332. Determined to avenge her brother, his sister Gylle de Burgh persuaded her husband Robert FitzRichard de Mandeville to murder the Earl, assisted by John de Logan and others.

The conspirators struck at Carrickfergus on 6th June 1333. The English crown inflicted severe punishments on the murderers, while the Earl's wife and daughter were taken to England to safety. A further result of the murder was a bloody feud that developed between Earl William's retainers and the de Mandevilles.

William's estates were taken over by Walter's brother Edmond Albanach de Burgh from Connacht, who called himself MacWilliam forthwith, and declared his independence from the English crown. He founded the *Mac William Íochtar* (Lower Mac William) line, who also became known as the Mayo Burkes. This family was to adopt Gaelic customs and lifestyle.

Edmond de Burgh, who was Earl William's uncle, was also the founder of the William Burke line in County Limerick. An illegitimate son of an earlier de Burgh, presumably named Uick, founded the Clanricade line, also known as *Mac William Uachtar* (Upper Mac William), or Galway Burkes. While the Mayo Burkes and the Galway Burkes divided almost the entire estates of the Earls of Ulster in Connacht among themselves, the estates in Ulster itself fell to local Irish-Gaelic magnates, among them the O'Donnells and O'Neills.

Meanwhile, the O'Doherty clan (Gaelic: Ó Dochartaigh) took Northburgh castle for themselves. Earl William's daughter married Lionel, Duke of Clarence, second son of Edward III of England. *De iure uxoris* Lionel was the new Earl of Ulster. Although his power was now restricted to the south-east of Ulster, his estates still yielded a fair amount of income.

The Duke of Clarence also presided over the Parliament which passed the Statutes of Kilkenny in 1366. As from now, all relations between Anglo-Normans and Gaelic Irish – marriage, concubinage, and adoption – were strictly prohibited by law. Neither the Anglo-Normans themselves, nor the Irish servants of their households, were permitted to speak Gaelic. Anglo-Normans were forbidden to wear Irish costume, or bear Irish names. However, this attempt to prevent the Gaelicisation of the Anglo-Norman nobility met with no success.

[After Foster, Robert F.: *The Oxford History of Ireland*, Oxford 2001]

THE 14th AND 15th CENTURIES

Brian MacMahon was a difficult man to get on with. He was of violent character, and extremely ambitious at that. Brian was clan chief of the MacMahons and kinglet of Airgialla[79]. His plan was to ally himself with Somairle MacDonnell, galloglas commander of the O'Neills of Tyrone. Somairle had hereditary claims to the Lordship of the Isles and was thus considered a suitable wedding candidate for MacMahon's daughter. The trouble was that the galloglas constable was already betrothed (or even married) to the daughter of the O'Reilly chieftain.

Somairle had to be persuaded to get rid of his spouse, and so in 1365 MacMahon invited the constable to *Rath Tulach*, his place of counsel. After much drinking, the two men took to quarreling. MacMahon slung his arms around Somairle, rendering the latter immobile, and had his hands tied behind his back. The helpless MacDonnell was thrown into a nearby lake.[80]

This heinous deed caused the O'Neills to suspend their own incessant quarreling and in a rare act of unison to invade Airgialla together with MacDonnell's former command under its new constable Turlough Mor MacDonnell. Airgialla suffered considerable damage, but the elusive MacMahon managed to make good his escape. The O'Neills made Neill MacMahon new chieftain of the MacMahons in 1368.[81] Brian MacMahon hurriedly offered Neill half of his estates if he promised to forgo his claim to the chieftainship.

Brian MacMahon also offered the MacDonnells part of his estates in compensation for Somairle MacDonnell's untimely death. The Macdonnells and Neill MacMahon remained unimpressed however. Neill MacMahon joined forces with a galloglas constable by name of Alexander MacDonnell, and both moved against Brian MacMahon. Brian defeated the enemy force, and both Neill MacMahon and Alexander MacDonnell were killed. Brian MacMahon himself was eventually killed by a disgruntled kinsman in 1372.[82]

In the later Middle Ages the Irish provicial kings gradually developed from lawmakers and founders of monasteries to warriors and warlords. In the year 1395 a remarkable encounter occurred between Gaelic chieftains and the King of England: Richard II was one of the very few medieval English monarchs to visit Ireland.[83] The presence of his interpreter, Thomas Talbot by name, enabled the King to confer with the local Gaelic-Irish magnates in person.[84] Two of the Irish-Gaelic chiefs to pay their respect to King Richard were Philip MacMahon of Oriel and his brother Aedh.[85] The brothers had brought along the constable of their galloglas, a man named Thomas MacCabe of Clogher. At the Dominican priory of Drogheda, the monarch and the leader of galloglas met.

Another person of interest was Shane MacDonnell, chief of the MacDonnells. He had written to Richard II from Armagh expressing his wish to enter royal service.[86]

During the first half of the 15th century, galloglas had rarely made appearances outside Ulster and Connacht. One exception of note were the galloglas who under one Gregory MacRyry (*sc.* MacRory) took part in Maurice FitzGerald's attack on Youghal in 1428. This Gregory Macryry had been the constable of Turlough O'Connor's galloglas force in Connacht.[87]

In the second half of the 15th century galloglas still mostly restricted their activity to Ulster.[88] The first formal compact exchanging land against military service was probably agreed between Turlough O'Donnell King of Tyrconnell (r. 1380-1422) and the chief of the MacSweeneys Fanad.[89] It was agreed that whenever the king commanded his army in person, the latter would supply two men for every "quarter" of land received. A fine of two cows was fixed for every man that failed to show up when summoned (one animal for the warrior himself, and one for his armour).[90]

In 1423 the Gaelic chieftains of Ulster attacked Meath. The O'Donnell and O'Neill contingents were accompanied by the MacSweeney Banagh galloglas. These were commanded by Mulmurry (Gaelic: *Maolmhuire*) MacSweeney, constable in the O'Donnell army. In northeastern Meath the Ulstermen were met by an English force which had marched from the Pale to stop them. In the ensuing vicious engagement Mulmurry MacSweeney

---

79 Alternative spellings are *Airghialla* and *Oirghialla*, from which *Oriel* is derived.

80 Smith, Brendan: *Crisis and Survival in late medieval Ireland. The English of Louth and their neighbours 1330-1450*, Oxford 2013, p. 52 f.

81 Schlegel: *The MacDonnells of Tyrone and Armagh*, p. 198.

82 A suborned galloglass is said to have killed a chieftain of the MacMahons in 1425.

83 Richard II visited Ireland in the years 1394 and 1395, and a second time in 1399. On his first visit he was accompanied by a force of c. 10,000 men, thereby forcing many Gaelic chiefs into submission. Smith, Brendan and Frame, Robin: *Ireland and the English world in the late Middle Ages*, Basingstoke 2009, p. 149.

84 During his stay, King Richard made the chief of the O'Connors Don constable of Roscommon Castle.

85 Curtis, Edmund: *Richard II in Ireland 1394-95, and Submissions of the Irish Chiefs*, Oxford 1927, p. 39.

86 Cannan and Ó Broghain: *Galloglass*, p. 50. It is worthy of note that some Irish chieftains refused to show up, among them the O'Donnells of Tyrconnell, and the O'Dohertys.

87 One year after the Youghal fighting, Maurice FitzGerald was made 1st Earl of Desmond in the wake of a local feud between the Barrys and the Cogans. He is credited with inventing the system of coyne and livery. Lydon, James: "The Scottish Soldier in medieval Ireland", in: Simpson, Grant G.: *The Scottish soldier abroad 1267-1967*, Edinburgh and Maryland 1992, pp. 1-15 (p. 10).

88 In 1361 and 1362 a certain Donaldus Gall acted as a leader of mercenaries in the service of the Lordship of Dublin's government in the Wicklow Mountains. He was undoubtedly a galloglass, and so were his men. Lydon: *Scottish soldier in medieval Ireland*, p. 10.

89 The MacSweeney Fanad's stronghold was Rathmullan Castle, of which nothing remains today. McInerney, Luke: "The Galloglass of Thomond", in *North Munster Antiquarian Journal*, Vol. 55 (2015), pp. 21-45 (p. 28).

90 Heath, *Armies of the Middle Ages*, p. 16.

Tynekill Castle

engaged and killed an English knight in single combat.[91] The English broke and ran, leaving behind one hundred dead.[92] The Irish took a rich amount of plunder; only after they had extorted high tributes from Dundalk and the surrounding towns did they begin their march back north.[93]
In 1425 John Talbot, Lord Lieutenant of Ireland, captured several high-ranking Irish magnates. One of them was a galloglas constable of the MacDonnell clan.[94]
The galloglas spread out from Ulster to the south and south-west.[95] The Burkes of Galway, a gaelicized family of originally Anglo-Norman origin had already been employing galloglas since the end of the 14th century. The MacDonnells settled in Connacht, County Mayo, shortly after 1400 and acquired estates in Kilmaine.[96]

91 The *Annals of the Four Masters* incorrectly claim that the Englishman was the Lord Lieutenant himself.
92 Walsh, Paul: *Leabhar Chlainne Suibhne. An Account of the MacSweeney Families in Ireland*. Dublin 1920, p. 139.
93 Cannan and Ò Broghain: *Galloglass*, p. 41.
94 Schlegel, *The MacDonnells of Tyrone and Armagh*, p. 199.
95 Toirdhealbach MacSweeney was High Constable of Connacht. He was killed together with two of his brothers in 1397.
96 For a long time they were lords of Moycharra Castle and Ahalard Castle.

The MacSheehys also appeared in Connacht shortly after 1400, and frequently served as galloglas alongside the MacDonnells, to whom they were closely related.[97]
In 1419 the O'Kellys and their MacDowell galloglas fought the Burkes of Clanricard and their force of MacSweeney galloglas at the battle of Bel Atha Lig near Galway. Alexander MacDowell, constable of the MacDowell contingent, was killed together with two of his sons and a large number of galloglas.
Galloglas entered the service of the FitzGeralds of Desmond in Munster and the FitzGeralds of Kildare in Leinster at the beginning of the 15th century.[98] Around 1420, the MacSheehys came to Munster in the wake of the marriage between Mary, daughter of William Burke of Clanricard, and James Fitzgerald, 6th Earl of Munster. In the same year, a group of MacDonnell galloglas moved from the estates of the O'Kellys in Galway to Tynekill in Leinster[99]. It was here that John (Gaelic: *Eoin*) Carragh MacDonnell[100] built Tynekill Castle and entered the service of the English crown. John Carragh MacDonnell, "best captayne of the English"[101], died fighting at Offaly in 1466. He was succeeded by his son Turlough Òg MacDonnell.
The MacCarthys, who controlled Ireland's south-west, also employed MacSweeney galloglas.[102]
The MacCabes received land free of pay from the Maguires in Fermanagh in return for military service. The holders of the estates were also exempt from tenure and taxes, instead being obliged to fight whenever called upon.[103]
The clans of western Scotland supplied a constant flow of warriors for the many military conflicts occurring in Ireland: the galloglas. The same clans supplied the mercenaries fighting for the Scots magnates in the Lowland.

97 The MacSheehys also fought alongside the O'Donnels of Tyrconnel. John (Gaelic: *Eoin*) MacSheehy and Marcus O'Donnel were both killed at Lissedill while attempting to fight their way out of an ambush.
98 Marsden, John: *Galloglas. Hebridean and West Highland Mercenary Warrior Kindreds in Medieval Ireland*, Edinburgh 2003.
99 O'Laughlin, Michael: *The Families of Galway, Ireland*, Kansas City 2002, p. 17.
100 „John the Scabbed", according to English sources.
101 *Annals of Dudley Firbisse*, quoted after Borrowes, Sir Erasmus D.: *Tennekille Castle, Portarlington, and Glimpses of the MacDonnells*, Belfast 1854, p. 36.
102 A Donnell MacOwen MacSweeney is documented as bailiff of Blarney Castle in 1585.
103 Simms, Katherine: "Gaelic Warfare in the Middle Ages", in: Bartlett, Thomas and Keith, Jeffrey: *A Military History of Ireland*, Cambridge 1996, pp. 99-115 (p. 112).

A galloglass and two lightly-armed Irish warriors (so-called *kern*).

(Illustration by Sasha Lunyakov)

Ireland in c. 1450

These warriors were referred to as *caterans*.[104] While the Caterans did not settle outside their traditional homelands, the galloglas stayed in Ireland. Some even became wealthy landowners, for instance the MacSweeneys under the O'Donnells in Tyrconnell, the MacDonnells under the O'Neills, and the MacQuillans (at first under the Earls of Ulster).

Galloglas also became active in Scotland itself. This was due to the close relationship between the Lordship of the Isles and the MacDonnells of Antrim. Alexander MacDonald, Lord of the Isles, had been detained by James I King of Scots in 1429. The MacDonalds refused to accept this and found a charismatic leader in Donald Balloch MacDonald, who was aged only eighteen at the time. Donald Balloch managed to raise a force of 800 highlanders and galloglas (the latter mostly supplied by the MacDonnells of Antrim) and defeat a royal army under the Earls of Caithness and Mar at Inverlochy.[105]

In 1462 John MacDonald, Lord of the Isles, committed high treason by signing a treaty with the English crown against the King of Scots. He raised a powerful army of highlanders and galloglas, which he intended to place under the command of Donald Balloch. Some of the clan chiefs resented this decision however, resulting in Lord John's son Angus Óg Maconald being placed in nominal overall command, with Donald Balloch acting as his tactical advisor. The army took Inverness, but relations between the English and Scottish crowns began to improve, so that the Lord of the Isles was forced to withdraw his troops from Inverness.[106]

While these events were taking place around Inverness, Ireland had become drawn into the vicious conflict for the English throne between the houses of Lancaster and York which was to become known as the Wars of the Roses. Most Anglo-Norman barons backed the Yorkists, one high-ranking exception being the Butlers of Ormond. In 1462 John Butler of Ormond returned to Ireland with an army allegedly 5,000 strong with the objective of bringing the entire island back into King Henry VI's fold. Thomas FitzGerald, 7th Earl of Desmond marched against him, and in August 1462 the two forces faced each other at Pilltown. FitzGerald's army contained numerous galloglas. The battle was a bloody affair and ended in defeat for Ormond.[107] Thomas Fitzgerald undertook an expedition to Offaly in 1466, where he himself was defeated. In 1468 he was summoned before a parliament at Drogheda and charged with treason. He was found guilty and executed. It was not long until the Fitzgeralds of Desmond pillaged the English territories around Dublin (The Pale) with fire and sword, and, needless to say, galloglas.

In 1468 the new Lord Deputy John Tiptoft[108] attacked the Gaelic town of Cavan, which was situated in the centre of the territory controlled by the O'Reillys. In 1470 the O'Reillys struck back. Apparently with 2,000 warriors (among them probably MacCabe galloglas), they attacked Meath. The Bishop of Armagh and the Mayor of Drogheda, William Dawes, raised a scratch force of 500 archers, a handful of cavalry, and 200 axemen, and repulsed the intruders.[109]

It is not particularly surprising that during the entire Wars of the Roses (1455-1485) the English crown only provided frugal resources for its Irish possessions.[110] In general, the Plantagenets (and the early Tudors) do not seem to have cared overmuch for their Irish estates, much to the delight of the local Irish-Gaelic rulers, who were mostly left do do as they pleased. Even after the conclusion of the Hundred Years War with France in 1453, English monarchs (and nobles and merchants along with them) continued to dream of the great days of the old Angevine Empire with its large possessions on the Continent. The latter had by now shrunk to a few patches around Calais, and the Norman Channel Islands. The fate of these possessions carried much more importance at the English court than what was going on in Ireland.

We do not know much exactly how many galloglas fought in the armies of the various chiefs and barons during this time. In 1458 Edmond MacWilliam Burke commanded a force of sixty galloglas, sixty kern, and some cavalry from his own estates. In 1460, 280 galloglas attended the funeral of Henry MacCabe, the chieftain of the galloglas clan of the MacCabes.[111]

In the year 1490, the Gaelic-Irish chiefs and the mostly gaelicized Anglo-Norman barons in Connacht were able to field armies of the following strengths: 3,000 horse, 3,000 galloglas, and 15,000 kern.[112] At this time numerous galloglas, among them many leaders, were of Gaelic-Irish stock, while some also hailed from gaelicized Anglo-Norman families.[113]

---

104 Sadler, John: *Clan Donald's greatest defeat. The Battle of Harlaw 1411*. Stroud 2005, p. 89.

105 Seehase: *Der schottische Clan MacDonald*, p. 38.

106 Grant, I. F.: *Angus Og of the Isles*, Edinburgh 1969, p. 50.

107 Seehase, Hagen and Krekeler, Ralf: *Der gefiederte Tod. Der englische Langbogen in den Kriegen des Mittelalters*, Ludwigshafen 2001, p. 178.

108 Tiptoft, Earl of Worcester, was a bloodthirsty and notorious butcher. In England he had made a name for himself in various offices serving the Yorkists. His day of reckoning was yet to come however.

109 Seehase and Krekeler: *Der gefiederte Tod*, p. 187. The axemen may actually have been billmen, or galloglas.

110 King Henry VI himself was a notable exception to this rule. In 1429 he promised a crown subsidy of ten pounds to anyone willing to build a small castle in the territory of the Pale (measurements were specified). Johnson, D. Newman: "Later Medieval Castles", in: Ryan, Michael (ed.): *The Illustrated Archaeology of Ireland*, Dublin 1991, pp. 188-193 (p. 191).

111 Heath, Ian: *Armies of the Middle Ages*, page 17.

112 Conolly, S. J.: *Contested Island. Ireland 1460-1630*, Oxford and New York 2007, p. 14.

113 This may be concluded by examining their names. Heath, Ian: *Armies of the Sixteenth Century*, St. Peter Port 1997, p. 83.

Galloglass fighting a dismounted knight in Gothic plate armour.
(Photograph: Jessica Greenwood)

Galloglass wearing a barbute-style helmet.
(Photograph: Jessica Greenwood)

THE BATTLE OF KNOCKDOE IN 1504

Gerald FitzGerald, 8th Earl of Kildare was born in 1456 the son of Thomas FitzJohn FitzGerald, 7th Earl of Kildare, and his wife Jane FitzGerald, herself an offspring of the FitzGeralds of Desmond. His nicknames Garret the Great (*Gearóid Mór*) and The Great Earl (*An tIarla Mór*), both of which already existed during his lifetime, are indicative of the prominent position which he occupied in the Ireland of his time. He inherited his father's title in 1477 and was made Lord Deputy of Ireland in the same year. He retained this position even after King Henry VII mounted the throne in the events following the Battle of Bosworth, which had concluded the Wars of the Roses. Gerald FitzGerald chose to support several pretenders from the Yorkist camp in their struggle against the new king. In 1487 he even went as far as to dispatch an Irish army to England to depose Henry. These troops were mostly slaughtered in the Battle of Stoke in 1487, among them Kildare's own brother. Stoically, King Henry pardoned the Earl of Kildare, and even allowed him to remain in office. In 1488 the king sent a special envoy, Sir Richard Edgecombe, to keep an eye on the troublesome Earl of Kildare.[114]

Since 1477 the Earl had ruled the English domains in Ireland almost unmolested, his family's influence extending even beyond the borders of his territories. During this time, Ireland was virtually autonomous.[115] In 1492 however, the king stripped him of his title as Lord Deputy. In 1492 his numerous Irish enemies succeeded in deposing and removing him to London, where locked up in the Tower he awaited his trial for treason. Thanks to a masterful defence in front of the king, he was acquitted and reinstated as Lord Deputy in 1496.

After removing Kildare from office, King Henry VII had appointed as Lord Deputy Sir Edward Poynings, a capable English soldier. Poynings took a tough stance against rebels and employed galloglas on campaign.[116] In 1494 Poynings summoned a parliament to Drogheda, which decreed "Poynings' Law" of lasting fame: no Irish parliament was henceforth allowed to convene without royal assent. All Irish magnates were forbidden to wage war (or conclude peace) without the monarch's permission. Eventually Poynings and his English army were recalled however – the experiment had proved too costly. Poynings simply lacked the dynastic networks and political ties which would have been necessary to keep Ireland firmly under control.

In 1500 Gerald FitzGerald was able to quell a rebellion in Cork. The town's mayor Maurice Roche was hanged for his insolence.[117] In view of his royal office the Earl

**The two-handed sword
was a fearsome and effective weapon.**
(© Claíomh – Niamh O'Rourke 2011)

was granted a household troop of archers. Not content with this, the Earl also purchased half a dozen handguns from Germany, presumably the first of their kind to be imported to Ireland. The handguns were used to equip the bodyguards guarding his residence at Thomas Court in Dublin, a move which surely did not fail to impress the Dubliners. The Earl himself was very charismatic, and an experienced soldier who had learned his trade in years of campaigning. In 1472, at the age of sixteen, he had already commanded a small troop of 24 spearmen.[118]

---

114 Hayes-McCoy: *Irish Battles*, p. 55.

115 At the beginning of the Tudor period England's population numbered some three million, Ireland's about one million.

116 Lydon, *The Scottish soldier in medieval Ireland*, p. 11.

117 Smith, Charles: *The Ancient and Present State of the County and City of Cork*, vol. I, Cork 1815, p. 424.

118 The English settlers of the Pale did not rely on the crown for their own safety. In 1480 they founded the Fraternity of St George, consisting of thirteen high-ranking citizens. Once a year these men elected a captain who commanded a force of 120 mounted archers, 40 cavalry, and 40 pages.

Galloglas duelling.
(Photograph: Jessica Greenwood)

Opposite page:
Galloglas covered the retreat and thrived in heroic single combat.
(Illustration by Sascha Lunyakov)

As Lord Deputy he raised a small standing force of three hundred kern, galloglas and cavalry. At the end of the 15th century a captain of galloglas by the name of Barrett (Gaelic: Baróid, or Bairéad) fled from Tirawley in north-eastern Mayo and entered the service of the Earl of Kildare together with 24 of his subordinates.[119] Through local recruiting this small force soon increased to 120 galloglas. The core of the unit, the galloglas that had accompanied Barrett from Mayo, in all likelihood consisted of members of the MacDonnell clan.[120] They became the most important galloglas in Kildare.[121]

The Burkes were the most powerful family of Anglo-Norman stock in Connacht despite being thoroughly gaelicized. The Burkes of Mayo (or *Mac William Íochtar*) were almost constantly at loggerheads with the Burkes of Clanricarde (*MacWilliam Uachtar*), who were based in Galway. When the chieftain of the Burkes of Mayo died in 1503, Ulick Fionn Burke, Lord of Clanricarde took this as an opportunity to attack the O'Kellys, who were allies of the Burkes of Mayo.[122] Ulick destroyed three McKelly castles in the following year, causing Melaghlin MacKelly to appeal to the Lord Deputy for help. Somewhat ironically, the Earl's daughter Eustacia was married to Ulick Burke. Later chroniclers claim that the marriage was not a happy one, Ulick having an affair with the wife of the chief of the O'Kellys. Gerald FitzGerald thus had very personal motives when it came to dealing with this troublemaker. To add insult to injury, Ulick seized Galway, which since 1484 had belonged to the English crown. The Lord Deputy now had to act.

---

119 Hayes-McCoy, Gerard Anthony: *Scots Mercenary Forces in Ireland*, Dublin and London 1937, p. 36.

120 The Barretts were a Cambro-Norman family which had come to Ireland with the first wave of Norman conquerors. They first settled near Cork before moving to Connacht with John de Cogan in 1236. Henceforth they were to be found in the Tirawley district. A feud which had broken out between the Barretts and the Lynotts formed the background to the rather morbid ballad of *The Welshmen of Tirawley*.

121 The Barretts are attested in numerous documents until the end of the 16th century. Later, many Barretts served in the Irish regiments of the Spanish army.

122 Hayes-McCoy, *Irish Battles*, p. 55.

A galloglass awaits the enemy.
(Niamh O'Rourke 2011)

When Gerald FitzGerald, Earl of Kildare, set about punishing Ulick Burke in accordance with the authority he wielded as Lord Deputy, Ulick decided to resist. The affair had now turned from a private (and by no means legal) feud into open rebellion against the English crown. At least this was how the Earl of Kildare came to regard things. FitzGerald was able to rely on the support of Hugh Dubh O'Donnell, who had been growing increasingly uneasy at Ulick's rise in power. The latter was likewise able to call upon a number of allies: there were the O'Briens of Thomond (Ulick's mother was an O'Brien), whose chieftain was said to be a sworn enemy of all things English. The MacNamaras also sided with Ulick, as did the O'Carrolls of Ely and the O'Kennedys of Ormond, who in earlier times together with the Burkes of Clanricarde had supported Sir James Butler against the Earl of Kildare. The minor clan of the Mac I Briens of Arra also rallied around the Burkes.

The alliance forged by the Lord Deputy was even more impressive however. There was Hugh Dubh O'Donnell, and several lines of the O'Neills. Of the clans of Ulster, the Magennis, MacMahon, O'Hanlon and O'Reilly joined the Earl's colours. Of the Connacht clans, there were the O'Kellys, the Burkes of Mayo, the MacDermots of Moylurg, and chief O'Connor Roe together with his retainers. Gerald FitzGerald's force was completed by the O'Farrels and O'Connors of Offaly. The Bishop of Ardagh, William O'Ferral (Gaelic: *Uilliam Ó Fearghail*), provided an additional contingent. Altogether this force constituted one of the largest alliances of Irish magnates in the history of Ireland. To this force Fitzgerald added his own and the royal contingents he had at his disposal. Among the latter were the 120 archers of his bodyguard, the only true Englishmen to take part in the entire campaign.[123]

The Anglo-Irish and Irish warriors from the Pale were commanded by Sir Robert Preston, Viscount Gormanstown; Richard Nugent, Baron Delvin, was also present.[124] Other nobles included the Lords Barnewall of Trimlestown, Fleming of Slane, St Lawrence of Howth, the Plunketts of Dunsany and Killeen, and William Darcy of Platen, the "Great Darcy"[125]. To these added the contingents from Dublin and Drogheda, each led by their respective may-

---

123 In 1498 the Earl of Kildare had requested a contingent of 300 English archers and 60 handgunners from England, but there is no evidence that they were ever dispatched.

124 In 1496 Nugent had been something akin to commander-in-chief of the Pale's armed force. Two years later he failed to appear at a parliament however, and was fined 40 shillings for his absence.

125 Darcy was a personal friend of FitzGerald and had always grimly resented Gaelic influence on the Anglo-Irish. Oddly enough, he himself spoke Gaelic fluently and had married one of his daughters to a member of the O'Donnells.

ors.[126] Firearms were provided from the Earl's arsenal. No artillery was employed despite the fact that the Earl had previously made use of it in a number of sieges.[127]

Of rather greater strategic importance were the 120 galloglas of Barrett/MacDonnell and the 160 galloglas fielded by the MacMahons of Oriel. Together with the vassals and retainers and the Earl's household troops, they constituted a sizeable force.[128]

The army marched westwards from the Pale in August 1504. In O'Kelly territory they were joined by the contingents from northern Connacht, Ulster, and parts of the Midlands. According to the chronicle of the St Lawrences, a council of war was now held. The *Chronicles of Howth* inform us about the alleged topic of discussion.[129] Lord Delvin advocated immediate attack, wishing to be the first to throw a spear into the enemy ranks.[130] More cautiously, Lord Gormanstown pointed out that losing a single battle would put the entire Irish realm at risk. The Lords of Killeen and Trimlestown shared this point of view. After all, the enemy was superior in numbers (which was untrue). It is hardly surprising that St Lawrence of Howth finally reminded his fellow commanders that it was their duty to to fight determinedly and bravely. It would be advisable, he argued, to deploy in battle order under cover of darkness so that every man knew his place at first light. The Gaelic chiefs were likewise itching for a fight.[131]

The Earl of Kildare called for the constable of his galloglas and ordered him to open the battle since this would prove less of a strain to them than to the young warriors from the Pale. The galloglas commander felt flattered by this proposal and with manly words ("God's Blood!") assured his master that he could ask for no greater honour. Gripping his axe, he went to summon his men. The following day (or the next), two hundred enemy horsemen were sighted. The Earl's son, a seventeen-year-old youth, wanted to attack immediately but was held back. The Kildare force struck camp near Knockdoe on 18th August 1504.[132] The name of Knockdoe is an Anglicization of the Gaelic *Cnoc-Tuagh*, meaning "Hill of the Axes". Rarely was there a more befitting name for what was about to follow. On the morning of 19th August 1504 the Earl of Kildare's army deployed on the hill of Knockdoe facing west.

The archers were commanded by Viscount Gormanstown and Baron Killeen, the billmen[133] were led by St Lawrence of Howth, while the cavalry were led by Lord Delvin.[134] The billmen formed the centre while the archers stood on the wings. The right flank was protected by a low wall approximately two feet high. Since this would have impeded the movement of cavalry, the Earl placed his cavalry on the left flank. The Irish-Gaelic allies stood on the opposite flank. The Earl's galloglas stood with the billmen and presumably formed the first rank. After all, the Earl had promised his commander pride of place in the battle line (and the position most at risk). Garret Óg FitzGerald commanded the reserve, whose duty it was to protect the baggage train. According to estimates, the Earl's army numbered 6,000 fighters. Ulick Burke appeared on the battlefield slightly later. The battle array of his troops was simple: his foot soldiers formed a long continuous battle line, while his cavalry deployed on the left flank. Ulick would have had around 4,000 men under his command.

The galloglas of both armies glowered at each other across the field. The Earl MacDonnell's galloglas stood in the center of the battle line, while those of his Gaelic allies were positioned on the right flank. With the campaign taking place comparatively far from home, the Gaelic chiefs will have relied chiefly on their galloglas: the MacDonnells brought along the MacSweeneys, the O'Neills the MacDonnells. The O'Connors also fielded their MacDonnell galloglas. The Burkes of Mayo had their own MacDonnell and MacSweeney galloglas. On Ulick Burke's side, the other branches of the MacSweeneys were present along with other galloglas contingents.

Burke ordered the attack. His men had allegedly spent most of the night drinking and gambling, but this may have been a chronicler's later invention. While the Earl bided his time, Lord Devin was unable to restrain himself. True to his word, he galloped forward and transfixed a Burke with his spear.[135] It is however possible that this heroic feat was merely a polite way of circumscribing an otherwise unsuccessful cavalry charge. Ulick's galloglas advanced, their mighty war cry thrice ringing across the field. Many a warrior would have lost heart even at the sight and sound of the charging mercenaries, yet the Earl's archers stood firm. They loosed volley after volley at the advancing enemy ranks, whose momentum gradually began to wane. MacSweeney, the commander of the Burkes of Clanricarde's galloglas, called out for the Great Darcy to step out since he was the only opponent

---

126 In Dublin's case, by John Blake.

127 The Earl had employed artillery against Balrath Castle in Westmeath in 1488, and again against Dungannon in 1498. In the following year, he brought cannon to bear against the defences of several castles in Connacht.

128 Hayes-McCoy, *Irish Battles*, p. 58.

129 The chronicle was compiled in 1544 with the aim of glorifying the deeds of the St Lawrences of Howth and can therefore hardly be called impartial.

130 This vow is worth noting in that in 1498 the Irish Parliament had decreed that every Anglo-Irishman carry English arms. The throwing of javelins was Gaelic practice however.

131 Hayes-McCoy: *Irish Battles*, p. 59 f.

132 Evans, Martin Marix: *The Military Heritage of Britain & Ireland. The Comprehensive Guide to Sites of Military Interest*, London 1998, p. 230.

133 Billmen were armed with polearms similar to those carried by German halberdiers.

134 James, Jeffrey: *Ireland. The Struggle for Power. From the Dark Ages to the Jacobites*, Stroud 2017.

135 Burke, John: *A General and Heraldic Dictionary of the Peerage and Baronetage of the British Empire*, London 1832, p. 605.

The battlefield at Knockdoe.
(Photograph: Maximilian Bunk)

deemed worthy of a fight. Darcy accepted the challenge. MacSweeney succeeded in striking a heavy blow at Darcy's head, causing his opponent to fall to his knees. Baron Nangle of Navan stepped in for the stunned Darcy, seriously wounding MacSweeney.

The battle became a brutal head-on melée of individual single combat with neither side seeking to outmanoeuvre its opponents. The galloglas did what was was expected of them – they fought and died where they stood. After several hours the numerical superiority of the Earl's army gradually began to tell. Ulick Burke's cavalry had made a detour around the wall protecting the Earl's flank (as well as the galloglas of the Earl's Gaelic allies) and set to plundering the enemy baggage train. The men detailed to guard it had meanwhile joined the fray under their commander Garret Óg (which is to say, they had deserted their posts), leaving the baggage defenceless. Completely oblivious of what was going on on the battlefield Burke's horsemen gleefully took to looting the wagons. So great was their ignorance that one of them approached a warrior from the Pale asking him who had taken the Earl prisoner. In reply, one of the Dublin arquebusiers struck him across the skull with the stock of his weapon, dashing his brains out (as related by the sources).

Such troops as were left of Ulick Burke's army began to give ground and eventually retired from the field. Losses were staggering, some sources claiming as many as 2,000 casualties. The Earl's losses were likewise heavy, but comparatively fewer.

The victorious army marched to Galway, which readily opened its gates. Athenry also greeted the victors with gates wide open.

Gerald FitzGerald, 8th Earl of Kildare, was made a Knight of the Garter in the following year. Ulick Burke died in 1509.[136]

---

136 This does not mean that peace had finally established itself. In 1512 Aed Oge O'Donnell began to wage war against MacWilliam Burke. He is reputed to have levied 1,500 "axemen" in northern Ireland. Contemporary chronicles mention four "battles" of galloglas serving Aed Oge and his son Manus (cf. Heath, Ian and Sque, David: *The Irish Wars 1485-1603*, London 1993, p. 12).

On 6th June, a ship carrying Ferdinand of Austria, the later Archduke and Holy Roman Emperor, was swept to the southern Irish coast by adverse winds. He sojourned at Kinsale for several days before continuing his voyage. Here three Irish warriors await the illustrious guest at Desmond Castle.

(© Claíomh – Katherine Bond 2018)

The Battle of Knockavoe

The Battle of Knockavoe (Gaelic: *Cnoc-Buihdh*), fought on 15th June 1522, was the bloody climax of the prolonged and costly feud between the O'Donnell and O'Neill clans, in which the galloglas supplied by the MacSheehys, the MacDonnells and the MacSweeneys also played a major role.

Hugh Dubh O'Donnell (Gaelic: *Aodh Dubh Ó Domhnaill*) was chief of the O'Donnells and had held the title of King of Tir Chonaill (Tyrconnell) since 1505. There had lately been serious clashes with the O'Neills, but in the year 1511 Hugh Dubh O'Donnell believed that the situation had stabilized sufficiently for him to embark on a pilgrimage to Rome. In his absence, his son Manus was to rule the clan. In spite of his youth, Manus proved a remarkably adept ruler. Hugh Dubh O'Donnell returned after two years. In the course of his return journey, King Henry VIII had knighted him. On his return however, Sir Hugh was forced to realise that Manus flatly refused to step down. His insubordination was supported by the entire clan.

Sir Hugh turned to the Maguires for help, while Manus allied himself with the O'Neills. Around 1522, the alliances had changed, yet Manus O'Donnell still ruled the O'Donnell clan.

Over the years, the threat from the O'Neills had rematerialized. Chief Conn O'Neill's objective was no less than to conquer the O'Donnells, and he began to raise a powerful army. Apart from the O'Neills and their vassals, and galloglas of the MacSheehys and the MacDonnells, the Bissets and the MacDonnells of Antrim also joined Conn O'Neill's colours. Other allies were found in Munster and Connacht, and the Earl of Kildare himself sent Anglo-Irish soldiers and galloglas of the MacDonnells of Tynekill.

Without waiting for the entire army to assemble, Conn O'Neill took Ballyshannon, which was held by the MacSweeney Galloglas. Many galloglas and high-ranking members of the O'Donnell clan were killed in the fighting. Grown confident with his success, Conn believed Tyrconnell ripe for the taking, and had his army encamp near Strabane. The contingents from Connacht still had not arrived.

Many of Conn O'Neill's allies seem to have been driven solely by the lust for plunder. The army was a good deal larger than that of the O'Donnells, but it was also a rather rag-tag and piebald affair.

Manus O'Donnell's force consisted of men from the clans of O'Donnell, O'Gallagher, O'Doherty, O'Boyle, and MacSweeney. In the dead of night this force approached the enemy camp at Knockavoe and overpowered the sentries without giving them the opportunity to raise the alarm. Then the O'Donnells fell upon their unsuspecting opponents. The darkness made it hard for the fighters to distinguish friend from foe, but the hotch-potch nature of their army made affairs particularly difficult for O'Neill's men. When the fighting finally died down, 900 men of the O'Neills and their allies lay dead. Donnell Oge MacDonnell and many of his MacDonnell galloglas had been killed, as was Turlough MacSheehy along with many men from his command. The victors took the weapons of the slain as spoils and gathered a large amount of booty.

The battle did not spell the end of the conflict between the O'Donnells and the O'Neills. The results were far-reaching: the last MacEoin Bisset, chief of the Bisset clan, was killed fighting on the O'Neill side. This provided the MacDonnells of Antrim with the opportunity to extend their hold on Antrim. The bloody feud between the O'Neills and the O'Donnells was also a hard-fought contest between the galloglas clans of MacSheehy and MacSweeney. This rivalry was to continue for several decades.

[After Campbell, Kenneth L.: *Ireland's History. Prehistory to the Present*, London et al., 2014]

UNDER TUDOR RULE – THE FALL OF THE HOUSE OF FITZGERALD

Gerald Fitzgerald, 8th Earl of Kildare, died sometime around 3rd September 1513 while on a punitive expedition against the O'Carroll clan. He had been wounded by an arrow while watering his horse.[137]

Gerald was succeeded as Earl of Kildare and Lord Deputy by his son Garret Óg. Garret Óg was unfortunate in that at the same time, Cardinal Wolsey was appointed Lord Chancellor in London. Wolsey took a considerable amount of interest in Ireland and persuaded King Henry VIII to keep a close eye on the 9th Earl of Kildare. Several times Garret Óg found himself summoned to London and deposed, only to be eventually reinstated every time. His last journey to London in 1534 sparked off a rebellion. Rumours which had deliberately been spread claimed that the Earl had been executed. As a result, his son Thomas FitzGerald, Lord Offaly, dubbed "Silken Thomas" for his unfailingly impeccable turnout, rose in revolt.

It was open rebellion. Thomas' troops at first proved superior to the English, the rebels taking and briefly holding Dublin (though the castle remained in English hands). The Archbishop of Dublin was executed at Thomas' bequest. Meanwhile, Garret Óg had indeed died in London, and Silken Thomas was now the new Earl of Kildare.

An English army commanded by the new Lord Lieutenant of Ireland, Sir William Skeffington, was dispatched to settle the Irish problem.[138] Skeffington's heavy artillery breached the walls of Maynooth Castle, Silken Thomas's headquarters, and forced the garrison to surrender. In March 1535, the rebellion was over.[139]

Lord Leonard Grey succeeded Sir William as new Lord Lieutenant. Grey was not interested in prolonging the conflict and gave short shrift to his opponent. Silken Thomas was captured and sent to London.[140] On 3rd February 1537 he ended his life on the gallows at Tyburn together

Galloglass of the MacSweeney clan at Barryscourt Castle.
(© Claíomh – Michael Selby-Bennetts 2010)

137 Not all contemporary military conflicts were of political nature, as had been the confrontation between Ulick Burke and the Earl of Kildare. Many were simply forays in search of plunder. In 1513, the port of Killybegs was pillaged by the notorious pirate Eoghan O'Malley together with the crews of his three ships. Due to adverse weather conditions, they were however unable to make off to Connacht with their captives and booty. At the time, the constable of the MacSweeney Banagh was on campaign serving with the MacDonalds of Tyrconnell. In his absence, a youngster named Brian MacSweeney assembled all the local peasants and shepherds he could muster and attacked the pirates, freeing the prisoners. Eoghan O'Malley met his death at the hands of Brian MacSweeney. Another raid occurred in 1547; this time, the MacSweeneys were able to repel a landing force at Rathlin O'Beirne.

138 Skeffington was already seventy years old at the time. He was an expert artilleryman. Edwards, Ruth Dudley: *An Atlas of Irish History*, New York 1981, p. 97.

139 At about the same time, the chief of the MacAuliffes based in southern Munster was involved in a feud with several branches of the Fitzgeralds. Lord Clonglass was killed fighting for the Fitzgeralds, as were numerous galloglas of the MacSheehys. MacAuliffe had a number of MacSweeney galloglas fighting in his ranks. Mulmurry, son of Brian MacSweeney was killed.

140 Thomas had been promised safe conduct before surrendering.

with five of his uncles.[141] FitzGerald's galloglas were taken into royal service and proved themselves loyal.[142] Three hundred MacDonnell galloglas served in the English forces in Ireland in 1560. The same number is given by the sources in the years 1566 and 1570.

After his half-brother Thomas's death, the young Gerald FitzGerald became the 11th Earl of Kildare. In order to assert his claim to the earldom, several Irish families houses bound to the Fitzgeralds by family ties concluded an alliance, the so-called Geraldine League. With Lord

141 In 1539, the Earl of Ormond supplied 800 galloglas to the English crown against the FitzGeralds.

142 Seehase, Hagen: „Galloglas – irische Krieger des 13-16. Jahrhunderts", in: *Zeitschrift für Heereskunde* (No. 402), 2001, pp. 135-143 (p. 143).

A detailed rendition of a *cótun* on the de Burgo effigy at Ballinakill Abbey.
(Photograph: Dave Swift)

Helmet and mail coif as depicted on the de Burgo effigy at Ballinakill Abbey.
(Photograph: Dave Swift)

Ballinakill Abbey.
(Photograph: dougf, Creative Commons)

Opposite page:
Effigy of de Burgo warrior at Ballinakill Abbey near Glinsk.
(Photograph: Dave Swift)

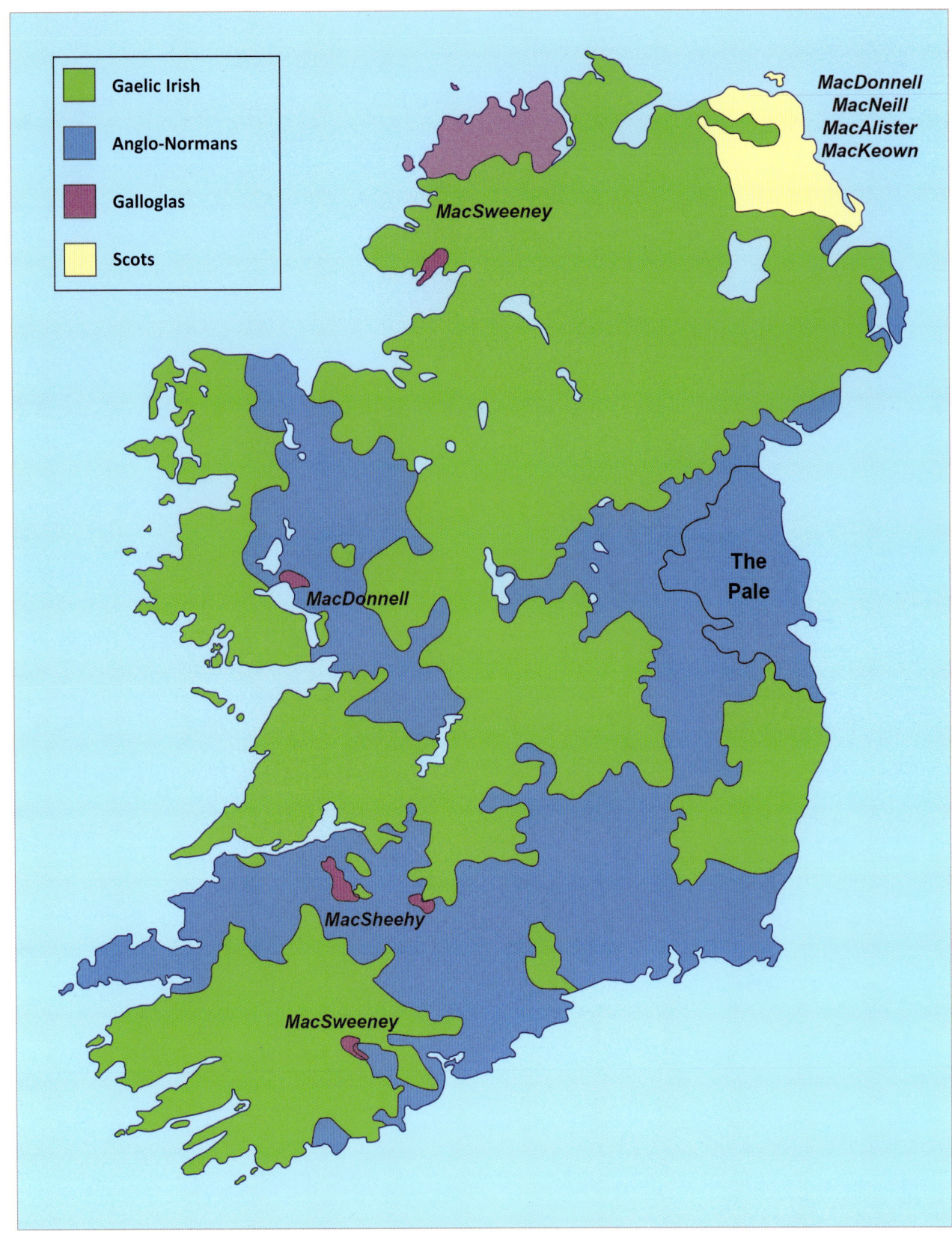

Ireland in the second half of the 16th century

Grey away in Cork, the O'Neills and O'Donnells raided the Pale and sacked Navan and Ardee. Grey hurried back and raised a force of 400 men. The Earl of Ormond contributed another four hundred fighters, among them horsemen, kern and galloglas.[143] At the battle of Belahoe, Lord Grey decisively defeated the Irish magnates. Gerald FitzGerald was able to escape to the Continent, and soon allegations were levelled at Lord Grey, whose sister was none other than young GeraldFitzGerald's mother. Grey denied all accusations against him, but to no avail. A royal death warrant sealed his fate, and he was executed on the headsman's block on Tower Green on 28th July 1541. After the FitzGeralds' demise the road for Henry VIII's proposed settlement of the Irish question ought to have been wide open.[144] To complicate things however, the King had just begun to quarrel with the Pope over his marriage, a conflict which was to finally lead to his break with the Church of Rome. In a diplomatic approach which was to prove successful, Henry had his new viceroy Lord St Leger negotiate treaties with the Irish magnates.

The Irish nobles consented to transfer their respective realms to the English crown and in turn to receive them as fiefdoms together with English titles. In 1541, a parliament assembled specifically for this purpose declared Henry VIII King of Ireland.[145] The King's policy of religious reformation, ruthlessly carried out in England, had undesirable consequences in Ireland however. The Irish's stubborn refusal to abandon their ancient religious faith soon became the bedrock of Irish national identity and in the centuries to come made the country a pawn in the various campaigns of European Catholic monarchs against England.[146] The rules of Henry's son Edward VI and his daughter Mary Tudor failed to make a significant impression on their Irish subjects, although Mary increased the number of English troops stationed in Ireland.[147]

Mary's successor Elizabeth I faced a difficult political legacy. The far-sighted Queen was quite clear about the potential which Ireland offered as a political playground for ambitious foreign powers. The following years saw the settlement of English colonists beyond the confines of the Pale, especially in Munster to the south-west. This area was the ancient battleground for the incessant rivalry between the FitzGeralds of Desmond and the Butlers of Ormond.

Ignoring the royal decree forbidding internal strife, these two old enemies now once again embarked on a private feud. In 1565 Gerald FitzGerald, 15th Earl of Desmond, had complained to a distant relative, Sir Maurice FitzGerald, Lord of Decies, over certain tenures and other income due as regular payments to the Earl of Ormond. Sensing trouble, Sir Maurice had informed Thomas Butler, 10th Earl of Ormond, nicknamed "Black Tom", of his cousin's discontent. During a subsequent skirmish at Affane near Waterford, the Earl of Desmond was wounded in the hip by a pistol shot and taken prisoner.[148] Ormond's force allegedly amounted to no less than one hundred cavalry and 300 galloglas and kern, while Desmond commanded 56 cavalry, 60 galloglas and the same number of kern. Both figures are quoted after the two opponents' official statements, which unashamedly played down the number of fighters actually involved in order to assuage the English officials entrusted with the subsequent inquiry.[149] The wounded Earl of Desmond was held captive by the Earl of Ormond until ordered by Lord Justice Nicholas Arnold to surrender his prisoner. After a brief spell in English captivity Desmond returned to Ireland, only to be taken prisoner once more and sent back to England, this time in the company of his brother, Sir John of Desmond. Sir Gerald was accused by the Privy Council of having kept more than 500 galloglas under arms. Desmond's reply that they had proved necessary to counteract local bandits and poachers was deemed unsatisfactory.[150]

In 1569, Desmond's deputy and cousin James FitzMaurice FitzGerald led the clan in open rebellion against the English crown (First Desmond Rebellion). FitzGerald considered himself the champion of the true Catholic faith, and besides had personal wrongs to settle – the English had confiscated parts of his estates and given it to the English St Leger family for colonisation. The entire southwest rose in revolt, partly due to the arrival of large numbers of English settlers.

At first, things did not go well for the rebels. James FitzMaurice FitzGerald attacked the castle of Thomas FitzMaurice of Lixnaw, Lord of Kerry. In a pincer movement, forces commanded by FitzGerald attacked Lixnaw from the west, while his ally John O'Connor led his MacSheehy galloglas in an attack from the east.

James FitzMaurice FitzGerald knew that FitzMaurice of Lixnaw's contract with his galloglas was due to expire, and believed the time to be perfect for an attack. However, Edmond MacSweeney, galloglas constable to FitzMaurice of Lixnaw, had no intention of remaining idle. In spite of the vast numeric superiority of James Fitzmaurice's force, to stand and fight was to Edmond MacSweeney simply a question of honour. With the aid of a certain

---

143 Moore, Thomas Sturge: *History of Ireland*, vol. 2, Paris 1840, p. 359.

144 The suppression of the revolt had cost the royal treasury the substantial sum of 40,000 pounds. Ellis, Steven G.: "The Tudor Borderlands 1485-1603", in: Morrill, John: *The Oxford Illustrated History of Tudor and Stuart Britain*, London et al. 1996, pp. 53-73 (p. 67).

145 Metzger, Franz: „Irland unter den Tudors. Von der Kolonie zum Königreich", in *Geschichte* 7/2015 (2015), pp. 40-42 (p. 41).

146 Under Henry VIII, Ireland received a permanent English garrison, which was however restricted to 500 soldiers before the year 1547. Ellis, "The Tudor Borderlands", p. 67.

147 From originally 300 soldiers in 1535, the number of troops was raised to 540 in 1543, and again increased to 1,200 in the 1550s. Heath and Sque, *The Irish Wars*, p. 19.

148 Heath, *Armies of the 16th Century*, p. 117.

149 Connolly, *Contested Island*, p. 157.

150 Berleth, Richard: *The Twilight Lords*, Lanham 2002, p. 69.

Two galloglas practising sword fighting.
(© Claíomh – James Doyle 2010)

Opposite page:
Galloglass standing guard outside a large "Tower House" in County Munster.
(© Claíomh – Dave Swift 2010)

Captain O'Malley and his force of sailors,[151] Edmond MacSweeney succeeded in soundly defeating John O'Connor's MacSheehy galloglas. Edmund MacSheehy and Murrogh Balb MacSheehy, two clan leaders, were killed in the fighting together with many other galloglas. Nevertheless, despite this reverse the military potential of James FitzMaurice's rebel army was impressive. At the rebellion's highpoint, the force allegedly numbered no less than 1,400 galloglas, 400 pikemen clad in coats of mail, 400 arquebusiers and 1,500 kern as well as a handful of cavalry.

In June 1569 James Maurice FitzGerald and his new ally the Earl of Clancarty took fortified Tracton Abbey and hanged the entire garrison. James FitzMaurice FitzGerald sought to negotiate alliances with several local Irish magnates (MacCarthy Mor, O'Sullivan Beare, and O'Keefe), and demanded that the City of Cork abstain from the heresy of Protestantism. It was obvious that these moves had in fact been masterminded by Irish Jesuits keen to bring all of Ireland back into the Catholic fold.

Already in September 1569, the backbone of the rebellion had been broken by the Lord Deputy Henry Sydney. He ordered Humphrey Gilbert, half-brother of the famous Sir Walter Raleigh, to hunt down James FitzMaurice FitzGerald. Gilbert conducted a campaign no less ruthless than FitzGerald's, mostly at the expense of the civilian population. Gilbert ordered the large-scale slaughter of civilians to shake the enemy's morale and deprive the rebels of their supposed hideouts. In December 1569, after the final surrender of one of FitzGerald's Gaelic allies, Gilbert received his knighthood from Sir Henry Sidney in the midst of a battlefield mayhem of slaughtered galloglas.

Meanwhile, James FitzMaurice FitzGerald had gone into hiding in the forests of Aherlow in Tipperary. He proceeded to raise a new army, and after Gilbert's return to England with 120 men took Kilmallock, which was

---

151 The O'Malleys were a seafaring clan from Mayo with a predilection for piracy.

Under the late Tudors, the brutality of political conflict was further supplemented by religious strife.
(© Claíomh – Niamh O'Rourke 2013)

thoroughly sacked. In February 1573, after being assured a royal pardon, he decided to surrender. His estates were confiscated, while he himself left Ireland.[152]

The victorious English queen did not prove as irreconcilable as might have been expected. The Earl of Desmond was released from captivity, and his estates and titles were restored to him. He was held under official arrest in Dublin, but Desmond had no trouble extricating himself, and returned home to his county. There the first man to greet him is said to have been Maurice MacSheehey, his constable of galloglas.

In the meantime, the English Lord Deputy Sir John Perrot had banned important aspects of Gaelic culture: as from now, Irish costume, poetry, and the Brehon Law were officially forbidden.

The resistance sparked by these measures was particularly pronounced among the galloglas of the FitzGeralds.

The English response was harsh: to clamp down on Irish resistance William Drury, Lord President of Munster in 1576, had seven hundred galloglas executed.[153]

The galloglas continued to resist, and they did so with a vengeance. For example, in 1576 a landowner named Edmund FitzDavey complained to the English authorities that his farmstead had been pillaged. The documents state that a certain Mortagh McEdmond McShey and his brother Morrough McEdmond together with 198 galloglas and 15 horsemen had attacked the farm in question.[154] In all likelihood, the "McSheys" were the MacSheehys.

Already in early 1570 Pope Pius V had issued his papal bull *Regnans in excelsis*, thereby excommunicating Queen Elizabeth I and the Privy Council. With the Church of Rome's explicit blessing, this edict made many Catholic rulers potential allies of rebellious Irish Catholics. This gave a boost of morale to all Irish magnates contemplating rebellion. James FitzMaurice Fitzgerald travelled across the Continent in search of potential supporters.[155]

---

152 In May 1570 the Earl of Ormond moved against Thomond with a sizeable force including 400 galloglas and expelled Connor O'Brien, 3rd Earl of Thomond. McInerney, Luke: *The Galloglass of Thomond*, p. 30.

153 O'Domhnaill, Rónán Gearóid: *Fadó: Tales of lesser known Irish history*, Kibworth Beauchamp. 2013, p. 43.

154 Pierse, John H.: *Pierse. The Pierse Family*, London 1950, p. 85.

155 Beckett: *Geschichte Irlands*, p. 62.

Monasternenagh Abbey (derived from Gaelic *Manister an Aonaigh*).
(Photograph: Maximilian Bunk)

Spain and France lacked interest, but the Pope was enthusiastic. The Holy See provided FitzGerald with 1,000 warriors with which to conquer Ireland and instal Giacomo Boncompagni, the Pope's nephew, on the throne of the High Kings. The campaign never materialized.

A new attempt was made in 1579, when on 18th July a small fleet carrying Italian, Spanish and a few Irish soldiers dropped anchor in Smerwick Harbour.[156] The invaders confidently announced that they would conquer Ireland, and a crusade against Queen Elizabeth I was solemnly declared. Eventually the entire clan of the FitzGeralds of Desmonds joined the invading force. The Earl himself, having been decreed a traitor by the English, took over command of the rebels. James FitzMaurice FitzGerald was killed in a minor skirmish, but this was no longer of any importance, since more and more Irish chiefs threw in their lot with the Earl of Desmond. The MacSheehy galloglas formed the military backbone of the revolt.[157] The Earl of Desmond set the tone of the rebellion by storming Youghal and massacring the entire English garrison. The English retaliated in kind by dispatching a punitive force, which numerous magnates (many of the Gaelic-Irish) chose to join in the hope for plunder.

On 3rd October 1579 the two forces met at Monasternenagh. 2,000 Irish rebels commanded by Sir John FitzGerald (a brother of Gerald FitzGerald), with 1,000 galloglas among them (the majority of these were of the MacSheehy), faced an English and Anglo-Irish force about half the size commanded by Sir Nicholas Malby.[158] Malby's soldiers were armed with calivers, muskets, pikes and halberds, and were supported by a small cavalry force. Undeterred by the withering fire of the English musketeers, the galloglas repeatedly charged the enemy line. The sheer momentum of their attacks penetrated the blocks of pikemen in several places. As the outcome of the battle hung in the balance, Malby ordered his cavalry to attack the flanks of FitzGerald's army. When the cavalry appeared in the enemy's rear, threatening to cut off their line of retreat into the woods beyond, Irish resistance collapsed, and FitzGerald's men took to

---

156 The combined force probably amounted to no more than 80 Spaniards, a handful of Irish, and 500 Italians; cf. Pierse: *Pierse*, p. 87.

157 Falls, Cyril: *Elizabeth's Irish Wars*, Syracuse 1997, p. 77.

158 Williams, Perry: *The Later Tudors. England 1487-1603*, Oxford et al. 1995, p. 295.

Monasternenagh Abbey.
(Photograph: Maximilian Bunk)

Carrigafoyle Castle.
(Photograph: Maximilian Bunk)

their heels. Fitzgerald's army sustained a large number of casualties during the rout – many galloglas were killed by musketry, having sustained comparatively few losses in combat at close quarters. Many wounded rebels who had taken refuge in nearby Monasternenagh Abbey were sought out by the pursuing enemy and killed.[159] Many high-ranking galloglas commanders had perished in the fighting, MacCarthy Mor losing a legitimate son as well as an illegitimate one; Tirlough MacSheehy and Sir John FitzGerald also lost sons. The implications were considerable – since the English crown had stripped the rebellious lords of their estates and many heirs lay dead on the battlefield, wide stretches of land were now available for settlement from abroad.

The most powerful stronghold of the FitzGeralds of Desmond, Carrigafoyle Castle, was placed unter siege from sea and land. Garrisoned by some fifty Irishmen and a few Spanish mercenaries, the castle surrendered shortly before Easter Sunday in 1580 after a heavy bombardment. On hearing the news, the defenders of nearby Askeaton Castle blew up their castle in order to avoid having to surrender it to the enemy. The rebels now increasingly resorted to guerilla warfare, applying hit-and-run tactics against the English.

In the meantime, the rebellion had spread to Leinster. On 25th August 1580 Fiach MacHugh O'Byrne defeated an English force under the Lord Deputy Arthur Grey, 14th Baron Grey de Wilton.[160]

On 10th September 1580 a small Spanish-Papal relief force numbering c. six hundred soldiers under Sebastiano de San Giuseppe landed at Smerwick, almost at the same spot where one year previously James FitzMaurice FitzGerald had set foot on Irish soil. A force commanded by Thomas Butler, Earl of Ormond, and Lord Grey de Wilton immediately surrounded the enemy force and prevented it from moving inland. In early November an English naval squadron brought fresh ammunition and supplies for Ormond and Grey's men, among them some urgently needed field pieces. These culverins opened fire on San Sebastiano's men, who were forced to surrender after a three-day fight. With the exception of a handful of officers, all prisoners were subsequently executed at Lord Grey de Wilton's orders. This disgraceful and brutal behaviour caused Queen Elizabeth to relieve Grey of his post in summer 1582 on a charge of excessive cruelty.

John FitzGerald was killed in a skirmish outside Cork in early 1582. At the end of April the Earl of Desmond was encamped at Kilfinnane with a small galloglas contingent. Due to the boggy environment and the damp weather, the Earl's old hip wound (sustained from a pistol ball at

---

159 Heath, Ian: *Armies of the 16th Century*, p. 21.

160 At the time, Grey commanded 3,000 of the altogether 6,000 soldiers which he had recruited in England.

Galloglass from the late period wearing a cabasset helmet. (© Claíomh – Dave Swift)

Affane) began to give him trouble. Finally he was in so much pain that walking became impossible. His men were busy making camp and preparing food when a stronger English force under Sir John Zouche attacked the camp. A few galloglas, among them their constable Maurice MacSheehy, bedded the helpless Earl on a blanket and dragged him to safety while the rest of the galloglas force covered the retreat. Forty were killed.[161]

Since John FitzGerald was dead and his brother nowhere to be found, the English unwisely decided to reduce the number of troops stationed in Munster. Thomas FitzMaurice of Lixnaw and his MacSweeneys promptly seized the town of Adare and took Lisconnell Castle, making short shrift of the garrison: the hapless English soldiers were simply thrown to their deaths from the battlements.

Captain Dowdal overtook and defeated FitzMaurice's column at Glenflesk. Two hundred men of FitzMaurice's force were killed; all supplies as well as 800 cattle and 500 horses were seized by the English as booty. This thrashing caused an anxious FitzMaurice of Lixnaw to appeal to his old friend Thomas Butler to intervene and ask for mercy on his behalf. In this he proved successful.

---

161 Cannan & Ó'Brógháin: *Galloglass*, p. 52.

Clodah Castle.
(Photograph: Marko Tjemmes)

Thomas Butler of Ormond was now appointed commander of the English forces operating in Munster, receiving the official title of "Lord General of the Forces in Munster". A reasonable man, he was inclined towards diplomacy rather than brutality. With the help of a number of allied Irish chieftains, Desmond's troops were expelled from Tipperary and Waterford and driven into the rough mountains of Kerry. Aided by a handful of English soldiers, the MacCarthy Reagh clan began to inflict increasingly painful losses on the FitzGeralds. Thus the MacCarthys Reagh hoped to cast off the yoke of their nominal overlords, the FitzGeralds and MacCarthy Mór.[162] The new chieftain, Florence MacCarthy (Gaelic: Fínghin mac Donnchadh Mac Cárthaig) claimed to have personally slain two of Desmond's most important galloglas constables, Gorey MacSweeney and Morrice Roe.[163]

Desertion was rife in Gerald FitzGerald's army. His forces began to wane, the last officer of name being no MacSheehey but a member of the MacSweeney clan. He flatly refused to desert his master and was promptly killed by his men for his pains. The Earl of Desmond and the last of his followers were finally killed by members of the Moriarty clan in Glanagenty Valley in 1583.[164] Owen Moriarty presented Desmond's head as a trophy and received a generous financial reward from the delighted English.[165]

The suppression of the rebellion had cost the English crown the astronomical sum of 500,000 pounds.[166] The intangible costs were to prove no less dear. Due to the religious divides and the atrocities committed by English commanders before Thomas Butler took command, the Desmond Rebellion, as it came to be called, constituted a highpoint in brutality. As a consequence, many Anglo-Irish Lords of the Pale became increasingly alienated from the English motherland and kept faith with the old Catholic religion. These men, referred to as "Old English", differed profoundly in their attitudes from the new settlers who had come across the Irish Sea, the so-called "New English".

Enormous stretches of land in Munster had become ownerless, 160,000 hectares having been confiscated by the English crown. The "Munster Plantation" began in 1585.

162 Gaelic: *Mac Carthaig Mór*.
163 In south-western Ireland, the MacSweeneys had erected Clodah Castle near Crookstown.
164 Falls, Cyril: *Elizabeth's Irish Wars*, Syracuse 1997, p. 150 f.
165 Owen Moriarty was to meet his own end on the Triple Tree at Tyburn.
166 Palmer, William: *The Problem of Ireland in Tudor Foreign Policy 1485-1603*, Woodbridge 1994.

Lisnacullia Castle.
(Photograph: Mike Searle)

However, the high hopes placed in this initiative by the English government soon proved to be unjustified – only between 3,000 and 4,000 families responded to the call. Among those followers of the Earl of Desmond who had been disposessed and driven from their estates were the galloglas of the MacSheehy clan. Their home had been at Rathkeale, the chieftain residing at Lisnacullia Castle. MacSheehys had also lived in the valley of the River Awbeg. From this area they were also expelled.

Tirlough MacSheehy was expelled from his estates. This measure was met with resistance from the nobility and even the Protestant Lords. It was argued that although the MacSheehys had once been savage highlanders, they had now become quite civilized. But the crown was determined to make an example of this rebellious mob. Tirlough's son Murrough with three hundred of his men ambushed and robbed a merchant train near Mallow. He was arrested and imprisoned for life at Dublin Castle.[167] After these incidents the MacSheehys and their Irish kern moved north across the Irish Midlands and eventually reached Ulster.

In the south of Ireland, the galloglas had now entered history if one discounts those individuals serving the English crown. The English were terrified of a Spanish expedition to Ireland, which surely would have caused a general rising. These fears in London and Dublin were not at all unjustified. Had the renowned and battle-hardened Spanish *tercios* gained a foothold in Ireland and been given the chance to apply their tactics against the local English forces, the outcome would not have been hard to guess. The brutal and merciless treatment of the survivors of the Spanish Armada who found themselves stranded on the shores of the Irish coast was a direct and predictable result of this paranoia. For instance, when one Spanish vessel ran aground in Tirawly, County Connacht, the local baron, William Bourke of Ardnerie, had the unfortunate survivors slaughtered to a man. Apparently a galloglass named Meleghlen MacCabb (MacLaughlin MacCabe?) with his axe killed eighty Spaniards alone.[168]

However, it was not the Spaniards who were to cause Queen Elizabeth considerable trouble in Ireland. It was once again the Scots.

---

167 Berleth, Richard: *The Twilight Lords*, p. 209.

168 Johnson, Samuel and Oldys: *The Harleian Miscellany*, London 1809, p. 49.

QUEEN ELIZABETH I AND THE LORDS OF THE NORTH

When Shane O'Neill travelled to London to meet Queen Elizabeth in 1562, he brought with him his servants and a galloglas bodyguard. The Irish prince and his warlike entourage were looked upon askance and with some bewilderment by the elegant English courtiers.[169] A visitor from China or South America could not have created a more exotic impression at the English court.

At any rate, it was obvious that Her Majesty was in no way put out by the prospect of receiving even slightly awkward visitors, and Shane O'Neill was definitely a man to be reckoned with.[170]

Shane O'Neill (Gaelic: Sean Donngaileach O`Neill) was born around the year 1530 the younger son of Conn O'Neill, 1st Earl of Tyrone, or Tír Eógain (as seen from English and Irish perspectives respectively). And here the problems began: with his instatement as Earl by Henry VIII in 1542, Conn had recognized the suzerainty of the English crown and the jurisdiction of the Dublin parliament.[171] Whether he did so purely for formal reasons was immaterial since it certainly never occurred to the O'Neills to play by the rules set down by the English.

Conn's first wife had been Lady Alice FitzGerald, daughter of Gerald FitzGerald, 8th Earl of Kildare and the victor of the Battle of Knockdoe.[172] One of their sons was Felim Caoch O`Neill, who was chosen as his father's successor. However, within weeks after Conn and King Henry had met, Felim was dead. He had been involved in a lasting feud with his father's most formidable galloglas constable, Gillespic MacDonnell.[173] A javelin hurled from the hand of a MacDonnell galloglass struck him down, thereby creating a large number of new problems.

Conn's second spouse was Sorcha O'Neill, daughter of Hugh Oge O'Neill, chief of the O'Neills of Clandeboye. Whether Shane himself was a son from his father's first or second marriage has remained a matter of debate among historians to this day. He was passed over by his father in the wake of Felim's death (as were several other siblings), and was forced to yield any birthright there may have been to an illegitimate son of his father's: Matthew, whose mother Allison Kelly was a blacksmith's widow from Dundalk, was ten years Shane's senior, and was duly recognized by the English king. When Conn O'Neill was made Earl of Tyrone, Matthew was given the title of Baron of Dungannon. He was ostentatiously supported by the Dublin administration, but his followers among the O'Neills remained few. Matthew was killed by supporters of his half-brother Shane in 1558. The men who dealt the blow were members of the O'Donnely family by whom Shane had been raised as a child.

Conn himself died in the following year, and the question of who would succeed him once again presented itself. Shane's followers acclaimed him King of Tír Eógain and chieftain of the O'Neills, but in order to become the new Earl of Tyrone Shane was dependent on the approval of the English crown. Shane and Brian, Matthew O'Neill's eldest son and heir, were summoned to London. Both men duly set out, but as Brian was making his way from Newry to Carlingford on 18th pril 1562, he was set upon by Turlough Luineach O'Neill and killed, possibly at the instigation of his uncle Shane O'Neill.[174]

Thomas Radclyffe, 3rd Earl of Sussex and Lord Deputy of Ireland, had long since begun to mistrust Shane. Some sources claim that he even paid an assassin to have him murdered, but this did not happen. After Brian's death Radclyffe mustered a punitive expedition, and this force was surprised on the border between Tyrone and Monaghan by Shane and his followers. On 18th July 1561, the English rearguard numbering 400 men was confronted by O'Neill at the head of 120 cavalry and several hundred galloglas and Scottish mercenaries, so-called Redshanks. 50 Englishmen were killed and the rest of the force dispersed, before the English main body of 800 men under Sir George Stanley were able to turn back and drive off the O'Neills. To the Irish, the battle was to be known as "The Battle of the Red Sagums", supposedly alluding to the English soldiers' attire.[175]

In contrast to her rash Lord Deputy, the prudent Queen Elizabeth considered discretion the better part of valour and duly gave diplomacy preference over warfare. The meeting described above took place on 6th January 1562, and the Virgin Queen proved that she was in fact much smarter than the boorish Northern Irish warlord facing her. She readily confirmed his position as clan leader of the O'Neills, but this was irrelevant since according to English law this title did not even exist. Queen Elizabeth however was careful to never officially instate Shane O'Neill as Earl of Tyrone.

Soon enough Shane O'Neill was once again up in arms, this time even employing arquebusiers armed with firearms. In 1563, he once again submitted to English rule.[176] After all these intrigues and repeated rebellions, Elizabeth was growing rather tired of Shane O'Neill. Meanwhile Hugh O'Neill, a younger son of Matthew O'Neill, was

---

169 The meeting was also witnessed by the ambassadors of the King of Sweden and the Duke of Savoy. O'Neill was accompanied by the constable of his galloglas, a member of the MacSweeney clan.
170 Hayes-MacCoy: *Irish Battles*, p. 68.
171 Conn had even converted to Protestantism.
172 Lydon, James: *The Making of Ireland. From Ancient Times to the Present*, Routledge 1998, p. 117.
173 Schlegel, Donald M.: "The MacDonnells of Tyrone and Armagh. A Genealogical Study", in: *Seanchas Ardmhacha* vol. 10, No. 1, 1980-1981, p. 205.

174 Falls: *Elizabeth's Irish Wars*, p. 89 f.
175 Heath: *Armies*, p. 17.
176 Heath and Sque: *Irish Wars*, p. 4. Among the English forces engaged in putting down Shane's rebellion were members of the MacDonalds of Antrim.

A heavily-armed MacSweeney galloglass.
(© Claíomh – Niamh O'Rourke 2011)

growing up in England. The Queen had her eye on him and considered making him the new Earl of Tyrone in his uncle's stead.

Yet in Tyrone itself the political situation was a complex one. Among Shane's enemies were the O'Donnells of Tyrconnell, the Maquires of Fermanagh, and the O'Reillys of Cavan. Above all loomed the powerful MacDonalds of Antrim, who with the help of their Scottish relatives had undertaken several campaigns westwards into O'Neill territory. In the time of Shane's father Conn the MacDonnells of Antrim had been considered the greatest danger to the power of the O'Neills, and for this reason Queen Elizabeth had authorized punitive expeditions against Antrim in the years 1551, 1555, and 1556.

What made the MacDonalds of Antrim so dangerous was the fact that they were capable of mobilizing large numbers of warriors from the Scottish west coast and the Hebrides at very short notice. In contrast to the galloglas these "redshanks" had no Irish roots (they were also referred to as "New Scots"). These mercenaries habitually only served for three months before returning to their Scottish homelands. Armed with small bucklers called "targes" and their one-handed swords they were more nimble than the heavily-armed galloglas, but in the mid-1600s the two-handed claymore was also still in fashion, which could inflict wounds anything as terrible as those struck by the galloglas' heavy war-axes. The sheer number of redshanks available was giving the members of the Privy Council in London considerable headaches. It was reckoned that northern Ireland would soon be swarming with up to 7,000 Scots.

If the Privy Council was anxious, then so too was Shane O'Neill. Since his political ambitions extended to no less than full control over all of Ulster, the MacDonnells of Antrim were just as dangerous to him as the English. Consequently, there were now no less than three factions contesting for control of northern Ireland: the English crown, the MacDonnells of Antrim, and Shane O'Neill. In

On 2nd May 1565 Shane O'Neill defeated the MacDonnells of Antrim at the Battle of Glenshesk.[178] Among his about 2,000 fighting men were 40 redshanks and 120 Scottish bowmen. Interestingly, both contingents were commanded by Brian Carrach MacDonald, a brother of James MacDonald of Dunyveg, who fought on the opposing side. Shane O'Neill's force also contained between 100 and 200 horse, and 250 galloglas. Among the redshanks fighting for the MacDonnells of Antrim were many MacLeods and MacNeills.

At dawn, Shane O'Neill had his galloglas begin their uphill attack without previously having his archers and javelinmen skirmish with the enemy. The attack achieved surprise,[179] and secured victory for Shane O'Neill. The enemy lost 700 dead.

O'Neill's men managed to take a number of valuable prisoners from among the MacDonnells of Antrim. Sorley Boy (*Buidhe*) MacDonnell was captured,[180] and James MacDonald of Dunyveg, chief of Clan Donald South, was badly wounded.[181] The defeat at Glenshesk caused the MacDonnells of Antrim to seek the support of the English crown.

The methods employed by Shane O'Neill in bringing his troops up to strength bordered on the revolutionary. Up to then, carrying arms and warfare in Ireland had been both duty and privilege of the free-born. In 15th and 16th entury Ireland, Irish-Gaelic communities clearly distinguished between free-born and serfs, the latter working their lords' land. They were not permitted to bear arms. Shane O'Neill however proceeded to arm these men, and had them trained in the use of weapons: "He armeth and weaponeth all the peasants of his country"[182]. Shane O'Neill's relations with the Scottish Highland clans also permitted him to recruit large numbers of redshanks.

Eventually however, O'Neill began to get too big for his boots. He seriously contemplated proposing to Mary Queen of Scots and asked the King of France to dispatch an expeditionary force, writing to a French cardinal to ask for his support in the matter. The new Lord Deputy Sir Henry Sidney promptly received orders from England to deal with the over-ambitious Irishman. His troops were reinforced by 300 arquebusiers from Berwick and 700 recruits from the counties of western England. He was also ordered to recruit 200 infantry and 200 horse locally. The campaign was to commence at the beginning of the harvest season in order to maximize the damage to O'Neill and his troops. The English reinforcements were to gather on the Isle of Man, where the Lieutenant of the

This galloglass wears a heavily waxed *cotún* to ward off the damp.
(© Claíomh – Dave Swift 2010)

the royal palace at Richmond, Queen Elizabeth was beginning to view the MacDonnells of Antrim as a possibly useful instrument. To fight both groups simultaneously was impossible even by English standards. Meanwhile, large groups of mercenaries were gathering in Ulster – besides the ubiquitous galloglas, there were now redshanks, and the Bonnaghts, who were almost entirely of Irish-Gaelic stock, had become almost as significant as the previous two categories of mercenaries.[177]

---

177 Hayes-MacCoy: *Irish Battles*, p. 73.

178 Heath and Sque, *Irish Wars*, p. 4. The event is also referred to as the Battle of Glentaisie. Glenshesk is one of the nine Glens of Antrim.

179 Hill, J. M.: *Fire and Sword. Sorley Boy MacDonnell and the Rise of Clan Iain Mor*, London 1993, p. 90.

180 Seehase: *Der schottische Clan MacDonald*, p. 60.

181 He died several weeks later a prisoner of Shane O'Neill.

182 Hayes-MacCoy: *Irish Battles*, p. 74.

Ordnance Edward Randolph was to take over command. After linking up with Sidney's force, the plan was to reinstate Calvagh O'Donnell in Tyrconnell, and the chief of the Maguires in Fermanagh. Both men were Irish magnates who had been deposed by Shane O'Neill. This, it was reckoned, would increase local support, however feeble, for the English cause.

How had the above situation come about? In 1557 Shane O'Neill, not yet chieftain of the entire O'Neill clan, had attacked Tyrconnell, which was ruled by Manus O'Donnell. Two O'Donnell spies had managed to make their way into the O'Neills' camp and discovered the presence of Shane O'Neill's personal bodyguard of sixty galloglas. Other information gathered on the composition of O'Neill's army was to prove extremey valuable, as shortly afterwards the O'Donnells were able to defeat Shane O'Neill in battle.

In 1559 however, Shane O'Neill was able to capture Manus O'Donnell's eldest son Calvagh O'Donnell, together with his Scottish wife Catherine MacLean. Shane O'Neill himself was married to Calvagh O'Donnell's daughter Mary. Poor Mary soon died, allegedly of a broken heart due to her husband's harsh treatment of her father. Having received a heavy ransom and promises of good conduct, Shane released Calvagh in 1561, but Mary's stepmother Catherine MacLean had meanwhile become Shane's lover and remained with him.[183] Calvagh O'Donnell turned to the English crown for support. When his father Manus died in 1563, Calvagh became chieftain of the O'Donnells. He immediately attempted to shake off the O'Neill yoke, but to no avail.

Now, in 1561, the situation looked promising. Sir Henry Sidney was able to incorporate Edward Randolph's English reinforcements into his army at Lough Foyle. The latter were a strong force consisting of 200 cavalry, 1,200 archers and arquebusiers from the Pale, and a further 100 horsemen, 300 galloglas and 92 musketeers (or artillerymen) from Desmond.[184] The English army drove O'Neill's forces from western Ulster, and control of Donegal once again passed to Calvagh O'Donnell. Randolph remained in Derry as commander of the local garrison, while Sidney marched back south, making his way through Connacht. Sidney had hardly turned his back when Shane O'Neill returned in force and attacked the Derry garrison. The English managed to repel the attack, but Randolph was killed in the fighting. Shane O'Neill's élite galloglas likewise suffered heavily. In the spring of 1567 the English garrison's powder magazine blew up, the survivors abandoning the town. Hugh O'Donnell, the new chieftain of the O'Donnells (Calvagh had died in 1566), was not put out by this reverse and instead began to raid O'Neill territory. The fuming Shane now raised an army of considerable size and marched west into O'Donnell country.

Hugh O'Donnell's scouts had informed him of O'Neill's approach. Together with a small force he was encamped in an old fort at Ardingary (near Letterkenny) on the west bank of the River Swilly. The O'Neill force, approaching from the east, forded the river at Farsetmore (Gaelic: *Fearsad Suilighe*). Since this stretch is determined by the tide, the river was running low on the morning of 8th May 1567. Hugh O'Donnell had despatched messengers to assemble his dispersed forces, and ordered his son, also named Hugh, to delay the enemy until he was ready to fight.

While the elder Hugh assembled his foot soldiers and led them across marshy ground to a safe position, Hugh the younger led his cavalry to the attack. His horsemen clashed with O'Neill's cavalry. Many noblemen were killed in the fray, until the numerical superiority of O'Neill's horsemen gradually began to tell against the O'Donnells. Hugh O'Donnell saw that his father had taken up a favourable position and broke off the fight, retreating towards his own infantry. By now the reinforcements were beginning to arrive: the first to appear were the MacSweeneys Doe led by their constable Murrough MacSweeney, followed by the MacSweeneys Fanad, commanded by the chieftain's sons. The last to arrive were the MacSweeneys Banagh under the command of Maolmuire MacSweeney. Irish chroniclers tend to sympathise with the O'Donnells and play down the size of the forces available, claiming that the O'Donnells had only 400 troops at their disposal. This is hardly credible, since the galloglas and their retinue alone numbered four hundred, and the O'Donnells were a warlike clan so will have fielded a much larger number of hardy and experienced fighters[185]. O'Neill had ordered a rest for his men, and now the time had come for the O'Donnells to settle old scores. The MacSweeneys fell upon the startled O'Neills, who scattered before the onslaught. Shane O'Neill escaped and was guided to safety across the Scarrifholis ford by men of the O'Gallaghers from Tyrconnell, who were old enemies of the O'Donnells.

For once, Shane O'Neill seems to have been at a loss over his next move. He eventually invited the MacDonalds of Cantire[186] to Ireland. Why he did so, is not entirely clear. It is possible that he acted on the advice of his prisoner Sorley Boy MacDonald. Alexander Óg MacDonald, Sorley Boy's brother and chief of the MacDonalds of Cantire, accepted the invitation and sailed to Ireland accompanied by a large number of his warriors. Together with fifty of his own men, Shane O'Neill entered the MacDonald camp at Cushendun on 2nd June 1567.

What exactly brought about what happened next is impossible to determine. Either a trap had been sprung,

---

183 In 1563 Catherine became Shane's third wife. The altogether ten sons that Shane had with his wives all became notorious leaders of mercenaries known as the "Wild MacShanes".

184 Hayes-MacCoy: *Irish Battles*, p.78.

185 Ibid., p. 81.

186 Modern Kintyre.

Dunluce Castle.
(Photograph: Marco Tjemmes)

or the negotiations got out of hand. The Scots with their heavy claymores set upon O'Neill and his warriors and slaughtered them to a man. Shane's body was wrapped in a tattered shirt and cast into a well. His head was dispatched to Dublin, constituting a pleasant surprise to everyone present.

Shane O'Neill was succeeded by Turlough Luineach O'Neill as clan chieftain. This man turned out to be a little more dependable than his troublesome predecessor, at least when he was sober. Sorley Boy MacDonald once again assumed his former political position among the MacDonalds of Antrim.

Turlough held the peace until September 1574, when he rose in revolt against the English crown. By June 1575, Walter Devereux, 1st Earl of Essex, had crushed the rebellion.[187] In 1581, the chief of the O'Neills once again made a nuisance of himself by fighting against the O'Donnells of Tyrconnell. Turlough allegedly had at his disposal a force of 700 cavalry, 2,500 redshanks, 1,500 galloglas, and an unknown number of kern.[188] The skirmishing eventually petered out without too much harm done, but the conflict resurfaced in 1583. Turlough O'Neill was a violent man, and a heavy drinker.[189] What made him even more of a liability was the fact that he now counted a powerful Scottish clan chieftain among his relatives. James MacDonald of Dunyveg, dying a captive of Shane O'Neill, had left a widow, Lady Agnes Campbell, who of all people decided to marry Turlough.

After Shane O'Neill's death, Sorley Boy had briefly returned to Scotland. Returning with six hundred redshanks, he swore never to leave Ireland again. It is worth remembering that Sorley Boy's claims to the leadership of the MacDonnells of Antrim (whether judging by English,

---

187 At the time, Turlough O'Neill is said to have had 200 horse, 1,000 kern, 400 galloglas, and 400 redshanks under arms; cf. Heath: *Armies*, p. 85.

188 These numbers are probably an exaggeration; cf. Heath: *Armies*, p. 85.

189 Morgan, Hiram: *Tyrone's Rebellion. The Outbreak of the Nine Years War in Tudor Ireland*, London 1993, p. 90. According to legend, Turlough killed three galloglas constables in the course of a single binge. Henceforth, galloglas were understandably reluctant to take service with an O'Neill force.

Galloglas and kern.
(© Claíomh – Niamh O'Rourke 2012)

Irish or Scottish standards is immaterial) were extremely thin. He had attained his current position through violence and sound military leadership alone, and he had not hesitated to dispose even of close relatives if it suited his ends.[190]

Let us take a brief look back:

There is a region in Antrim known as "The Route". This was home to the MacQuillans who around the year 1460 had purchased the remaining estates, castles and manors of the de Mandevilles. The area had formerly been known as Twescard, but had been given its present name by the MacQuillans. The name is derived from the word *rout*, meaning something akin to a private army. The area was indeed of strategic significance: when James V King of Scots had briefly befriended the MacDonald (or MacDonnell) clan, the risk of a Scots invasion of Ulster had been very real. The lands of the MacDonalds of Antrim could very well have served as a bridgehead for the Scottish campaign. The English government in Dublin had not remained inactive in the face of this danger and despatched several punitive expeditions against The Route. During one such campaign in 1550, Sorley boy was taken prisoner and taken to Dublin. Here he remained a prisoner in Dublin castle for twelve months, before being exchanged against a number of English captives seized by his brother James MacDonald of Dunyveg. Sorley Boy managed to take the constable of Carrickfergus Castle prisoner and received a high ransom in exchange for the man's freedom. He then set about driving the MacQuillans, who were former allies of the MacDonnells, from The Route. In 1558 the chief of the MacDonnells of Antrim duly appointed Sorley Boy "Lord of the Route", but left it to him to conquer the territory for himself should he wish to do so. Sorley Boy raised a force of redshanks in Scotland, landing in Marketon Bay in 1559. Battles were

---

190 This was not going to change. Sorley Boy's elder brother Coll had also stayed in Antrim, his son Gillespie Fiacal marrying a girl from the Irish O'Quin clan. As a part of the wedding celebrations, a form of bullfight was staged, in the course of which Gillespie was injured. He was taken to Rathlin Island for medical attendance, where he died, allegedly poisoned at Sorley Boy's orders. Stevenson, David: *Alasdair MacColla and the Highland Problem and the Seventeenth Century*, Edinburgh 1980, p. 34.

fought at Bonamargy and Beal a Faula. The MacQuillans were forced to yield, Sorley Boy seizing the strategically important Dunluce Castle.[191]

In 1571 Sir Thomas Smith received from the English crown a legal title to 150,000 hectares of land in eastern Ulster for colonisation. Informed of this development, the chief of the O'Neills of Clandeboyne torched every large building and settlement in the region. When the English colonists arrived, they were promptly attacked, forcing the English to abandon the scheme.

Sorley Boy had played an active part in foiling the English plans. In order to further his political career at the English court, the Earl of Essex had offered to conquer and colonise Ulster at his own expense. In 1573, Sorley Boy reached an agreement with Sir Thomas Smith, who promised to support Sorley Boy's claims to The Route if Sorley Boy converted to Protestantism. Essex began to fear for his plans and allied himself with Turlough Luineach O'Neill. He succeeded in defeating Sorley Boy at Castle Toome but was forced to withdraw to Carrickfergus because he was unable to exploit his victory due to the small size of his force and a shortage of supplies.

Essex then ordered an attack on Rathlin Island, where the most important of Sorley Boy's retainers and family had sought refuge, and where the coffers were kept. A force commanded by Sir Francis Drake and Sir John Norris landed on the island and took Rathlin Castle. On 26th July 1575, with Drake's ships patrolling the waters around the island, Norris had the entire garrison and the civilian population of the island summarily slaughtered.[192] Sorley Boy was forced to helplessly look on and watch the massacre of his relatives from the mainland. Altogether 700 people fell victim to this atrocity, most of them members of the MacDonnells of Antrim. In retaliation, Sorley Boy annihilated the English garrison of Carrickfergus Castle, which had unwisely ventured from the safety of the walls to fight against his men in the open.

In 1583, many MacDonnells of Antrim took service with Turlough Luineach O'Neill. With Sorley Boy's manpower running low, the MacQuillans undertook an attempt to regain possession of The Route. Having allied themselves with Sir Hugh MacPhelim O'Neill of Edenduffcarrig and reinforced by two companies of English musketeers from the Pale led by a Captain Chatterton, the MacQuillans deemed themselves strong enough to stand up to Sorley Boy. Led by Edward and Roderick MacQuillan[193], the force attacked Sorley Boy, but the old warrior was not so easily beaten: at the battle of Slieve-na-Aura in April 1583, Sorley Boy once more exhibited remarkable military talent. The enemy cavalry and galloglas were lured into a frontal attack across apparently solid ground, only to find themselves literally bogged down and face to face with the lightly armed, fast-moving redshanks. The battle became a one-sided affair, with Sorley Boy allegedly convincing the constable of the MacAulay of the Glens galloglas, who arrived when the fighting was at its height, to change sides and fight for him instead of the MacQuillans. In 1584 Sorley Boy and a large force of Scottish mercenaries once again raided Antrim. Sir Henry Bagenal, the governor of Carrickfergus Castle, tried to contain the threat but was repulsed. After this final clash Sorley Boy settled down to enjoy the spoils of his long military career. The English were only too glad to leave him alone, and he died at a ripe old age in 1589 or 1590.[194]

---

191 Wright, Rev. George Newenham: *A Guide to Giants Causeway and the North-East Coast of the County of Antrim,* London 1823, p. 67-69.

192 This unmitigated massacre was not only the moral low ebb of this famous English sea dog's career, but also of the entire English Lordship government.

193 Patterson, Raymond Campbell: *The Lords of the Isles. A History of Clan Donald*, Edinburgh 2008, p. 89.

194 Sorley Boy was born between 1505 and 1510. His son Randal (or Ranald) MacSorley MacDonnell of Antrim inherited his father's title and estates. He was made Earl of Antrim by King James I in 1620.

GALLOGLAS FACE GALLOGLAS IN CONNACHT

Actually, the Lord President of Connacht, a Protestant Englishman by the name of Fitton, had planned to disband all private armies of local magnates and thereby deprive all galloglas of their livelihoods. In the end he not only failed but employed large numbers of galloglas himself.

Situated on the border between today's counties of Mayo and Galway, Shrule was a castle of considerable strategic importance. It had been erected in the year 1238 by the de Burghs. Since their descendants, the Burkes of Clanricarde and the Burkes of Mayo, were continually at loggerheads with each other, the castle saw much action. On 21st June a battle was fought beneath its walls in which not only Burkes fought Burkes, but also MacDonnell galloglas against MacDonnell galloglas.

The office of Lord President of Connacht, newly created in 1569, was a powerful one. Primarily, it was a military command allowing its owner to impose martial law, counteract rebellion by force of arms, and to have the final say even in civil litigation.

Sir Henry Sidney appointed Sir Edward Fitton, a radical Protestant, Lord President. Among his duties was the division of Connacht into English administrative areas, i. e. shires and baronies. He was further expected to determine the borders between Connacht and Thomond. The Gaelic, "mere" Irish magnates were advised to abandon their time-honoured Irish titles and to instead adopt new English ones, making them earls and barons. Needless to say, they were also encouraged to abandon not just their ancient titles but also their traditional Roman Catholic religion. This system became known as *surrender and regrant*. Another measure envisaged was the dissolution of all private armies[195], the galloglas among them, and the abolition of the coin-and-livery system. It was thought that these measures would increase the tax flow and facilitate tax collection.

Not only was Sir Edward an ardent Protestant, he also nursed a particular loathing for Richard Burke, 2nd Earl of Clanricarde. The latter was not universally recognized even among his own clan members, his rule being questioned by relatives on several occasions. His father, the first Earl of Clanricarde, had come by his title only by converting to Protestantism together with his family and retinue. Thus Sir Edward deeply mistrusted the 2nd Earl's loyalties. Conversely, other Irish lords disliked the 2nd Earl for his Anglophile leanings, and dismissively christened him *Sassanach*, Englishman.[196]

Richard Burke himself was considered a trifle odd even by his contemporaries. For example, he had divorced his first wife because he suspected her of witchcraft. His eldest

Shrule Castle.
(Photograph: Maximilian Bunk)

son, Ulick Burke by name, had attempted several risings against his father in the 1560s. These dynastic squabbles, which affected large parts of Connacht and Thomond, became known as the *Mac an Iarla* Wars.

With his administrative reforms, Sir Edward Fitton managed to rekindle the age-old conflict between the Burkes of Mayo and the Burkes of Clanricarde.

Fitton quarreled with Connor O'Brien, 3rd Earl of Thomond.[197] Although officially part of Munster, Thomond had been assigned to Fitton's jurisdiction, and Sir Edward had appointed a sheriff whom the Earl did not approve of (although the man himself was Irish). In 1569 the Earl of Thomond joined forces with James FitzMaurice FitzGerald, and in February 1570 he defeated Fitton's troops at Ennis, pursuing him to Galway, which he placed under siege. Sir Henry Sidney sent a relief force which was able to break the siege, but the unrest had spread: two sons of the Earl of Clanricarde, Ulick and John (nicknamed John of the Shamrocks), had joined the rebellion[198]. The Earl of Clanricarde himself hurriedly dispatched troops

---

195 As far as the English were concerned, these were any troops unauthorized by the Lordship government.

196 Translator's note: the word *Sassanach*, or *Sasanach*, has Germanic roots and is related to the Old English lexeme *Seaxan*, Saxon.

197 Connor O'Brien had been a close ally of Richard Burke. Both had suffered defeat at Spancel Hill in 1599.

198 Connolly: *Contested Island*, p. 161.

MacSweeney galloglas.
(© Claíomh – Shirley Lougheed 2010)

relatives of the MacDonnells of Antrim. Fitton also commanded the MacDonnells of Tynekill, led by Colla MacDonnell of Tynekill.[199]

Fitton failed in taking Shrule castle, which was held by the rebels, so he settled down to a siege.[200] Connor O'Brien, 3rd Earl of Thomond, the Burkes of Mayo, and the MacDonnells of Mayo combined forces to relieve the castle. The rebels were probably commanded by Shane MacOliver, a chieftain of the Burkes of Mayo.[201] Fitton had ordered his men to take up defensive positions around the castle. His troops included English musketeers, several guns, 300 horse, and a large number of galloglas, among them (as mentioned above) the MacDonnells of Tynekill and the MacDonnells of Knocknacloy. One battle (i. e. company) of MacDowell galloglas was also present. Among Clanricarde's force, his five battles of MacSweeney galloglas were the most important contingent. Shane Oliver ordered his galloglas and kern to attack. The musketry of Fitton's troops was not able to break the momentum of the charge, and the English force began to retreat towards their camp. Fitton now personally led his comparatively few cavalry into the fray. His horse was brought down, Fitton himself suffering facial injuries. The MacSweeney galloglas stoically held their ground, dying where they stood. Eventually the galloglas of the MacDonnells of Leinster, fighting on the English side, conceded defeat and retired, joyfully pursued by their relatives of the MacDonnells of Connacht. These developments prompted Shane MacOliver to break off the fight.[202]

Although Fitton's losses exceeded those of the enemy,[203] a number of favourable circumstances had enabled him to remain in possession of the field and declare himself the victor. A short while later, Shrule was taken and the entire garrison put to death.[204]

---

199 His real name was Calvagh MacDonnell, but he has gone down in history as Colla MacDonnell.

200 Fissel, Mark Charles: *English Warfare 1511 – 1642*, London and New York 2001, p. 209.

201 Falls: *Elizabeth's Irish Wars*, p. 108. Other sources give the commander's name as Walter Cluas le Doinin.

202 Shane MacOliver employed his galloglas to enhance his own political status, becoming the leader of the Burkes of Mayo in 1571. In contrast to most of his contemporaries, he was not disposed towards warfare and had the good of his people in mind. Despite such attitudes, he kept a large galloglas force under arms. He was made Baron Ardenerie in 1580, but died the same year.

203 The constable of the MacDonnell of Knocknacloy galloglas, Calvagh „Colla" MacDonnell, was killed.

204 For his services rendered to Her Majesty in the battle for Shrule in 1570, Ferragh MacDonnell of the Cloneen was given the castle itself and four quarters of the the surrounding countryside in 1585.

---

in aid of Fitton's beleaguered troops and vehemently denied any connection with his two sons' behaviour. He was quick to add that this rebellion was chiefly directed against himself, an allegation which Fitton was reluctant to accept. Fitton claimed that he had evidence of secret negotiations between the Earl and the chief of the Burkes of Mayo.

With a strong force, Fitton moved north from Galway. His army also included galloglas of the MacDonnells of Knocknacloy. The latter traditionally served the O'Neills of Tyrone, and occasionally crossed swords with their

On campaign ...
(© Claíomh – Katharina Temirati 2022)

The ruins of Shrule Castle. (Photograph: Maximilian Bunk)

In 1571, rebellion once again broke out among the Gaelic Lords of Mayo.[205] In the following year, two sons of the Earl of Clanricarde rose in revolt. A younger son of the Earl whose Gaelic name was *Seán mac an Iarla a Búrc* (who by English law was not inheritable) rebelled in 1572 and destroyed Athlone. He then laid waste to the middle of the island, leaving a trail of death and destruction. He destroyed a large number of castles in the region, pillaged the countryside around Galway and further north towards Roscommon. He then crossed the Shannon to plunder Westmeath before once again turning west to raid Connemara.[206]

After the rebellion of 1572, Sir Edward Fitton had finally had enough of Irish unruliness. Having always mistrusted the Earl of Clanricarde, he had him put in chains and locked up in Dublin Castle. The Earl was released after six months, and in order to underline his firm allegiance to the English crown he immediately hanged one of his sons, a nephew, the son of one of his cousins, one galloglas constable, and fifty other unfortunates.

---

[205] Jordan, Donald E.: *Land and Popular Politics in Ireland. County Mayo from the Plantation to the Land War*, Cambridge 1994, p. 21.

[206] Martyn, Adrian: *The Tribes of Galway 1124-1642*, Galway 2016, p. 146 f.

Manning the ramparts. (© Claíomh – Dave Swift 2012)

In 1576, things came to a head when the Earl's recalcitrant relatives once again rebelled. This time, the English were supported by the Burkes of Mayo. Irish pirate queen Grace O'Malley offered to support the Burkes of Mayo with two ships and 200 warriors.

In 1580, yet another son of the Earl of Clanricarde found himself with the hangman's noose around his neck. William mac an Iarla Burke had surrendered and been placed under arrest. The mayor of Galway, Nicholas Lynch, managed to get him pardoned, but the High Sheriff of Galway, William Oge Martyn, had him executed anyway. To be on the safe side, he had his men delay the mayor, who had been on his way to the place of execution with the document that would have saved William's life.[207]

Richard Burke, 2nd Earl of Clanricarde, died in 1582. John of the Shamrocks (John "na Seamer" Burke, Baron Leitrim) was ambushed and killed by his elder half-brother Ulick on 11th November 1583. Ulick became the 3rd Earl of Clanricarde and remained loyal to the English crown.

---

[207] Martyn was a veteran of the Battle of Shrule Castle. In 1579, he had undertaken a vain attempt. to storm Rockfleet Castle in order to seize Grace O'Malley. In December 1586 he had galloglas constable Edmond MacSheehy executed.

A galloglass awaits his chance to strike at the enemy.
(© Claíomh – Niamh O'Rourke 2016)

THE NINE YEARS WAR

Hugh Maguire, who had rebelled against the English crown, had fortified a position covering two fords across the River Erne at Belleek. His force was between 900 and 1,200 strong. About one hundred of these men were cavalry. Maguire placed between 400 and 500 of his force – musketeers, archers, and galloglas – in the fieldworks commanding the fords, and held the rest in reserve.

The date was 10th October 1593. Maguire's army was opposed by Sir Henry Bagenal (or Bagnall) with 400 English soldiers, and Hugh O'Neill, Earl of Tyrone, with 200 horse and 600 Irish infantry. Since Maguire's redoubt ran along a ledge created by a bend in the river, Bagenal positioned his musketeers on the flanks, from where they were able to take the enemy under fire from two sides.[208] He then had his infantry attack across one of the fords. His force was organized in two lines, the second of which was accompanied by the cavalry. The defenders of the redoubt fled before Maguire was able to send reinforcements. Maguire lost three hundred dead, while the enemy only lost three dead and 20 wounded.[209] The action was subsequently known as the Battle of the Erne Fords.

The Earl of Tyrone retired early from the battlefield, claiming that a leg wound had forced him to seek medical assistance.[210] Tyrone declared this injury sufficient proof of his allegiance to the English crown, while some spies reported that he had secretly met Maguire, his son-in-law, before the battle.[211]

During the pursuit of Maguire's force, Bagenal encountered a lone galloglass lurking in the woods. The latter saw his chance to kill the enemy commander and struck out at Bagenal with his axe. If the blow had not been deflected by a branch of a nearby tree, Bagenal would undoubtedly have been killed. Thanks to his arboreal saviour, he was only wounded.

According to English law, Hugh O'Neill was the legitimate heir of his grandfather Conn O'Neill, 1st Earl of Tyrone. After Shane O'Neill's violent death, Turlough Luineach O'Neill had been declared chieftain of the O'Neills by the clan's elders, but by English legal standards such an appointment was completely null and void.

Despite this situation, the English made no move to depose Turlough, even though he had killed Hugh's brother Brian, the legitimate heir of Conn O'Neill originally backed by the English crown.[212] Apart from his rebellion in 1574-75, Turlough O'Neill kept a low profile in his northern Irish territories however, and so no more was said or done about it.

Born around the year 1550, Hugh O'Neill was raised a ward of the English crown, spending most of his childhood in the Hovenden household in the Pale. He also spent some time in England itself, the Earl of Leicester acting as one of his influential patrons. Having returned to Ulster in 1568, he was received into the entourage of the Lord Deputy, Sir Henry Sidney.

During the Desmond Rebellion, Hugh fought in the English armies, doing the same in the struggle against Sorley Boy MacDonnell in 1584. In the following year, he was admitted into the Irish House of Lords, assuming the title of 2nd Earl of Tyrone. After a spell at the English court in 1587, he received an official legal document granting him his grandfather's estates as a fiefdom. Hugh was wise enough not to challenge Turlough O'Neill openly, but he secretly succeeded in whittlling away at his support inside the clan. His profound knowledge of English politics and law were to prove valuable assets in what was to come.

His shock of russet hair had earned Hugh the nickname "Red Hugh". His first wife was Katherine O'Neill, but the marriage was dissolved in 1574 due to a prohibited degree of relation. Hugh married Siobhan O'Donnell, who died in 1581. The widower asked Sir Henry Bagenal, commander-in-chief (*Marshal*) of the English army in Ireland, for permission to marry Bagenal's sister Mabel. Mabel was still under age, and Bagenal refused. Not taking no for an answer, Hugh paid Mabel a visit, and the couple eloped. A short while later they were married at Dungannon, where Hugh O'Neill had his residence.

At some stage the Earl of Tyrone must have reached the decision to rebel against the English crown. We do not know when exactly the decision was taken, but the reasons are clear enough: while the already long-existent English rule over Ireland and the presence of powerful Anglo-Irish lords do not appear to have contributed to Hugh O'Neill's grievances, he obviously found it impossible to stomach the gradual replacement of traditional Irish law, the *Brehon Law*, with English law.[213] Irish traditions and customs were also increasingly being superseded by English ones, and English administration was taking a firm hold.

In Munster and Connacht, the Lord Presidents (who were effectively military governors) wielded a large amount of power. In accordnace with English practice, these two provinces had been divided into shires in which sheriffs enforced English laws. Such a procedure was now also envisaged for Fermanagh. One of Hugh's daughters from his first marriage was married to Hugh Maguire, the Gaelic Irish lord of Fermanagh.

---

208 O'Neill, James: "Tyrone's proxy war 1593-4", in: *History Ireland* (March/April 2015), pp. 14-17 (p. 14).
209 Heath: *Armies*, p. 22.
210 Hugh Maguire was also wounded.
211 Brigden, Susan: *New Worlds, Lost Worlds. The Rule of the Tudors 1485-1603*, London et al. 2001.
212 Brian and Hugh were both sons of Matthew O'Neill and Siobhan Maguire.

213 Beckett: *Geschichte Irlands*, p. 72.

In spring 1593, Captain Humphrey Willis was appointed Sheriff of Fermanagh[214]. Hugh Maguire drove Willis out however, attacked Sligo in May, and in the following month invaded Roscommon at the head of 1,000 men. On 23rd June, a curious action was fought against the force of Sir Richard Bingham, Lord President of Connacht.[215] The field of Rathcroghan was covered in dense fog, when both columns ran into each other. Since the mist made it impossible for the English musketeers to employ their weapons to any effect, Bingham was forced to retire.[216] The archbishop of Armagh, Edmund MacGauran, was killed in a skirmish near Skearnavart. MacGauran was considered by many of his contemporaries as having been the driving force behind Maguire's rebellion.[217]

Summer passed, the Lord Deputy, Maguire and Tyrone exchanging letters negotiating truces and promises of safe conduct, but with no tangible results. Meanwhile, Turlough Luineach O'Neill appointed Hugh O'Neill captain of Tyrone and Tanist (Gaelic: *Tánaiste*), thus making him his heir and future successor. A short while later, the O'Neills made Hugh O'Neill chief of the clan.

In September, Hugh Maguire resumed his campaign, moving against the town of Monaghan and pillaging the county. Marshal Bagenal assembled 150 horse and 900 infantry, and asked Tyrone for military assistance. On 24th September Bagenal arrived at Enniskillen, which with the exception of its castle had been burned to the ground by Maguire's force. His men had occupied the castle, and the nearby ford across the Erne at Lisgoole had been heavily fortified.

Tyrone and his force joined Bagenal, who immediately wished to force a crossing of the Erne. Tyrone advised against it, and Bagenal was forced to look for another crossing upriver. The ford at Belleek was also occupied by Maguire's forces, and defended by fieldworks. The ensuing action, the Battle of the Erne Fords, has been described above.

Tyrone returned to Dungannon. His brother-in-law Bagenal wished to march to Tyrconnell, but Bingham was unwilling to dispatch troops from Connacht. Finding the enemy positions at the Lisgoole ford deserted, Bagenal assumed that he had crushed the rebellion and dismissed his troops on 22nd October.

Sir William FitzWilliam, Lord Deputy of Ireland,[218] was of the same opinion when he wrote to the Privy Council that Maguire's rising had been successfully dealt with. However, Maguire was far from beaten. The losses sustained at the Erne Fords had served to kindle his resistance rather than break it. In the winter of 1593 the English captain John Dowdall marched along the Erne, and finally seized Enniskillen Castle on 2nd February 1594, killing the surviving garrison.

On 22nd May 1594 the forces of several Irish Lords began to lay siege to the castle. The Lords whose forces were involved were Hugh Maguire, Cormac MacBaron O'Neill (a half-brother of Hugh O'Neill, Earl of Tyrone), and "Red Hugh" O'Donnell, Lord of Tyrconnell. They were supported by 1,200 warriors brought over from Scotland by Donald (Dòmhnall) Gorm MacDonald and Rory (Ruairidh) Mór MacLeod of Harris.

The Irish erected fieldworks cutting off the garrison's access to the river and mounted nightly attacks on the walls. The English garrison's desperate calls for help reached Dublin, and the Lord Deputy ordered the rapid dispatch of a relief force.[219] On 4th August 1594, a contingent of 46 (or 76) cavalry and 600 infantry led by Sir Henry Duke and Sir Edward Herbert departed from Cavan.[220] Three days later, Maguire and Cormac Macbaron O'Neill attacked the English column at a ford across the River Amey, eight kilometres south of Enniskillen at Drumane. The head of the English column, which was divided into three contingents with the baggage train filling the gaps between the individual bodies of troops, was delayed by musketry from the northern bank. The English centre and rearguard were scattered by the attack of Cormac MacBaron's pikemen. A counter-attack by the English block of pikes drove the Irish musketeers off, gaining a moment's respite for the English. Duke and Herbert knew that only a retreat towards Sligo would extricate their force from the trap. The victorious Irish aided the English escape by concentrating on plundering the English baggage. The victuals and supplies gathered gave the battle its name: the Ford of the Biscuits.

The English had lost 56 dead and 79 wounded.[221] Despite the defeat of the relief force, the Enniskillen garrison held firm. The Scottish clan chiefs eventually returned home, leaving 300 warriors behind to continue the siege with MacDonnell.

When Sir William Russell, the new Lord Deputy, landed in Ireland, he was met by Tyrone, who offered him every means of support to raise the siege of Enniskillen Castle. After a twelve-day march Russell reached Enniskillen. In spite of the apparent peacefulness of the surrounding countryside, every single English scout had failed to

---

214 In 1591, Hugh Roe MacMahon, cief of the MacMahon clan, had resisted the installation of an English sheriff in Monaghan. He was subsequently charged with treason and executed. Hill, George: *The Fall of Irish Chiefs and Clans and the Plantation of Ulster*, 2004, p. 48.

215 When Bingham received the submission of the most important Gaelic-Irish lords at Donomona Castle in 1588, Justin MacDonnell, the leader of the MacDonnell galloglas, had been one of the first to pay his respect. Nevertheless, Bingham had him hanged a few months later because he had hidden survivors of the Spanish Armada. Bingham's behaviour caused the Irish-Gaelic lords to complain about a death sentence they considered unlawful (Falls, *Elizabeth's Irish Wars*, p. 170).

216 O'Neill, „Tyrone's proxy war", p. 14.

217 O'Sullivan Beare, Philip. *Ireland under Elizabeth*, Dublin 1903, p. 69-71.

218 In 1587 Fitzwilliam as governor of Fotheringay Castle had been instrumental in the execution of Mary Queen of Scots.

219 O'Neill, „Tyrone's proxy war", p. 16.

220 Perret, Bryan: *The Battle Book. Crucial Conflicts in History from 1469 BC to the Present*, London 1992, p. 107 f.

221 Heath: *Armies*, p. 22.

The Battle of the Erne Fords.
(Contemporary illustration)

return, nor had any messenger dispatched to the castle ever made his way back. Nevertheless, Russell was confident enough to call off the dispatch of 2,000 reinforcements from England.[222]

Meanwhile, the crafty Tyrone regularly attended the gatherings of rebellious Irish lords in Ulster. Some he even bullied into joining him.[223] Art MacBaron O'Neill, another of Tyrone's half-brothers, set about pillaging the countryside with virtual impunity. The English forces, who were busy dealing with the situation in Fermanagh, were incapable of stopping him.

By April 1594, the English were growing suspicious. Numerous officials were under no illusions about Tyrone actually being the mastermind behind the rebellion. He was drilling his infantry in modern tactics and and importing large amounts of lead, claiming he wished to renew the roof tiles of his castle at Dungannon. He acquired a large shipment of gunpowder in Scotland, and was also producing it in Dungannon itself. Muskets and arquebuses were purchased in Scotland and Spain, some were even imported from as far as Poland. What he needed most

---

222 O'Neill: „Tyrone's proxy war", p. 16.
223 Magennis of Iveagh and O'Hanlon of Orior were among these unfortunates.

was well-drilled musketeers, and ironically these were provided by the English crown. The Lord Deputy, believing that there would be war with Turlough O'Neill, had sent Tyrone six military instructors. Presumably of Anglo-Irish stock, these men were known as "butter captains", supposedly so because they and their assistants were paid with victuals. The butter captains' job had been to instruct six companies of altogether six hundred musketeers, but Tyrone constantly exchanged well-drilled men with new recruits so that he effectively had a much larger force at his disposal than the six hundred men originally envisaged.[224] Tyrone also kept one troop of horse under arms whose pay, equipment and rations were financed by the English crown.[225]

Tyrone even attempted to clothe his men in uniform attire. In the early days of the conflict, red clothing was the hallmark of Tyrone's troops. His tactics did not really cater for galloglas, while his allies employed them in large numbers.[226]

On 16th February 1595 Tyrone openly placed himself at the head of the rebellion by leading an attack on Blackwater Fort. In 1575, the English had constructed a fortified bridge across the river. O'Neill's tactical foresight soon recognised the danger this access represented to the County of Tyrone, and he decided upon a show of force. With his inauguration as "The O'Neill" emulating the ancient Gaelic Kings of Ulster and the storming of the last strongholds still held by the supporters of Turlough Luineach O'Neill, Tyrone now openly challenged English rule over Ireland.

While O'Neill constantly modernized his troops' training and equipment, the English were slow to react. The Royal Irish Army was reinforced by freshly recruited troops from several English counties and troops recently returned from an expedition to Brittany. The latter were certainly veterans, but there were not enough officers available to take command.

To remedy these problems, English commanders frequently took the fateful decision to fill the gaps in the ranks with local Irish recruits. Operations usually followed the traditional scheme of placing garrisons, many of them completely isolated, in enemy territory. Reconnaissance patrols and foraging parties were regularly ambushed and massacred by the rebels. Any reinforcements marching across country invariably found themselves fighting battles under extremely unfavourable conditions since it was the Irish who chose the battleground. Nearly all military actions fought in the early stages of the Nine Years War resulted from English attempts to establish and supply garrisons on the southern border of the O'Neill territory.

Hugh O'Neill now laid siege to Monaghan Castle. The English commander Sir Henry Bagenal marched from Dundalk via Newry to relieve the English garrison. His force numbered 1,750 troops, most of them raw recruits bolstered by a small number of experienced troops. As a prelude to the battle of Clontibret, O'Neill ambushed the advance guard of the English army near Monaghan. The rebels had taken up positions in the woods lining the road to Crossdale and opened fire on the English column. There was no fighting at close quarters however, and the English eventually reached Monaghan Castle, having lost 12 dead and 30 wounded. Bagenal relieved the garrison, posting fresh troops and providing fresh supplies. Two days later, on 27th May 1595, the English troops set out in the opposite direction.[227] Bagenal chose a more southerly route leading through Drumlin and Clontibret, parts of which were determined by hilly country, moors, and forests. Not long after their departure, the English column came under fire in another ambush laid for them not far away from the Pass of Clontibret. O'Neill's army, numbering around 4,500, consisted of contingents provided by the O'Neill, MacMahon and Maguire clans, reinforced by Scottish redshank mercenaries mostly serving as archers. The MacDonnells of Tyrone were also present, but these troops no longer fought in the traditional galloglas manner, instead fighting as musketeers and pikemen. Heavy musketry decimated the English ranks in the ensuing running battle. O'Neill's cavalry charged, showering the enemy with javelins. The horsemen were supported by small groups of musketeers and Scottish archers. O'Neill himself was almost killed when he became involved in a duel with James Seagrave, an officer of horse from the Pale. Seagrave and a few of his men forded the river and made for O'Neill and his entourage with couched lances. He managed to unhorse O'Neill with his lance, and the latter was only saved by his "jack-of-plate" armour (a brigandine type of corselet), a personal gift from Lord Chancellor Sir Christopher Hatton. O'Neill's standard bearer, Donal Ballagh O'Cahan, the son of the O'Cahan chief, severed Seagrave's arm, and O'Neill himself dispatched him with a thrust of his dagger. Eighteen other English horsemen were killed in the melée.

At dusk the Irish attacks finally subsided, and in the gathering gloom Bagenal took up a position on a hill named Ballymacowen. Although the English expected a renewal of the Irish attack, this did not occur, presumably for lack of gunpowder.[228] At dawn, English reinforcements arrived from Newry. The battle was over.

In June 1595 Sir John Norris arrived in Dublin with 2,900 soldiers and several field pieces. Norris held a royal warrant providing his command independence from the Lord Deputy in Ulster. The English commander believed that

---

224 Heath and Sque: *Irish Wars*, p. 13.
225 Ibid., p. 16.
226 English observer John Dowdal's assertion that the galloglas had meanwhile become regular pikemen was therefore inaccurate, although he may have been right regarding the O'Neill galloglas from the Blackwater Valley. Handling the pike required a considerable amount of physical strength.

227 O'Neill, James: *The Nine Years War 1593-1603. O'Neill, Mountjoy and the Military Revolution*, Dublin 2017, p. 51.
228 O'Neill's troops had used up fourteen kegs of gunpowder (i. e. 1,400 pds.), the English ten.

Moyry Castle.
(Photograph: Marko Tjemmes)

his reputation as an efficient and merciless butcher along with his undeniable previous military successes would soon spell the end of the rebellion. He marched north, established his headquarters at Newry, and proceeded to fortify Armagh Cathedral.

On receiving the news of the enemy artillery, O'Neill destroyed Dungannon Castle and took the field. Instead of concentrating his forces he skilfully dispersed his troops, relying on minor strongholds such as the Crannógs on Lake Marlacoo, where he was able to rely on the local support of the O'Hanlons and the MacDonnell galloglas. Norris did not dare to venture northwards beyond the Blackwater. His situation became increasingly precarious as he considered it too risky to retire across the Moyry Pass. In the end, the English commander evacuated his force by ship and sailed back to Dublin.

As more English troops were sent to Ireland, companies were brought up to strength with up to twenty Irishmen per company. The English commanders were themselves well aware that this might prove a liability, but continued the practice anyway. Norris meanwhile intended to take up winter quarters in Armagh, which he revictualled in September 1595.[229] Norris then marched to Dundalk to collect a number of draft horses. As he made his way back to Armagh, the Irish struck.

The Battle of Mullaghbrack took place on 5th September 1595. Between 1,700 and 2,000 English soldiers (many Irishmen among them) were attacked by an Irish force numbering c. 4,000. The Irish had attempted to occupy a pass ahead of the English column but failed. The Irish cavalry then fell on the English rearguard consisting of cavalry and a small force of musketeers. Norris, together with his brother Thomas and Henry Bagenal, succeeded in repulsing the Irish attack. The Irish infantry (among them numerous redshanks) wreaked havoc in the English ranks until Norris' cavalry together with a force of infantry counterattacked and drove them off. The English lost twelve dead, Irish losses were slight.[230]

Both sides now agreed on a truce until New Year's Day 1596. In a letter, O'Neill declared that he was not seeking support from Spain (which in fact he was), and Norris was inclined to believe him. The fighting of the year 1596 was to focus on Connacht, to which the rebellion had meanwhile spread.[231]

On 3rd April 1597 Thomas Burgh, 3rd Baron Burgh, was appointed new Lord Deputy of Ireland. In early July he embarked on a campaign to Ulster with 3,000 infantry

---

229 McGleenon, C. F.: "The Battle of Mullabrack 5th September 1595", in: Seanchas Ardmhacha: *Journal of the Armagh Diocesan Historical Society* vol. 13 (No. 2), Armagh 1989, p. 90-101 (p. 92).

230 Heath: *Armies*, p. 23.

231 In the same year, Mabel O'Neill, wife of Hugh O'Neill and sister of Sir Henry Bagenal, died. O'Neill had had affairs with two Irish gentlewomen, causing her to leave him. Hugh O'Neill married a fourth time, his new spouse being Catherine Magennis. Historians and novelists have tended to exaggerate Mabel's part in the conflict between her husband and her brother. Stylized as "Helen of Ulster", her actual role was in fact fairly insignificant.

and 500 horse. His force reached the ford crossing the Blackwater at two o'clock in the morning. O'Neill had fortified the opposite bank with trenches and fieldworks, and placed four wall guns at strategic posts. Musketeers covered the flanks.

De Burgh's soldiers were mostly inexperienced recruits, so the Lord Deputy decided to boost his men's morale by personally leading the attack. At the head of a troop of Gentlemen Volunteers, he stormed across the ford, catching the Irish off guard.[232] The Irish were so surprised that they did not have time to discharge the wall guns. The defenders took a number of casualties from the English musketeers, and before long the entire English force had forded the river. Skirmishes continued into the night, but the Irish withdrew on their main force, and O'Neill decided not to interfere. De Burgh dismantled O'Neill's defences and replaced them with much stronger fortifications.[233] On 2nd October, O'Neill attacked these defences, but the Irish were unable to dislodge the English troops. De Burgh died on 14th October 1597, his duties being temporarily adopted by Lord Justices Gardiner and Loftus.[234]

In November 1597, things came to a head between the MacDonalds of Antrim and the English force garrisoning Carrickfergus Castle. The governor of Carrickfergus, Sir John Chichester, had planned to overwhelm Sorley MacDonald, son of Sorley Boy, by seeking negotiations and then capturing him and his entourage when they arrived. The shrewd Scot was not fooled by Chichester's ruse, and appeared with a large number of armed retainers. In the ensuing fight, Chichester was killed. James MacSorley MacDonald had Chichester decapitated and dispatched four gallopers to present the grisly trophy to the Earl of Tyrone. After O'Neill had inspected the gift, a group of galloglas employed poor Chichester's head for a spontaneous game of football.[235]

On 30th December 1598 Queen Elizabeth appointed her declared favourite Robert Devereux, 2nd Earl of Essex, Lord Lieutenant of Ireland. Robert was son to Walter Devereux, 1st Earl of Essex (d. 1576), and had gathered military experience while campaigning in the Netherlands.

Hugh O'Neill had seen several Lord Deputies come and go. Adhering to his defensive strategy, he had so far managed to beat back every single English attack on Ulster. Although the rebellion had long since spread to other parts of Ireland, Ulster remained O'Neill's top priority. It is possible that he hoped to hold Ulster until the Queen died, since there was reason to believe that an agreement could be reached with Elizabeth's designated successor, James VI of Scotland.[236] However, the King of Scots was keen to avoid any rash moves which might have endangered his prospects south of the border. He thus began to reduce the flow of redshank mercenaries from Scotland to Ulster – henceforth, O'Neill would have to do without these fierce and efficient warriors.[237]

O'Neill turned to other places for support. His next goal was to involve Spain. Although the proposed Spanish invasion was slow in coming, the Spanish had sent military instructors who apart from basic military skills taught O'Neill's troops the tactics of the Spanish army. The mighty Spanish *tercios* became the model of the Earl of Tyrone's Irish army. Despite the fact that so far he had been successful applying the hit-and-run tactics at which the Irish excelled, the spreading of the rebellion invited the possibility of one day having to face the English army in open battle. The Earl of Tyrone was determined to fight this battle with troops modelled on continental European armies of the day, not with the traditional *battles* of the galloglas.

---

232 Gentlemen Volunteers were members of the gentry who accompanied and fought with a unit of their choice without pay or a specific command. Motivation ranged from a sheer lust for adventure to the wish to arouse the attention of influential political personalities. They frequently filled gaps in the officers' ranks and thus quickly gained a chance for social and political advancement. Such volunteers were also found in other armies of the day and in later times, e. g. in the Spanish army.

233 Heath: *Armies*, p. 23.

234 Hayes-McCoy: *Irish Battles*, p. 115.

235 Palmer, Patricia: *The Severed Head and the Grafted Tongue. Literature, Translation and Violence in Early Modern Ireland*, Cambridge 2014, p. 13. The story of this gruesome football match may indeed be apocryphal and merely intended to emphasise the brutality of the galloglas, of which Tyrone only employed a small number. There is a macabre sequel to the episode: When James MacSorley's brother Randal MacSorley visited Chichester's tomb at Carrickfergus many years later, he is said to have remarked that he wondered whether anyone had had the sense to bury the head along with the rest of the body. After all, it had been him who had cut it off.

236 James VI of Scotland would become King James I of England.

237 O'Neill himself was not entirely blameless in this development. He had ditched a mistress, a girl of the MacDonald clan. This was not well received across the Irish Sea.

THE GALLOGLAS' LAST STAND – THE BATTLE OF THE CURLEWS IN 1599

A ship from Dublin lay at anchor in the port of Rathmullan in north-eastern Ireland. It was the year 1587, and not far from Rathmullan fifteen-year-old Hugh Roe O'Donnell had wedded Rose, daughter of Hugh O'Neill.[238] Young Hugh was invited aboard the Dublin vessel for a cup of wine. O'Donnell gladly accepted (after all, he was Irish), and came on board. He was promptly seized and bound, and the ship's crew hurriedly set sail for home.

The plan had been hatched by the Lord Deputy of Ireland, Sir John Perrot, who wished to prevent an alliance between the O'Donnells and Hugh O'Neill, the new Earl of Tyrone.[239]

Hugh Roe O'Donnell had been born in 1572 the son of the Irish-Gaelic Lord of Tyrconnell, Sir Hugh O'Donnell, and his second wife Ineen Dubh.[240] Among his siblings were Donnell, Rory, and Cathbarr O'Donnell. In Sir Hugh's later years, the siblings began to quarrel over their father's succession. The English crown supported Donnell O'Donnell, and dispatched several companies of the Royal Irish Army under John Connill to add force to his claims. While the MacSweeneys Banagh under Donnchadh MacSweeney declared their allegiance to Donnell O'Donnell, the MacSweeneys Doe and MacSweeneys Fanad opposed him. Ineen Dubh, fighting furiously for her imprisoned son's cause, employed a force of redshanks, who soundly defeated Donnell O'Donnell's supporters at Doire Leathan on 3rd September 1590.[241] Donnell O'Donnell was killed. Hugh Roe O'Donnell managed to escape from his Dublin prison in 1591, but was soon caught and once again put under lock and key.

Hugh Roe O'Donnell was not discouraged. Together with his fellow prisoner Art O'Neill and his brother Henry O'Neill, he prepared for another escape attempt. One measure was to raise sufficient money to bribe the local English officials into turning a blind eye. On 6th January 1592, a cold and clear winter's day, the men made their escape and set out on a fifty-kilometre journey to a manor situated in Glenmalure Valley in the Wicklow Mountains. This house in Ballinacor belonged to Fiach McHugh O'Byrne, who was privy to Hugh Roe O'Donnell's escape plan. It was a close run – Art O'Neill lost his life on the way, while in the bitter cold Hugh O'Donnell lost two of his toes to frostbite.[242]

After his return to Ulster and the resignation of his father, Hugh Roe O'Donnell became the uncontested leader of the O'Donnell clan and was henceforth known as "The O'Donnell", Lord of Tyrconnell. After driving the English sheriff[243] and his men from Tyrconnell, he led two campaigns against Luineach O'Neill in 1593. His aim was to force Luineach to resign his leadership of the O'Neills and instead to submit to Hugh O'Neill.

Hugh Roe O'Donnell and Hugh O'Neill both possessed determination and conceivable military ability. Unfortunately, Tyrconnell's economic and military resources did not match those of Tyrone. In comparison to O'Neill, O'Donnell lacked sufficient funds, international relationships and insight into English military affairs, which produced an altogether much more conservative military system in the O'Donnell clan. Galloglas were held in high esteem by the O'Donnells, and the rank of constable carried considerable prestige. The galloglas commanders were among the most important men in the chief's entourage, and part of the power behind the throne. The MacSweeneys Fanad were able to field 120 galloglas, as did the MacSweeneys Doe. Being a smaller clan, the MacSweeneys Banagh could only muster sixty galloglas.

Like Maguire's, Hugh Roe O'Donnells operations bought the time for Hugh O'Neill to prepare his own moves. At this early stage, the Earl of Tyrone was careful not to show his approval of O'Donnell's actions, let alone his support. When Hugh Maguire began his rebellion in Fermanagh in 1593 and Hugh O'Neill challenged Turlough Luineach O'Neill's authority, Richard Bingham was Lord President of Connacht. In February 1594, he was taken ill at Athlone and unable to travel to Dublin. In September of the same year Brian Oge O'Rourke and Hugh Roe O'Donnell attacked the town of Sligo, but were repulsed with heavy loss. In March 1595 Bingham drove O'Donnell's troops from Roscommon, but O'Donnell returned in April with a large force. Lacking sufficient troop numbers to counteract the threat, Bingham was merely able to push the enemy back to Longford. In June, his brother George was murdered by his own standard bearer Ulick Burke, a cousin of the Earl of Clanricarde. Burke had plotted together with the garrison of Sligo Castle, who promptly gave themselves up to Hugh Roe O'Donnell. Bingham wrote to Dublin asking for six companies of foot and fifty horse to retake Sligo and Ballyshannon. No reinforcements were available since the English forces had their hands full fighting Hugh O'Neill, Earl of Tyrone. Bingham

---

238 It is also possible that they had only become betrothed to each other at this time.
239 Morgan: *Tyrone's Rebellion*, p. 128.
240 Ineen was the daughter of James MacDonald, 6th Laird of Dunnyveg, and Lady Agnes Campbell.
241 Ineen Dubh had her own redshank bodyguard whose men hailed from all over Scotland, the men from the Crawford clan being the most numerous. The force is said to have altogether numbered between 80 and 100 men.
242 Apparently this was the only ever successful breakout from Dublin castle.
243 The sheriff was the same Humphrey Willis who had previously aroused Hugh Maguire's anger.

Ballinafad Castle at the foot of the Curlew Mountains.
(Photograph: Maximilian Bunk)

saw himself confronted with allegations questioning his loyalty. He was summoned to Dublin, but fled to England because he feared for his life.[244]

In 1595 Hugh Roe O'Donnell was able to conquer large areas of Connacht. On 24th December he forcibly enthroned Tibbot MacWalter Kittagh Burgh (Gaelic: *Tiobóid mac Walter Ciotach Bourke*)[245] as chief of the MacWilliams Iochtar (or Burkes of Mayo). O'Donnell had his warriors surround the clan's meeting place, and this short-sighted and violent move did much to alienate many Irish magnates from the rebel cause.

On 2nd August 1597, Sir Conyers Clifford narrowly escaped Hugh O'Donnell's warriors after his attack on Ballyshannon Castle had been beaten back.[246] On 4th September 1597 he succeeded Richard Bingham as Lord President of Connacht.

Brian Oge O'Rourke's leadership of the O'Rourkes was challenged by his brother Teigue, who was forever asking Hugh Roe O'Donnell and Tyrone for support. Angered by his brother's political intrigues, Brian Oge O'Rourke declared his allegiance to the English crown in February 1598. Lord President Conyers Clifford now backed Brian's position, but in June 1598 Brian again changed sides as in the late summer the focus of operations shifted to Munster.

In April 1599 Robert Devereux, 2nd Earl of Essex, landed in Ireland at the head of an army of 17,000.[247] He marched to relieve the fort at Maryborough[248] which was besieged by a force of Irish rebels under Owny MacRory O'More. Having been driven off by Essex at Maryborough, O'More attacked Essex's force on 17th May at the Pass of the Plumes. Although the English stood their ground, the Earl's army was soon becoming decimated by disease and desertion. Essex was forced to recognize that his own troops would soon no longer be numerous enough to deal with the rebellion efficiently. He also managed to squander precious military resources in pointless sideshows, e. g. by besieging Cahir Castle in Munster in May 1599. Almost at the same time, a small English force of 450 to 500 infantry[249] and a few dozen cavalry under Sir Henry Harrington was defeated by an Irish force of roughly equal size under Phelim MacFeagh O'Byrne at Wicklow on 29th May.[250]

Essex saw that his strategic options were limited. He turned to Sir Donough O'Connor from Sligo, a sworn enemy of the O'Donnells, and encouraged him to recapture those parts of his territory in Sligo previously lost to Hugh O'Donnell. Sligo itself was an excellent starting point for an attack on Ulster, since the ford at Ballyshannon c. 35 kilometres north-east of Sligo offered easy access to Donegal, the heart of the O'Donnell country.

O'Connor's brother-in-law Theobald Burke was vice-commander of an English naval squadron sailing from Galway to Sligo, where it would await O'Connor's arrival. O'Connor however was stuck in Collooney castle, which had been placed under siege by Hugh Roe O'Donnell and 2,000 of his warriors. Essex had no choice but to come to the beleaguered O'Connor's aid, since O'Connor was one of the very few Irish allies on which the English were still able to fully rely. Essex ordered Sir Conyers Clifford to march from his headquarters at Athlone to assist O'Connor with 1,500 infantry[251] and 200 horse.

Among O'Donnell's field commanders were John O'Dogherty of Inishowen, Owen MacSweeney, and

---

244 In England preparations were being made for a large expedition against Ireland. Bingham's knowledge and military expertise were in high demand, and he was appointed Marshal of the Royal Irish Army at the end of 1598. Having sailed to Ireland at the head of 5,000 men, he died there on 19th January 1599.

245 His younger sister Sabrina was later to marry the chief of the MacSweeney Banagh.

246 Heath and Sque: *Irish Wars*, p. 6 f.

247 Essex had 16,000 infantry and c. 1,300 horse under his command (cf. Curtis, Edmund: *A History of Ireland. From Earliest Times to 1922*, London/New York 1988, p. 185).

248 Today's Portlaoise.

249 One of the five companies engaged consisted of turncoat Irish rebels, while the others were mostly made up of inexperienced recruits.

250 Heath and Sque: *Irish Wars*, p. 7.

251 The sources vary considerably regarding troop numbers.

In broken, wooded terrain the traditional combination of kern and galloglas was still very effective.
(© Claíomh – Rob Hunt 2010)

O'Gallagher of Donegal. O'Donnell left a force of between 200 and 300 cavalry under his cousin Niall Garve O'Donnell to continue the siege of Collooney Castle, and dispatched between 400 and 600 men under MacSweeney of Fanad and Tibbot MacWalter Kittagh Bourke to Sligo in order to prevent the landing of Theobald Burke's ships. Hugh Roe O'Donnell himself marched to Dunavaragh with 1,500 warriors, where he was met by the local chiefs Conor MacDermott and Brian Oge O'Rourke. O'Rourke and O'Donnell were old rivals, and it remains unclear whether O'Rourke agreed to fight under O'Donnell's command.

The joint rebel forces moved to prepare an ambush in the Curlew Mountains, which the English would have to negotiate on their march from Athlone. The Curlew Mountains are a shallow mountain range with occasionally marshy terrain reaching from Boyle in the south to Ballinafad in the north.[252] Brian Oge O'Rourke led a vanguard of between two and four hundred men to the Curlews. His men immediately set about felling trees to block the English route of advance.[253] On receiving the news of the English approach, O'Rourke had his men man the barricades. In the hot afternoon sunshine of 15th August 1599, Clifford's force[254] reached the Curlew Mountains. The English soldiers were exhausted, hungry and poorly equipped, and in urgent need of rest. Clifford, who was eager to pass the obstacle and continue his march on Sligo, had received false information according to which the pass had not been occupied. He immediately decided to seize the opportunity and march on. On his orders, the English army advanced into the pass.

Clifford's force consisted of 200 cavalry and between 21 and 28 companies of foot (1,400 to 1,900 soldiers).[255] The advance guard was led by Sir Alexander Radcliffe, the main body ("main battle") by Richard Lord Dunkellin, and the rearguard by Sir Arthur Savage.[256]

---

252 The mountain tops reach a mere 260 metres above sea level.

253 According to other sources, O'Rourke's men were already poised in the Curlews. Some sources claim that the MacDermotts were the first to engage the English on the barricades. The battle took place in MacDermott territory.

254 Older accounts of the battle claim that a MacSweeney who had been snubbed or insulted by Hugh Roe O'Donnell abandoned the rebel cause and accompanied Clifford on his march into the Curlew Mountains (cf.. D'Alton, Edward Alfred: *History of Ireland*, vol. III, London 2012 (reprint), p. 153).

255 A source considered fairly accurate renders Clifford's strength as 511 pikemen and 985 musketeers and calivermen. Officers were not counted.

256 Heath: *Armies*, p. 25. In fact the main body was the smallest contingent.

Whenever the enemy line broke, the kern moved up to fall on the enemy with sword and javelin.
(© Claíomh – Rob Hunt)

The Irish put the English soldiers under fire as soon as these had reached the barricade. However, the rebels swiftly withdrew so that the English were able to continue their march into the pass. The path was a mere two metres across and consisted of stepping stones on otherwise soft ground. The track was lined by woods on the one side, and by bog on the other. The further the English ventured, the more withering the Irish fire from the adjoining woods grew. Many English soldiers lost their nerve and turned tail.

On this occasion, the Irish fielded musketeers, archers, and javelineers (the latter possibly of the MacDermott clan)[257]. The engagement lasted for one and a half hours, until the English musketeers ran out of powder. The wagons carrying the gunpowder supplies were stuck at the end of the column and due to the confined space of the battleground could not be moved forward.[258] Morale was becoming brittle in the English front line. The commander of the vanguard, Alexander Radcliffe, began to lose control as many of his men turned and ran, colliding with reinforcements coming up from behind. Confusion and panic spread as the main body lost its cohesion and many of its soldiers likewise began to take to their heels. Sensing the beginning rout, the Irish infantry advanced. The situation was an ideal one for the galloglas, and led by Brian Oge O'Rourke in person, 160 galloglas proceeded to carve up the English with sword and axe.[259]

Clifford, who was desperately trying to rally his men, was felled by an Irish pikeman. The Irish pursued the English soldiers, and it was only thanks to the valiant English cavalry which held open the line of retreat that complete disaster was averted. Led by Sir Griffin Markham, the English horse attacked uphill across stony and marshy

---

257 Light throwing spears were known as darts, heavy specimens were classified as javelins.

258 Heath: *Armies*, p. 25.

259 O'Rourke's galloglas were probably of the MacCabe clan.

Charles Blount, 8th Baron Mountjoy.
(contemporary engraving)

Lord Mountjoy's galloglass bodyguard c. 1601.
(© Claíomh – Dave Swift 2014)

terrain which was in fact entirely unsuitable for cavalry. Nevertheless the English horsemen managed to stem the tide of pursuers long enough for the English army, which had become a panic-stricken rabble, to make good their escape. The English horsemen sustained casualties, Markham himself suffering a fractured arm.[260]

The remains of Clifford's force were pursued to Boyle, where they took shelter in the local abbey. Many English soldiers had lost their lives, casualties being given as between 120 and 200 dead, eight of Markham's cavalry among them. No Irish figures exist, but losses would have been much lighter. Clifford's body was decapitated according to Gaelic custom and delivered to Hugh O'Donnell, whose main force had been nearby without becoming engaged. While Clifford's head was taken to Collooney Castle as a means to demoralize the defenders, MacDermott had Clifford's body sent to Lough Key Abbey for burial.[261] The Irish-Gaelic lords had always treated Clifford with a certain amount of grudging respect. A short while later O'Connor and his men surrendered Collooney Castle and joined the rebels.

As a consequence of the Battle of the Curlew Mountains, desertion among the Irish serving in the English Army soared. Meanwhile, O'Donnell made Ballymote Castle his headquarters.

Hugh Maguire took part in an expedition to Thomond in 1599 and in the following commanded Tyrone's cavalry during raids into Leinster and Munster. His luck ran out on 18th February 1600, when his force was confronted outside Cork by an enemy corps commanded by Sir Warham St. Leger. Maguire killed his enemy but succumbed to his

---

260 Colum, Padraic: *A Treasury of Irish Folklore*, New York 1982, p. 202.

261 Irish tradition contains some macabre details, according to which MacDermott wanted to keep Clifford's body in order to exchange it for Irish prisoners. The Irish-Gaelic Lords allegedly offered Clifford's head to the English governor of Boyle for interment.

> ### The Battle of Yellow Ford, 14th August 1598
>
> Sir Henry Bagenal marched westwards of Armagh to revictual the English garrison at Blackwater Ford. His force consisted of 3,900 infantry, 320 horse, and five field pieces. The infantry was organized into six regiments. On the march, two regiments formed one line, each flank protected by groups of musketeers and cavalry. Bagenal himself commanded the second regiment of the advance guard. The country the English were about to march through was hilly, densely wooded and interspersed with bogs, which made it ideal for ambushes. Guessing the way the enemy would take, O'Neill had trenches and fieldworks prepared along the way. He had at his disposal 4,500 infantry and between 600 and 800 horse (according to irish sources; English sources give Irish numbers as large as altogether 8,000). Hugh Roe O'Donnell had sent 3,000 men to support O'Neill.
>
> On 14th August 1598 Bagenal's column came under attack from five hundred Irish musketeers. Bagenal sent forwards a screen of musketeers and cavalry to engage the attackers but these skirmishers were unable to drive the Irish off. A field piece of the second English line had become lodged in the mire, and the men were delayed by their attempts to dislodge it. One of the gun carriage's wheels broke, and the Irish succeeded in killing the draft oxen. Meanwhile the English vanguard had marched off, and communication between the English units became disrupted. After four hours, Bagenal was forced to call a halt behind Yellow Ford in the face of a rampart and ditch which O'Neill had erected between two stretches of bog. The fieldworks erected by the Irish were 400 metres in length and barely one metre in height, but the top of the rampart was lined with thorny brush. The rampart was manned by 40 Irish soldiers armed with four wall guns. Instead of attacking the obstacle head on, the English wisely chose to employ their cannon, and managed to blow a breech into the defences. Then Sir Richard Percy's regiment advanced to seize the Irish position. The soldiers had hardly crossed the ditch when orders from Sir Henry Bagenal arrived ordering them to retire and await the arrival of the second English contingent. O'Neill exploited the ensuing confusion, and ordered his pikemen to attack. The infantry was supported by forty cavalry, led by Tyrone in person. When Bagenal was killed by a bullet in the head, his regiment fled. Sir Thomas Wingfield, commander of the fourth regiment, now assumed overall command and ordered Henry Cosby, the officer in command of the third regiment, to fall back. He dispatched a messenger ordering the rearguard to hold the ford at all costs.
>
> Ignoring Wingfield's orders, Cosby had his men advance in order to receive the remains of the shattered vanguard. In danger of being overrun, his troops were saved by Wingfield's timely intervention. The English main body and rearguard were eventually able to retreat in good order.
>
> English losses were high, estimates varying between 800 and 2,700 killed. Apart from Sir Henry Bagenal, between 13 and 23 captains had perished in the fighting. Many soldiers had been killed when four kegs of gunpowder (200 pounds) had exploded after being touched off with the match of one of Cosby's musketeers. The Irish managed to capture several English colours, three hundred Irish soldiers from the English force changed sides. Any English wounded found by the Irish were slaughtered without mercy. O'Neill lost around two hundred dead and six hundred wounded. The Irish pursued the retreating English force to Armagh and laid siege to the town. After three days of negotiation, the English were permitted to march off, but were forced to leave behind their weapons and ammunition.
>
> (After Heath, Ian: *Armies of the Sixteenth Century*, St Peter Port 1997)

own wounds only hours later. His foster father, his confessor, and all of the officers of his mounted corps were also among the slain.[262]

Lord Essex ignored Queen Elizabeth's explicit orders to remain at his post. He sailed for England on 24th September 1599, reaching London four days later. There the Earl burst into the Queen's private chambers, catching Gloriana only half-dressed. The over-confident Essex had finally overreached himself and lost all claim to the Queen's benevolence. His Irish campaign had been an unmitigated disaster. After an inquest by the Privy Council Essex was placed under house arrest. He was succeeded in Ireland by a diehard veteran, Charles Blount, 8th Baron Mountjoy, who was appointed Lord Deputy in 1600.[263]

---

[262] Another piece of unwelcome news for Tyrone was that Conn MacShane O'Neill, son of the Shane O'Neill whom Tyrone had imprisoned on an island in Killetra (the most inhospitable and impenetrable part of Ulster), had escaped his captors and joined the English forces.

[263] Between 1586 and 1598 Blount had served with the English armies in Brittany and the Netherlands.

TWILIGHT OF THE GALLOGLAS

A Lord's Galloglass rode at his lord's side, carried his helmet, and was always prepared to defend him with his life. In accordance with his special duties, he received a higher salary than ordinary galloglas. To be a Lord's Galloglass was both duty and privilege, and most Irish-Gaelic lords employed Lord's Galloglass; even Tyrone, who was not particularly fond of them, was no exception in this respect.

One of these brave men even served Sir Charles Blount, 8th Baron Mountjoy, as he was about to improve the Royal Irish Army's training and fill its ranks with reliable and hard-fighting men.[264]

Since there was still a pronounced lack of English recruits and the number of men liable to serve with the colours in the Pale was also limited, Mountjoy was still forced to recruit native Irish into the English ranks.[265] In order to confuse Tyrone as to his true strategy, Mountjoy was careful to only field a fraction of all troops available at any time. Adopting a combination of scorched-earth policy and the establishment of strongholds in enemy territory, Mountjoy sought to finally break the back of the rebellion. This he did with mounting success.

Sir Henry Docwra followed this principle when he established an English garrison at Derry on 15th May 1600. Between 20th September and 13th October of the same year several skirmishes occurred in the Moyry Pass between Tyrone's troops and English forces commanded by Lord Mountjoy.[266] The Battle of the Yellow Ford had left Tyrone master of the entire province, with the English being forced to abandon the forts along the Blackwater, and Armagh Cathedral. Newry had constituted their most advanced postion.[267]

The actions at the Moyry pass had inflicted heavy losses on the English, and fortunately Mountjoy had received Irish reinforcements commanded by Sir Thomas Burke, son of the Earl of Clanricarde.

Only with great difficulty was Mountjoy able to force the pass, and to protect this vital thoroughfare he erected Moyry Castle at the northern end of the pass, which was designed to accomodate heavy artillery.[268]

In the fateful year 1600, Niall Garve O'Donnell changed sides. On 8th October 1600 O'Donnell together with English troops led by Sir John Bolles and a Gaelic contin-

Ballintober Castle.
(Photograph: Maximilian Bunk)

---

264 The galloglas of the MacDonnells of Tynekill formed a small but very reliable source of military support for English military presence in Ireland.

265 In May 1601, the Pale was able to muster 477 kern, 372 mounted archers and 335 cavalry including the warriors supplied by the local Irish-Gaelic chieftains loyal to the English crown. Of the 1,250 men mustered at Newry in June 1601, only 593 were English (cf. Heath and Sque: *Irish Wars*, p. 33)

266 Duffy, Christopher: *The Fortress in the Early Modern World 1494-1660*, London and New York 1996, p. 144.

267 Hayes-McCoy: *Battles*, p. 132.

268 Fry: *Castles of Britain and Ireland*, p. 225.

gent commanded by Arthur O'Neill[269], the second oldest son of Turlough Luineach O'Neill, seized Lifford, whose garrison did not put up a spirited defence. Summoning a force of the redshanks originally recruited by his mother, Hugh Roe O'Neill hurried to retake Lifford, but was repulsed. Niall Garve's force included galloglas.

At the end of October, the Anglo-Irish garrison made a sortie from Lifford and deployed for battle outside the walls in order to repel the besiegers. Niall Garve O'Donnell and Hugh Roe O'Donnell's younger brother Manus O'Donnell[270] engaged in single combat with Garve's lance penetrating Manus's armour and wounding him fatally. Later Niall Garve O'Donnell and his men together with English soldiers defended the town of Donegal, which was under siege from Hugh Roe O'Donnell.

After a series of several setbacks, Hugh O'Donnell marched south to Kinsale in autumn 1601. Shortly afterwards, Niall Garve O'Donnell's troops took the strategically important town of Ballyshannon. Although the Irish rebels were able to capture English guns on several occasions, they only rarely employed artillery themselves, the siege of Ballintober Castle in 1599[271] being a notable exception.

The rebels were bent on copying both English and Continental warfare, most prominently tactics involving pikemen and musketeers. Galloglas did not feature in this new kind of warfare however.[272]

On 21st September 1601, Tyrone's long-cherished wish came true, when a Spanish expeditionary force arrived in Ireland. It was nowhere near the size Tyrone had hoped for however, and had landed very far away from his own operational bases. Don Juan de Aguila had disembarked at Kindale in Munster with a force of 3,800 infantry, but failed to move in Tyrone's direction. Instead, the Spanish commander chose to fortify his position. On 26th October Mountjoy appeared at the head of a thoroughly reorganized and well-trained English force and surrounded the Spanish fieldworks.

Tyrone was left with no choice but to gather his and Hugh O'Donnell's forces and race across Ireland to engage Mountjoy's army with Spanish assistance. On Christmas Eve 1601, the Irish were confronted by an English force and defeated, suffering approximately 2,000 casualties. In accordance with Spanish drill regulations and the instructions of his Spanish allies, Tyrone had had his men fight in the open in the style of the Spanish Tercios. This exposed them to English fire, and in contrast to the Spanish veterans, Tyrone's men broke under the ordeal.[273] While Tyrone and the remains of his army retreated to Ulster, O'Donnell boarded a Spanish ship three days later. He died soon after in Spain without seeing his native Ireland again. On 2nd January 1602 the Spanish garrison of Kinsale surrendered and was permitted to leave with its colours and guns.

Between February and December 1602, Sir George Carew brutally suppressed the last pockets of resistance in Munster, storming Dunboy Castle in 17th and 18th June. In the same month, Lord Mountjoy mounted a campaign in Ulster. At some point in 1602, Donough MacSweeney of Banagh changed sides and joined Niall Garve O'Donnell. During an expedition to Fermanagh, their troops were confronted by a force of Maguires, and a contingent of MacCabe galloglas. In an extremely bloody engagement, the chief of the MacCabes, Brian MacCabe, was taken prisoner.[274] Hugh Roe O'Donnell's brother Rory O'Donnell surrendered in December 1601.[275]

The winter of 1602-1603 was unusually harsh in Ireland.[276] The inclement weather broke the back of the rebellion. With Tyrone's formal submission on 30th March 1603 the Nine Years War came to its end, only six days after Queen Elizabeth I had passed away at Richmond.[277] Her successor James I offered very favourable peace terms.

Hugh O'Neill was able to retain his estates and title of Earl of Tyrone. What eventually caused him to leave Ireland together with Rory O'Donnell, the new Earl of Tyrconnell, and a large number of retainers (the so-called "Flight of the Earls") is a matter of conjecture. Their estates and those of many of their vassals were confiscated as a consequence. Intended for use as remuneration for the faithful service of those Irish nobles who had remained loyal and fought against Tyrone during his rebellion, not all were satisfied with their share. Sir Cahir O'Doherty felt he had been cheated of his reward and rose in revolt, but with this move merely managed to forfeit all of his estates. Finally, the lands were distributed among English and Scottish colonists. This move spelled the end of ancient Gaelic-Irish society with its kings and clan chiefs, at whose courts poets and priests had gathered, and where galloglas had been held in high regard.

What remained? Some galloglas families succeeded in changing their trades from mercenaries to gentleman farmers, rising in an increasingly anglicized society's local gentry. When Alexander MacColla MacDonell of Tynekill

---

269 Sir Arthus O'Neill had never got on well with his father, which may have been one of the reasons for his support of Hugh O'Neill.

270 McGurk, John: *Sir Henry Docwra (1564-1631), Derry's Second Founder*, Dublin 2006, p. 85.

271 In this case Hugh Roe O'Donnell employed a gun of Spanish manufacture.

272 Janin, Hunt and Carlson, Ursula: *Mercenaries in Medieval and Renaissance Europe*, Jefferson and London 2013, p. 96

273 Not even every English regiment present was actually engaged. Tyrone's force was supported by a small Spanish contingent of between 120 and 200 men and 300 MacDonald redshanks, of which only 31 are said to have survived. Apart from a few individuals, no galloglas were engaged (Heath: *Armies*, p. 26 f.).

274 He received a Royal Pardon, and represented his clan at the Fermanagh Jury in 1603. A close relative of his, Captain Seamus Óg MacCabe, emigrated to Spain.

275 Heath and Sque: *Irish Wars*, p. 7.

276 Newark and MacBride: *Warlords*, p. 273.

277 Tyrone was not the last prominent rebel to lay down his arms. Brian Oge O'Rourke surrendered several days after Tyrone.

Doe Castle, County Donegal.
(Photograph: Maximilian Bunk)

died in 1577, he was considered the most wealthy galloglas descendant in all of Ireland. His brother Yellow Hugh (*Aodh Buidhe*) MacDonnell was the last of the MacDonnell chiefs of Tynekill to have personally fought as a galloglass. His son Fergus lived a rather more unexciting life as Lord of Tynekill with 4,000 hectares of land and the right to hold a market once a week, and a yearly trade fair of two days.[278]

Donal MacSweeney of Fanad had been constable of Rory O'Donnell's Galloglas. When O'Donnell left Ireland together with the Earl of Tyrone in 1607, MacSweeney of Fanad, who had remained in Donegal, publicly declared him a traitor. Either his instinct had served him well, or whether by sheer good luck – he received an immediate tenure of more than 800 hectares, and a magistrate's chair. He was later reprimanded by the King's Counsel for his habit of presiding over court hearings dressed in his old coat.[279]

---

278 Cannan and Ó'Brógáin: *Galloglass*, S. 56-57.

279 Ibid., p. 56.

ENTER MULMURRY MACSWEENEY

It was left to the MacSweeneys to provide the galloglas with a memorable exit from the stage. Eoghan Óg MacSweeney was chieftain of the MacSweeneys of Doe from 1570 to 1596. He sheltered and aided the escape of survivors of the Spanish Armada, and in 1590 he received the rebel Sir Brian O'Rourke into his house. His nephew Mulmurry (Gaelic: *Maolmhuire*) succeeded him as chieftain in 1596. Mulmurry married Mary O'Donnell, sister of Hugh Roe O'Donnell, but they had no children and the marriage was annulled in 1593. Around the year 1599 Mulmurry was once again married and father of several children. Legend has it that Mulmurry's daughter Eileen jumped to her death from the battlements of Doe Castle because her father Mulmurry had murdered her lover Turlough O'Boyle. This heart-rending tale certainly sounds dramatic enough but is entirely untrue. Mulmurry MacSweeney only inhabited Doe Castle between 1596 and 1598, a time when his eldest child cannot have been older than six years. Turlough O'Boyle died in the Battle of Scarrifholis, which took place in 1650, long after Mulmurry's death.

In 1598, in the middle of the Nine Years War, Mulmurry MacSweeney changed sides and cast in his lot with the English, allegedly because Hugh Roe O'Donnell had made a pass at his wife. Knighted by the Earl of Essex in July 1599, Sir Myles MacSweeney Doe landed at Lough Foyle with an English fleet in May 1600. The English squadron was commanded by Sir Henry Docwra, who would soon have plenty of opportunity to marvel at MacSweeney's volatile character. Only two months later Mulmurry aka Sir Myles MacSweeney attacked Docwra's troops and made off with 160 horses. MacSweeney's attack had probably been planned and carried out in consultation with Hugh Roe O'Donnell. The English finally managed to get hold of Mulmurry and clapped him in irons on board an English warship. The vessel was due to sail for Dublin, and undoubtedly Mulmurry would have stood for his life, but legend has it that he was visited by a mysterious lady, who had the grace to leave open a hatch on her departure, through which Mulmurry made his escape. Despite the season being unsuitable for bathing, Mulmurry jumped overboard and swam ashore "before any man or boat sent after him could overtake him". It is highly probable that Mulmurry MacSweeney was the only MacSweeney chieftain from Tyrconnell to accompany Hugh Roe O'Donnell on his march to Kinsale. He is believed to have been the commander of O'Donnell's rearguard.

In April 1603 Henry Docwra was able to announce the capture of Doe Castle. At this stage the Nine Years War had already ended. Mulmurry MacSweeney finally submitted and received a Royal Pardon from King James I in October 1603.

A document from 23rd November 1604 has come down to us confirming Royal Grace to Mulmurry MacSweeney and several of his followers. In 1606 the MacSweeneys ejected Rory O'Donnell's men from Doe Castle, with Rory O'Donnell seizing it back in the following year. At the time, a certain Niall MacSweeney was the leader of the MacSweeney clan. In autumn 1608 the so-called "Lifford Jury" convened, which declared the abscondent Earls (among them Rory O'Donnell) traitors and ruled that all of Tyrconnell be handed over to the English crown. Among the jury were Donal MacSweeney of Fanad and Donough MacSweeney of Banagh.

Mulmurry MacSweeney was also tried for treason. Somehow he managed to persuade the authorities to drop the charges against him however, and in 1610 he was granted a further 2,000 acres of land near Dunfanaghy with the right to hold markets every Tuesday and a one-day fair twice a year.[280]

In 1615, Mulmurry found himself in dire straits one last time. Documents were found proving that he and his son Donough were involved in a plot to free the young Con O'Neill from Dungannon Castle. Con O'Neill was the son of Hugh O'Neill and had been left behind when his father fled Ireland in 1607.[281]

In 1630 Mulmurry MacSweeney's lifetime tenure of his estates and his heirs' entitlement thereto was once more confirmed. He died a short while later.

This late descendant of an ancient galloglas dynasty has become surrounded by legend, and yet folklore does not flatter him. Many stories relating the feats of Mulmurry MacSweeney border on the fantastical, or the bizarre. He allegedly earned himself the nickname "Myles of the Yellow Stick" by regularly lathering a certain stick in his possession with butter. When asked about this curious habit, he claimed that the devil was imprisoned in this stick in the guise of a beetle!

During O'Doherty's Rebellion in 1608 a force of rebels under a certain Shane MacManus O'Donnell retreated to Tory Island.[282] Here a certain Mulmory MacSweeney was in charge of defending the small local castle against the English. Hoping for the enemy's mercy, he is said to have treacherously murdered his comrades-in-arms one by one before being himself killed.[283]

---

[280] Ronayne, Liam: *Donegal Highlands. Paintings and Stories from Northwest Donegal*, Donaghadee 2004, p. 81.

[281] Con O'Neill was later released, but died under mysterious circumstances in Brussels in 1617.

[282] Bardon, Jonathan: *The Plantation of Ulster*, Dublin 2012, p. 105.

[283] Lenihan, Padraig: *Consolidating Conquest. Ireland 1603-1727*, Abingdon 2014, p. 44.

GALLOGLAS – A WARRIORS' TRADITION

The galloglas were originally recruited from the warlike inhabitants of the western Scottish Highlands and the Hebrides. As previously shown, these warriors travelled or migrated to Ireland in several waves, even entire clans leaving their Scottish homelands in the wake of political and military conflict to seek new homes in Erin.

The galloglas tradition was passed down from father to son. This was as common in Gaelic-Irish society as it was in Scotland, where occupations continued for generations within the same family. In Gaelic Ireland physicians, chroniclers, and harpers could hope for estates and other rewards from their lords. As warriors, the galloglas were no exception, and thus they belonged to the upper classes of Irish society. It was also common for a galloglas clan to establish a lasting relationship with a specific Irish aristocratic family, with loyalties often reaching across several generations.[284] Thus not only a warrior's profession but also his loyalties were unquestioningly passed on to his male heirs. Physical features also seem to have been inherited by subsequent generations of galloglas: while sources hostile to the galloglas abound with descriptions of their cruelty and savage nature, other chroniclers are bewildered by their unusual appearance. All sources agree however in that these men were extraordinarily tall and strong. These features can possibly be attributed to the Scandinavian origins of many galloglas, and their privileged social status which gave them access to food of higher nutritional value than many contemporaries could normally expect to receive.

The contract between an Irish magnate and his galloglas commander (or constable, as he was more frequently known[285]) provided the employer with the agreed number of galloglas in return for tracts of land and other social and economic benefits. If the constable was unable to provide the fixed number of warriors, he was obliged to pay a compensation of two cows for each warrior short of the agreed amount – one cow for the man himself, and one for his arms and equipment. As high-ranking officers, the constables themselves could hope for tax exemption and fishing rights, and often they would receive valuable horses or hunting dogs as particular tokens of their lords' favour. At table, it was considered an exceptional honour for a galloglas commander to sit at his chieftain's right side. Relations could become very close; having served their lords with devotion over several generations, the MacSweeneys eventually all but became a sub-clan of the O'Donnells of Tyrconnell. A similar realtionship existed between the MacSheehys and the Earls of Desmond.

MacSweeney tradition has it that they had been free mercenaries before taking service with the O'Donnells of Tyrconnell. Such non-committal business relationships were not restricted to early times however, as many galloglas offered their services in groups or individually, the term of contract generally lasting around three months.[286] Many galloglas constables did not hold tenures, but they were generally better paid than their subordinates. On the other hand, the MacDonnells of Tynekill possessed large estates in County Laois, as did the MacSweeneys in County Donegal. If a constable owned a sufficient amount of land, he was able to recruit warriors even from outside his own galloglas clan.

McSwynes Castle, County Donegal.
(Photograph: Maximilian Bunk)

---

284 Cannan and Ó Brógháin: *Galloglass*, p. 13.
285 Gaelic-Irish: *consabal*; the word is derived from the Latin word *comes stabuli*, i. e. master of the stables.
286 Ibid., p. 25.

ORGANISATION, COMMAND, AND LOGISTICS

The military unit in which the galloglas fought was called *corrughadh*, which English sources invariably translate as "battle"[287]. When contemporary writers refer to four hundred-strong "battles", this number remains impressive enough even if we consider that only between one third and one half of these men were actually true galloglas. Each galloglass was accompanied by at least one retainer, while two companions seem to have been the norm. These men served their master while learning the warrior trade, and accompanied him into battle, where they served as skirmishers. This concept was similar to that of the European knight being served by his squires, yet compared to the French *lances fournies* and the German *gleven*, these fighting communities remained very small. According to a source from 1575, a constable commanding 100 galloglas was permitted to pocket the equivalent of up to thirteen galloglas' salaries if his company fell short of this number of men (so-called "deadpays")[288], as well as the monetary equivalent of the rations and supplies for six men. He was also entitled to one riding horse and one hack for every three months' service.[289] From this we may conclude that a *corrughadh* numbering between eighty and ninety galloglas seems to have been the norm. The constable's rank was hereditary. He was expected to fight alongside his men in the first rank, and was accompanied by a piper and a standard bearer. It was not unusual for the constables of opposing galloglas units to engage in heroic single combat.

A constable's salary was tenfold that of an ordinary galloglass, but how much pay did galloglas actually receive? In 1553 a galloglas was paid four pence a day, by 1568 this amount had doubled. However, it was much more common to pay galloglas in kind, e. g. cattle, butter, meat, etc. The generally accepted practice seems to have been that a galloglass received three cattle for three months' service – one as his salary, two as campaign rations.[290] This was in keeping with other contemporary armies: English soldiers, whether serving in Ireland or elsewhere, also received beef rations since this was considered the best method to maintain their physical stamina.

Galloglas and other Irish warriors commonly drank milk or ale, but were also excessively fond of whisky, the latter being a popular drink in all levels of Irish society. English chroniclers were disgusted by the lack of restraint both Irish men and women showed when it came to consuming the beverage, often ending up "drunk as beggars".

A common phenomenon in European military history was to burden the civilian community with the costs of the military establishment, and professional soldiers in particular. This usually manifested itself in the form of taxes and contributions. In Ireland this specific fiscal system was referred to as *buannacht* (its anglicized form being "bonaght").

Gaelic-Irish society was rigid in its hierarchical structure and generally impermeable regarding social advancement. Its economy was chiefly based on the subsistence of the individual. This explains at least in part why salaries were paid in the form of victuals and accomodation. Although the galloglas were professional soldiers, they were of course not quartered in barracks like the soldiers of the standing armies which were to emerge later. It was common for the lord to billet his galloglas and their servants in his subjects' houses. Apart from providing accomodation, these unfortunates were also required to feed these proud and unruly individuals. Neither Gaelic chiefs nor Anglo-Irish lords or the English crown were unduly troubled by the inconveniences and burdens this placed on the individuals and families concerned.

This billeting and victualling system was known as "coin and livery". Sir John Davies, Attorney General of Ireland from 1606, deplored coin and livery as criminal and barbarous. In practice, a galloglass (or some other soldier) was forced upon a town dweller's or farmer's household, which was obliged to feed and shelter him along with his retinue. Some galloglas were not content even with this, since a certain William Clinch from Newcastle, County Dublin, complained that his galloglass lodger had stolen no less than thirteen cows![291]

Theft, physical and sexual assault, and other serious encroachments on the life of the landlord and his kin were frequent but hardly ever punished. In contrast to this, neglect of military discipline was met with draconic measures. If a galloglass failed to take good care of his equipment, he was fined by his constable. Serious offences were punishable by death: in 1558, a galloglass

---

287 Modern military terminology still refers to specific units as „battalions", a French derivation.
288 A constable of a battle of kern was only allowed to keep the salary of eight men.
289 Heath and Sque: *Irish Wars*, p. 11.
290 Cannan and Ó'Brógháin: *Galloglass*, p. 27.

291 Ibid., p. 29.

These two galloglas are wealthy enough to afford equipment of excellent quality.
(© Claíomh – Dave Swift 2010)

Irish warrior types.
The two figures at left are galloglas.
(Illustration by the German artist Albrecht Dürer, c. 1521)

Opposite page:
A Lord's galloglass attending a ball at the court of an Anglo-Irish baron.
(Illustration by Sascha Lunyakov).

from the Earl of Desmond's retinue was nailed to a shield because he had drawn his weapon in camp despite explicitly having been forbidden to do so. A short while later, another galloglass from the same contingent was strung up because he had stolen a coat of mail.[292]

In battle, the galloglas were often the only soldiers suitable for the long and exhaustive and terribly gory fight at close quarters. Galloglass duelling with galloglass was a common sight, and the hazardous duty of forming an army's rearguard was also often performed by galloglas. They acted as their lords' personal bodyguard, the Lord's Galloglass taking pride of place. It was fairly common for a Lord's Galloglass to take his master's place in a formal duel. A Lord's Galloglass received double pay and a double ration of meat. After all, an extra helping of beef was considered essential for his imposing appearance and strong physical condition.

The role of the Lord's Galloglass is perhaps best illustrated by the following episode: in 1586, a force of redshanks commanded by Alastair MacSorley MacDonnell was marching through Inishowen when it was caught up and confronted by English troops led by Sir Nicholas Merriman. Alastair MacSorley challenged the English commander to a duel, and was met by Merriman's Lord's Galloglass wearing his master's attire. The galloglas managed to wound Alastair MacSorley, but it was not a crippling blow. Alastair MacSorley succeeded in killing his enemy. Now Merriman himself stepped up, and fighting with sword and targe wounded Alastair MacSorley.

One of the absurd accusations levelled at Lord Grey was that he had been on all too friendly terms with rebellious Irish lords. After all, he had travelled through Thomond and Connacht accompanied by a single axe-armed galloglas![293]

---

292 Ibid., p. 30.

293 Moore: *History of Ireland*, p. 383.

Galloglas operated together with light-armed kern.
(Photograph: Jessica Greenwood)

A galloglass defends the entrance to a Crannóg.
(© Claíomh – Nathan Barber 2010)

OVERVIEW OF THE PRINCIPAL ELEMENTS OF GALLOGLAS ARMS & ARMOUR

The gallowglas who originally hailed from the Western Highlands and Isles of Scotland and largely settled in Ireland over the thirteenth and fourteenth centuries served Irish chieftains in the role of professional mercenary heavy infantry. By the fifteenth and sixteenth centuries they were firmly embedded in Irish society. Asides their offensive weaponry they were customarily armed with an iron helmet, a long mail shirt, a mail collar and a base-layer aketon, customarily worn under the mail, of stuffed textile or leather padding.

Throughout the late medieval period in Ireland, and in the wider European world, helmets of iron and various forms of body armour were worn by nobles, professional soldiers, and the more well to do when they were pressed to perform their feudal duty on campaign or in city militias. In Gaelic and Anglo-Irish Ireland, the iconographic evidence indicates that these affordances of protection were worn by the chiefly classes and their families as well as by the professional military ranks of galloglas. As the ruling elite, the former habitually performed the light cavalry role in late medieval Ireland while the latter were cast as resolute professional heavy infantry. With the obvious exception of the western seaboard and isles of Scotland, much of the combination of arms and armour used by galloglas was somewhat unique from a wider European view point. As with the cavalry, galloglas were typically armoured in a padded *cotún* or aketon, a mail *lúirech* shirt, a *sgabal* of mail around the throat and over the shoulders, and, of course, a *clogat* or helmet.[294] For nobles this ensemble could be augmented with the addition of a round wood and leather covered targe or shield, as well as the quintessential spurs. Gaelic-Irish cavalry famously did not routinely make use of stirrups until near the end of the period. Due to their defined heavy infantry role and preponderance to utilise two handed weaponry, galloglas did not habitually make use of either spurs or shields in the battle line.

While galloglas had been originally introduced from the Western Highlands and Isles of Scotland in the mid thirteenth to fourteenth century, they were firmly ensconced in the fabric of Irish medieval society by the fifteenth and sixteenth centuries. Both nobles and galloglas operated in tandem with a third – and by far the most numerous – component in Gaelic-Irish medieval armies: the lightly armoured kern warriors whose role it was to provide the indispensable flexible and fast moving light infantry needed in a tribal world where cattle-raiding was the most prevalent sport. With the darts, javelins, skein and sword as offensive weaponry kern were the ideal hit and run skirmishers.[295] Oft times when kern (or light cavalry) would be hotly pursued retreating from one *tuatha* to the safety of neutral or home ground – ideally carrying away a great prey of the enemy stores – the text book tactic was to deploy galloglas to act as a protective screen at a narrow topographical feature such as at a pass or a ford. From such a screen the possibility of counter attacks could be launched by the defenders – and all from the relative safety of 'a castle of bones, rather than a castle of stones'[296] – the galloglas ideally grimly holding their ground against all comers. At least that was the theory… In the upcoming paragraphs we shall look at the most prominent arms and armour elements in the panoply of these warriors.

Armour

Helmets

In the late medieval period and moving into the sixteenth century a broad observation of the sculptural, pictorial, written and archaeological evidence presents us with three broad categories of typology for protective helmets worn by galloglas and native nobles in the Gaelic-Irish late medieval world and – each of which can be further potentially broken down into further diverse subcategories with some overlap naturally occurring with the Anglo-Irish culture. The three main categories are here named Type 1, Type 2 and Type 3. Broadly speaking these three groups refer to respectively: the high centre crowned Irish bascinet, other late medieval 'skulls' and pot helmets etc with a low crown, and finally later sixteenth century fully developed burgonets and morions. Whatever the type though, one contemporary source is particularly terse with reference to how the helmet should be able to function as illustrated by this detail of a contract of service between the O'Donnells of Tyrconnell and their Mac Sweeney galloglass:

> "And Clann Suibhne say they are responsible for these as follows … that there should be no forfeit for a helmet deficient except the galloglass's brain [dashed out for want of it]; and no fine for a missing axe except a shilling, nor for a spear, except a groat, which shilling and groat the Constable [captain] should get, and Ó Domhnaill had no claim to make for either."[297]

---

294 Harbison, Peter: "Native Irish Arms and Armour in Medieval Gaelic Literature 1170-1600", in: *Irish Sword*, Dublin 2014, pp. 183-193.

295 Nicholls, Kenneth W.: *Gaelic and Gaelicised Ireland in the Middle Ages*, Dublin 1972, p. 84.

296 Ó Cléirigh, Cormac: "Irish frontier warfare – a fifteenth century case study", in: *ACTA 22. Kongress der Internationalen Kommission für Militärgeschichte XXII*. Edited by Heeresgeschichtliches Museum/Militärhistorischen Institut, Vienna 1997, pp. 179-194, here: p. 184.

297 Walsh, Paul (ed.): *Leabhar Chlainne Suibhne. An Account of the MacSweeney Families in Ireland*, Dublin 1920, p. 45.

This galloglas wears a Type 1b fluted helmet. (© Claíomh – Katharina Temirati 2022)

In 1543 Sir Anthony Sentleger observed 'as to ther footemen, they have one sorte, whiche be harnessed in mayle and bassenettes... and they be named galloglasse'[298]. Type 1 is the Irish bascinet with its distinctive combination of a deep close fit and high crown with medial ridge and centrally pointed apex. It is the most prevalent helmet type in our sources and the only type of the three categories to survive on the Irish archaeological context. As with all European helmets in this class the bascinet appears to have had its origins in the shallower brow length conical profiled helmets of the centuries preceding and overlapping with the advent of galloglass service in Ireland. Evidence is scanty for the first century of galloglass activity in Ireland but these early galloglas must have utilised a range of contemporary types including the conical or round topped helm – with or without nasal – and various other forms of iron 'war-hats' and 'skulls' then generally in vogue. In terms of dating, bascinets in Europe were generally in use from the middle of the fourteenth century[299] and continued in use until the evolution and subsequent decline of the heavy 'great bascinet' – i.e. bascinets with additional collar plates to rear and front – in England in the middle of the fifteenth century.[300] Despite this general trend in England, for example, iconographic evidence in sculptural and pictorial form from Ireland, as well as from the Western Isles of Scotland, indicates the presence of the bascinet as an enduring part of the warrior's panoply until as late as the second last decade of the sixteenth century.[301] A 1399 illumination depicting the mounted and fully garnitured native Leinster ruler Art MacMurrough-Kavanagh[302] would appear to indicate that such helmets had origins going back at least as far as the end of the fourteenth century. With at least two centuries of apparent continual use this would appear to make the bascinet the helmet mode in late medieval Ireland with the greatest longevity. Confirming this, the dating of such helmets rendered on funerary monuments also stretches over much of the fifteenth and sixteenth centuries in Ireland, but appears

---

298 Hayes-McCoy, Gerard Anthony: *Scots Mercenary Forces in Ireland*, Dublin and London 1937, p. 10

299 Capwell, Tobias: *Armour of the English Knight 1400-1450*, London 2015, p.66.

300 Capwell, Tobias: *Armour of the English Knight 1450-1500*, London 2021, pp. 6-7.

301 Harbison, Peter: "Native Irish Arms and Armour", in: *Medieval Gaelic Literature* 1170-1600", Pl. 18.

302 GGilbert, John T.: *Facsimiles of the National Manuscripts of Ireland* (vol. 3), Public Record Office of Ireland, Dublin 1879, p XIII, Pl. XXXIII.

The grave monument of Felim O'Connor at Roscommon Abbey. (Photograph: Maximilian Bunk)

at its most prevalent c. 1450 – 1570.[303] There is also some evidence for bascinet like helmets on non funerary effigies from before this time – the most convincing of which is the crested bascinet on an armoured Butler knight at a cloister arcade in Jerpoint, Kilkenny c. 1400.[304]

An examination of contemporary fifteenth and sixteenth military effigies in stone of nobles of The Pale (the English controlled area around Dublin including parts of Kildare, Meath and Louth) and elsewhere in Anglo-Irish medieval Ireland reveals that bascinets with attached moveable visors[305] were *de rigueur* as the most frequently seen protective headgear in those parts of Ireland imbued with that culture. Conversely we see very little evidence in the sources for the use of visored helmets by Gaelic nobles and none for galloglas – hence we shall not look any further at the visored version in this study. However the iconographical evidence of the higher echelons of Gaelic military society that survive, indicate that open-faced bascinets, i.e. those bascinets portrayed without visors, appear to have been the most prevalent native Irish mode of head protection, above all other helmets for much of the late medieval period and well into early modern times. For ease of reference, in my typology I refer to the bascinet with moveable visor as the Type 1a and to the open-faced bascinet as Type 1b. Type 1b bascinets may have a finished surface which is faceted or not, while Type 1a helmets thus far appear without this variation.

In Ireland the Type 1b open-faced bascinet has been traditionally best exemplified by medieval sepulchral survivals such as the galloglass sentinels at the O'Connor tomb at Roscommon Abbey[306], the effigy on the O'Cahan Tomb at Dungiven Co Derry[307] and the effigy of a mailed De Burgo warrior at Ballinakill Abbey at Glinsk, Co Galway[308] alongside various other bascineted 'heads' that survive e.g. at the churches at Clonfert and Kilcorban (both Co

---

303 Higgins, Jim: "Medieval Sculptures from Carran Church Co Clare and their significance", in: Shannon Archaeological and Historical Society (ed.): *The Other Clare 16 (April)*, Shannon 1992, pp. 21-26, here: p. 22.

304 Hunt, John: *Irish Medieval Figure Sculpture 1200-1600*, Dublin 1974, pp. 177-178, Pl. 117.

305 Rae, Edwin C.: "Irish Sepulchral Monuments of the Later Middle Ages", in: Royal Society of Antiquaries of Ireland (ed.): *The Journal of the Royal Society of Antiquaries of Ireland* (100/I), Dublin 1970, pp. 1-38, Pl. 14.

306 Ibid., Pl. 6a.

307 Hunt: *Irish Medieval Figure Sculpture*, pp. 130-131, Pl. 168.

308 Ibid., p. 150.

Galloglass wearing a fluted 1b type helmet.
(© Claíomh – Arthur Boyton 2022)

Galway), Carran (Co Clare) and the recently recovered Scattery Island example.[309] As may be expected there are many fine Western Highland sculptural examples too.[310] Examination of these effigies reveals that many of these bascinets generally had a single overt central crease, or medial ridge, from brow to nape but otherwise presented a smooth surface. At the brow it is also a common Irish feature that the ridge ends in a relatively shallow 'V' shaped projection which dips down – langet like – at the front of the helmet between the eyes. Occasionally, such as with the example of Kilninian in Mull,[311] that a full nasal guard is also present. Like English – and especially Scottish – bascinets, the Irish bascinets appear to be relatively short when compared with their continental equivalents, typically reaching to the jaw-line, although some only reach to the cheek bone.[312] However, unlike the typical English or continental bascinet, whose sides ran down sharply and diagonally backwards away from the brow,[313] the Gaelic bascinet tended to be presented

---

[309] Reilly, Gavan: "Stolen medieval carvings to return to Clare after 150 years", The Journal, 20 June. Available at: https://www.thejournal.ie/stolen-medieval-carvings-scattery-island-958260-Jun2013/ (Accessed: 30 November 2021)

[310] SSteer, K. A. and Bannerman, J. W. M.: *Late medieval monumental sculpture in the West Highlands,* (The Royal Commission on the Ancient and Historical Monuments of Scotland), Edinburgh 1977.

[311] Ibid., Pl. 25C.

[312] Capwell: *Armour of the English Knight 1400-1450*, p. 56.

[313] Ibid., p. 66.

The Lough-Henney helmet (reconstruction by White Rose Armoury).
(© Claíomh – Michael Selby-Bennetts 2010)

with more or less straight sides affording better relative cheek protection. The integration of greater cheek protection in Type 1b bascinets is logical given the apparent intended absence of a visor. Several of the Irish sculptural helmets feature a taper inwards towards the base of the helmet at the neck giving a very neat close-fitting appearance – the Glinsk helmet is a particularly good example of this feature.[314] Like some Type 2 helmets, there is some evidence that a small minority of the hewn bascinets once bore (removeable?) crests, e.g. at Carran Church, but this is inconclusive.[315]

A sub-group of the Type 1b helmets depicted on monuments including the late fifteenth century Roscommon Abbey galloglas on the right side of the tomb as you face it i.e. numbers 5–8[316], the Carran Church head, and the – presumed early sixteenth century – Glinsk warrior's helmet, had a faceted or fluted surface. The best example of these is the Glinsk effigy as it is rendered on a larger, and moreover – a closer to life-size – scale and demonstrates more details of the close fitting Type 1b faceted bascinet such as the neat and graceful taper of the helmet from the brow to the neck. It can also be discerned that the characteristic facets are all slightly dished, and the ridges

---

314 Hunt: *Irish Medieval Figure Sculpture*, p. 150.
315 HHiggins: *Medieval Sculptures from Carran Church Co Clare and their significance*, p. 21.
316 O'Connor, Kierean and Shanahan, Brian: *Roscommon Abbey. A Visitor's Guide*, Boyle 2013, p. 44.

Occasionally such round helmets (which were also referred to as "*skulls*") had attached rondels to protect the wearer's ears and cheeks.
(© Claíomh – Katharina Temirati 2022)

are slightly raised granting a somewhat gothic finish to the whole. The Glinsk bascinet features six longitudinal facets when viewed frontally, and given the even distribution and spacing of the facets a likely total of a dozen can be deduced around the helmets circumference.[317] Outside of Ireland faceted or fluted surfaces on bascinets are rare whether in monumental or artefact form.[318]

As it now stands, there are currently five helmets, of late medieval type, kept between the national collections on the island of Ireland. In terms of morphology these helmets all conform to the Type 1 bascinet in general form. The order of sequential acquisition is as follows: the Lough Henney helmet (County Down), the Clashnamuck helmet (County Laois), the Monea helmet (Co Fermanagh) and two helmets recently yielded from the River Shannon in the west of Ireland.

The Lough Henney helmet is the best known of the extant iron bascinets so far found on the archaeological record in Ireland. First exhibited and published in the 1850s the helmet had been yielded from Wright's Island, a crannog in County Down, most likely in the mid 1830s. The helmet stands 30 cm high and features a central pointed crown and its lower half is more or less a straight 90 degrees to its base. Fine rivet holes set out in pairs are evenly distributed on the lower edge – most likely to secure a liner and/or less likely to secure an aventail of mail. At the front are two enclosing cheek plates and between them a nasal which is riveted in place, the latter join tidily masked by a copper alloy mount with projected 'hook'. The whole gives a fairly enclosed frontal visage more like a barbute than an open faced bascinet. The oculars are in tighter compass than seen on the Irish effigies and are decorated with bevelled castings of copper alloy which are held in place with rivets of the same material which are recessed, perhaps these latter were designed to mount semi pre-

---
317 Crawford, Henry S.: "The Burke Effigy at Glinsk, Co. Galway", in: Royal Society of Antiquaries of Ireland (ed.): *The Journal of the Royal Society of Antiquaries of Ireland* (vol. 37/3), Dublin 1907, p. 307 f., here: p. 307.
318 Capwell: *Armour of the English Knight 1400-1450*, p. 67.

While the man in the background wears a morion helmet, the man in the foreground has donned a casquetel.
(© Claíomh – Nathan Barber 2010)

cious stones or similar.[319] Although there is no exact fit for the Lough Henney in contemporary monumental representations some comparisons have been justly made in the past with the effigy of a Butler knight in the cloister of Jerpoint Abbey Co Kilkenny, although the oculars – or rather a monocular – are seemingly more open and while no nasal is present, a crest is visible on the latter. With its acute apex and straight lower sides, a closer fit for the silhouette of the Lough Henney helmet, would be the early to mid sixteenth century effigy at Kilninian, Mull, Scotland[320] but this latter lacks the deep enclosing cheek guards. The closest fit of all is the illuminated late sixteenth century 'Book of the De Burgos' depicting several of the chieftains of the MacWilliam-Burkes. The profile of one of the helmets depicted is akin to the Lough Henney and it even has what appears to represent a brass hook like feature between the eyes.[321] The De Burgo source dates from around the early 1580s while the Butler knight at Jerpoint dates from the previous century giving us a fairly wide provisional two hundred year span of c. 1400–1590 in terms of dating the Lough Henney helmet.

The second bascinet to appear on the Irish archaeological record is the Clashnamuck helmet which was found in the bed of the River Nore 'in mud, about three feet below the surface of the land'.[322] The location of the find was in the townland of Clashnamuck which is about three km east from the town of Borris-in-Ossory in Co Laois. The helmet's profile is generally intact – and there is certainly enough of its profile, including an elegant apex, to be certain of its typology – but it is in a fairly fragmentary state of preservation. The Clashnamuck bascinet can cur-

319 Bourke, Cormac: "A Medieval Helmet from Lough Henney, Co. Down", Lecale and Downe historical society, Dundrum (ed.): Lecale Miscellany 1990, pp. 5-7.

320 Steer and Bannerman: *Late medieval monumental sculpture in the West Highlands*, Pl. 25C.

321 Trinity College Dublin (no date): The book of the de Burgos. Available at: https://digitalcollections.tcd.ie/concern/works/rb68xg028?locale=en (Accessed: 30 November 2021).

322 Mulvany, William Thomas et al: Appendix No. V: *Notices of Antiquities Presented to the Royal Irish Academy by W. T. Mulvany*, Esq., M. R. I. A., on the Part of the Commissioners of Public Works' Proceedings of the Royal Irish Academy 1836-1869, 1850-1853(5), pp. xxxi-lxvi 1853, here: p. xxxix.

Close-up detail of a late 16th century morion helmet.
(© Claíomh – Rob Hunt 2010)

rently be seen on permanent exhibition at the National Museum of Ireland's archaeological museum on Kildare Street, Dublin.

The antiquarian and artist William F. Wakeman reported the finding of a third bascinet in 1873 in Co Fermanagh at the Maguire crannóg at Monea near the fine plantation castle of the same name. The helmet was discovered by a workman when 'digging into a portion of its shore'.[323] At the moment of writing the whereabouts of the Monea bascinet is unknown to this writer. From Wakeman's illustration, despite its evident dilapidation, its similarity to the Clashnamuck helmet is apparent.

The very recent finds of two bascinets in the River Shannon in the west of Ireland comprise a near intact helmet 'Shannon 1', yielded in 2020, and a second more fragmentary bascinet discovered in 2021, 'Shannon 2'. Both helmets have medial ridges clearly visible and neither has a faceted surface. The general profile of the well preserved Shannon 1 bascinet, the elegant taper of its base, and its sharp defiant apex speak of a medieval Irish bascinet of exceptional elegance and craft. Its visage reveals an air of authority with its grim oculars appearing in small compass on either side of the apparently short nasal guard. The perfection of the graceful left cheek guard is mirrored by a missing right one.

In Scotland and Ireland the apex is usually depicted set at the centre of the crown while on English effigies and on continental originals it is invariably set back to the rear. This latter feature would have facilitated the raising and shutting of a visor apparently not present on Shannon 1. The helmet's apex is set fairly centrally and although there is a small perforation at the high point, it is likely close to its original height. The upright height is close to that recorded for the Lough Henney.

Due to a build up of encrustation on Shannon 1 it is not yet clear whether the nasal is riveted to the helmet, as with the Lough Henney helmet, or whether it was raised entirely of one piece of iron. The nose guard appears shorter on Shannon 1 than the Lough Henney possibly because it was damaged in antiquity. The right cheek guard is completely missing and it is possible that it and part of the nasal were sliced off in a blow from a sharp cutting weapon like a sword or sparth axe. The remaining left cheek-guard indicates a close protective visage akin

---

323 Wakeman, William F.: "Observations on the Principal Crannogs of Fermanagh", in: Royal Historical and Archaeological Association of Ireland (ed.): *The Journal of the Royal Historical and Archaeological Association of Ireland*, vol. 4 (2) 2, Dublin 1873, p. 218 f., here: p. 318.

Galloglass wearing blued Gaelic bascinet.
(© Claíomh – Ruby Gallagher 2022)

to the Lough Henney – it is very similar in scale but unlike the former which has vertical edges to the cheek-guards at front, the extant Shannon 1 cheek guard gently slopes diagonally outwards to the chin.

One of the most noticeable aspects of the profile of Shannon 1 is the graceful tapering base. This is a first on the archaeological record in Ireland as the other three helmets found in the nineteenth century all demonstrated straight sides. Of all the Irish effigy helmet representations, the Glinsk effigy has the most obvious taper, but unlike the Glinsk helmet, Shannon 1 is not fluted and features definite oculars. Some sepulchral monuments in Scotland such as some from the Iona School e.g. the Killean effigy at Kintyre, and the Lough Awe School Kilmartin effigies bear a similar elegant and tapered outline the Shannon helmet but they appear open faced and do not share the same enclosed frontal with tight oculars and nasal guard.

Both of the Shannon helmets had some remains of leather binding strips at their respective bases likely to retain an organic liner. The Shannon 2 leather strip also featured visible peened rivets with accompanying roughly sub-rectangular washers. Based on contemporary iconography it would appear that the Shannon 1 helmet, at least, is similarly dated as the Lough Henney i.e. c. 1400–1590. Type 2 helmets in this Irish typology are what are often referred to as 'skulls' in contemporary English sources. Although such helmets are not yet represented on the archaeological record they are specifically mentioned by both Barnaby Rich and John Dymmok in the later sixteenth century. It is likely that the intended meaning of 'skull' in contemporary sources is fairly loose, and so therefore does not just include the simplest skull cap like steel 'secretes', but also a diversity of helmets which had a lower bowl which conformed closely to the head rather than the high pointed crown of the Irish Type 1 bascinet. Such helmets could include, but may not be restricted to, kettle helmets and other brimmed pots as well as the later peaked casquetels. Representations of skulls survive on Irish incised grave slabs as well as on sixteenth century contemporary pictorial sources. One of the most intriguing examples is either a peaked casque, or a skull with a protective curved protective bar to the fore, seen from the side on two sparth axe bearing figures on the tomb of Donat O'Suibhne at Sligo Abbey c. 1577.[324] Similar looking helmets are also represented worn by Irish cavalry on John Derrick's 1581 woodcuts.[325]

Dürer, in his famous 1521 watercolour, has his left-most (first) figure wearing a secret with rondels and what appears to be a hinged nasal guard. The combination of rondels and secret was common on the continent particularly in places like Germany and Switzerland but they are not recorded in the Irish corpus to date. Dürer's second figure is represented wearing a slightly more elaborate casquetel not too dissimilar in general style to the helmet of Guidobaldo I da Montefeltro of Urbino in the Wallace Collection: essentially a proto-burgonet – or 'Burgundian sallet'[326] – with a deep curved frontal peak combined with integral brow plate attached by rivets located at the temples and a series of three articulated overlapping lames affixed to the rear providing cover for the neck.

Type 3 in this Irish typology is a catch all for the later sixteenth century helmets which appear in written and pictorial sources and evidently see more and more widespread use in Gaelic Ireland as the sixteenth century trudges on. The range of helmets in this category is well documented elsewhere,[327] but in short, includes the four main helmet types that dominated the period in Western Europe: the 'Spanish morion' which went back as far as the second half of the fifteenth century,[328] the cabasset,

---

324 Hunt: *Irish Medieval Figure Sculpture*, p. 219.

325 University of Edinburgh (no date): The Image of Irelande by John Derricke. Available at: http://www.docs.is.ed.ac.uk/docs/lib-archive/bgallery/Gallery/researchcoll/pages/bg0061_jpg.htm (Accessed: 30 November 2021).

326 Oakeshott, Ewart: *European Weapons and Armour, Woodbridge 1980*, pp. 114-115.

327 Ibid., pp. 214-218.

328 Ibid., p. 114.

burgonet and comb morion. The former two had high crowns which frequently featured a pear stalk finial, while the latter two had high combs projecting over the crown from front to back. Although the National Museum of Ireland has a couple of morions in its collection, none are known to be provenanced from Early Modern era Ireland. However in addition to literary records making reference to the use of Type 3 helmets, contemporary pictorial sources place them in the use of the Gaelic-Irish – galloglas among them. By way of example, John Goghe's map of 1567 shows two out of the three Tyrconnell (approximating to modern Co Donegal) septs of MacSweeney galloglas represented by mailed and axe armed warriors in what are clearly comb morions. The third MacSweeney sept is incidentally represented by a wearer of a more traditional looking Type 2 skull with an apparent crest.[329] Confirming the wearing of imported helmets at the close of the period, Fynes Moryson states that 'the galliglasses are armed with Moryons'.[330]

Armour made of organic materials

As part of a visually arresting and culturally distinct set of military accoutrements for a Gaelic noble, or a professional warrior like a galloglass, the helmet would have been donned in conjunction with a panoply of various other items of protective garb associated with, what we might now call, the galloglass' 'personal protective equipment'.

The base layer of this ensemble went by various names including 'gambeson', 'aketon' and the Scots 'actoun'. In Irish sources this padded coat is most prevalently referred to as the *cotún*. The *cotún* could be worn as stand alone armour or could act as padding beneath mail to prevent iron mail links – broken or not – rending the flesh. Evidence from contemporary effigies and illuminations indicates that the appearance of the late medieval *cotún* took the form of a long knee length coat made of multi layered fabric. Appraising the iconographic sources it appears that some were split at the legs, but that some may not have been. Distinctive, longitudinally stitched narrow piping evidently characterised the outer shell of the garment with the function being to keep the protective layers and tailoring in place throughout. One written account of 1521 appears to describe *cotúns* worn by Highland Scots as 'a linen garment manifoldly sewed and painted or daubed with pitch, with a covering of deerskin'.[331] It stands to reason that fabric armour would be proofed from the elements with something like pitch or wax especially in northern European climes for the sake of the integrity of the armour, the health of the wearer, and as a ward against unnecessary encumbrance and discomfort. No original *cotún* survives in Ireland from the galloglass period of c. 1250–1600 and the preservation of equivalent garments is rare in national collections across Europe. From what little evidence we do have the outer shells of continental aketons appear to have been made with various materials including linen and even silk. The few originals that do survive in European collections also indicate the use of various materials layered in concert acting as an internal padding. Such materials could have included a myriad of rags, linen, grass, wool and cotton[332] – there must inevitably have been much variation of exact composition depending on maker, availability of natural resources and access to trade. It would seem reasonable to expect that the better sort of *cotún* would have conformed to contemporary European standards. Unfortunately there are very few extant examples even when the whole continent is assessed. One notable survivor is a fourteenth century *pourpoint* at Chartres in France which has a few characteristics in common with late medieval Highland and Irish effigies frequently exhibit similar vertical stitching. As a presumed noble's padded armour the Chartres garment has silk as an outer layer. The inner layers are composed of two main layers of linen and cotton wool – in each of these main layers two layers of linen sandwich one layer of the latter making a total of four layers of linen and two of cotton wool.[333] In Late Medieval Ireland silk and cotton wool were both relatively expensive imports so it could be considered more likely that linen or leather may have provided the shell of many *cotúns* while it could be speculated that the filler was comprised of a stratified combination of linen and wool. Evidence from the Alexander MacLeod tomb at Rodel[334] points to the possible simultaneous use of two *cotúns* – one over the other, and the two underlying a long mail shirt. Perhaps an old and worn *cotún* was retained while a new one was worn atop it. Or the top layer was in place to protect the base *cotún* or the mason

---

329 Swift, Michael: *Historical Maps of Ireland*, New Jersey 1999, pp. 22-23.
330 KKew, Graham (ed.): *The Irish Sections of Fynes Moryson's Unpublished Itinerary*, Dublin 1998.
331 McClintlock, H. F.: *Old Highland Dress and Tartans*, Dundalk 1949, p. 4.
332 Steer and Bannerman: *Late medieval monumental sculpture in the West Highlands*, p. 25.
333 Harlaut, Mathieu: The Company of Saynte GeorgeClothing Guide – Men version 1.1. Available at: https://companie-of-st-george.ch/publications/costume-guide/(Accessed: 10 February 2022). http://creativecommons.org/licenses/by-nc-nd/3.0/ for CC BY-NC-ND 3.0, p. 19.
334 Steer and Bannerman: *Late medieval monumental sculpture in the West Highlands*, Pl. 32B.

A galloglas attired in *léine* and *trews* stands guard. He wears a waxed cotún to ward off the damp.

(© Claíomh – Dave Senior 2009)

Gauntlets were not necessarily worn in pairs.
(© Claíomh – Katharina Temirati 2022)

may have intended the lower hem to represent the creased layers of an underlying *léine*. The effigies leave us with many questions and few answers.

Cotún sleeves are universally depicted in contemporary sources reaching the wrist. Evidence from Oronsay Priory[335], for example, indicates that some *cotúns* may have been embellished with decorative cuffs and hems, or alternatively, that undergarments with decorated cuffs may have been worn beneath the *cotún*. Integrated elbow and/or forearm reinforcements are also suggested by details of seemingly integrated straps – featured both above and below the elbow – on various sepulchral pieces including the effigy of Bricius MacKinnon on Iona[336] and the galloglas on the O'Conor tomb in Roscommon. On the Glinsk monument the forearms – in higher relief, and therefore perhaps not integral to the *cotún* representing separate vambraces – appear to be the reinforced part with the elbow and cuff seemingly made of a decorative armoured layer which could be a representation of anything from *cuir bouilli* leather or textile. Other *cotún* sleeves on monuments appear plain at the elbows including the effigy – possibly of Cooey na nGall O'Cahan – at St Mary's Abbey at Dungiven (Co Derry) dating the last quarter of the fifteenth century.[337]

Evidence for fastenings on the *cotún* is fairly scanty and there is the possibility that the *cotún* was often put on jumper-style, overhead. Where present, fastenings for *cotúns* may have been buttons made of cloth or otherwise, or 'points' made of various textiles or leather. From at least the mid thirteenth century the tips of the points could have been mounted with aiglets which were typically made of rolled lightly tapering tubular chapes made of thin copper alloy sheet.[338] Retaining iron rivets are sometimes present on the wider end of the chapes in some late fourteenth and early fifteenth century examples.[339] A Great Wardrobe account of 1343–44 refers to 216 aiguillettes for 9 aketons which would imply 24 aiguillettes per garment – some of these may have been attributed to fastening the cuffs.[340] Due to the apparent absence of fastenings on many of the effigies – despite a seemingly very good fit – another possibility we might

---

335 Ibid., Fig. 6.
336 Ibid., Pl. 8.
337 Hunt: *Irish Medieval Figure Sculpture*, Pl. 168.
338 EEgan, Geoff and Pritchard, Frances: *Dress Accessories 1150-1450,* London 2002, p. 281.
339 Ibid., p. 282.
340 Ibid., p. 286.

Many *sgabals* extended to the lower chest and terminated in points.
(© Claíomh – Katharina Temirati 2022)

entertain for closures could be the use of the 'crochet and loop' – what we would now call hooks and eyes.[341] In general in Europe, it appears that over the course of the fourteenth century hooks and eyes – alongside buttons – came into growing use to facilitate the close fits of the then fashionable silhouette hugging styles. When utilised with a heavy padded garment like a *cotún*, such a closure would have been all but invisible to the casual observer.[342] On Albrecht Dürer's famous 1521 illustration of Irish soldiers and peasants, the left most figure's *cotún* is interesting as while it is broadly speaking in typical Gaelic form with regard to its longitudinal stitch lines, albeit with unpleated flanks, there are no obvious buttons or ties with or without aiglets. So, again like the effigies, this seemingly well padded *cotún* possibly had a closure made up of discreet hooks and eyes? Yet another possibility is that closures may have been hidden simply because they were located to the rear or to the sides and necessarily operated by a third party in the case of the former. Also visible on Dürer's left-most figure's *cotún* is a possibly intergral – albeit unpiped – standing collar.

Usually the neck is hidden by a pissane of mail. The figure also sports a slash in the garment at the point where the dagger is suspended presumably from a belt underneath. By the sixteenth century it appears that long padded aketons had fallen out of fashion and use in most of Europe – if not quite a bit earlier – but the style endured well into the second half of the sixteenth century in both Gaelic Ireland and the Western Highlands. The *cotún* may have doubled up in times of relative military inactivity as a warm garment to ward against inclement weather of all sorts. Certainly the prolific wearing of it is confirmed, as according to the contemporary Elizabethan poet Edmund Spenser, the *cotún* was *'worne then likewise of footmen under their shirts of mayle, the which footmen they call galloglasses'*. Much as Spenser must have understood the practical purposes of such a garment in a military context, he however, evidently greatly disdained the persistence of their donning in daily life, remarking that both Irish horsemen and galloglas wore the *cotún* 'daylie at home, and in townes and civile places' which he regarded as 'a rude habite and most uncomely'.[343] Such a picture set by Spenser certainly paints a vivid picture of native Irish soldiery even in times of relative peace.

---

341 Cole, George S.: *A Complete Dictionary of Dry Goods and History of Silk, Linen, Wool & other Fibrous Substances*, Wichita 1890, p. 77.

342 Campbell, Kenneth L.: *Ireland's History. Prehistory to the Present*, London et al. 2014, pp. 40-42.

343 Hadfield, Andrew and Maley, Willy (eds.): *Edmund Spenser. A View of the State of Ireland*, Oxford 1997, p. 74.

Mail armour

In terms of armour made of iron, mail is overwhelmingly the mode associated with native (as well as some Anglo-Irish) nobility, as well as galloglas. Plate armour is mentioned at muster in at least one source[344] but its general absence in the Gaelic-Irish sources implies it was comparatively rare, although in Gaelic-Scotland plate leg armour does make an appearance now and again.[345] Foot armour i.e. sabatons whether mail or plate, do not definitively appear in the Irish material but are infrequent presences on some of the West Highland military effigies where the state of preservation allows for analysis. Evidence for gauntlets are equally sparse, thus whereas a great many of the contemporary late medieval Anglo-Irish effigies depict hour-glass gauntlets, Gaelic and Gaelicised monumental representations like Roscommon and Glinsk would appear to not have any hand protection whatsoever. That said, the possibility remains that relatively close fitting cuffless gauntlets made of organic material are being represented. In Oxford, the Ashmolean Museum's late Henrician illustration of Irish kern,[346] depicting one protagonist with a duellist's left hand plate gauntlet suggests that such hand protection was in circulation, and likely available in mail form[347] as well as articulated plate. Cuffed gauntlets of some form – possibly mailed, or something more akin to the plated and riveted Wisby style[348] – now unfortunately damaged over the intervening centuries – are attested to on the West Highland effigy of Bricius MacKinnon[349] which most probably dates to the late fourteenth century.[350] On another West Highland effigy, a more clearly defined gauntlet of probable hourglass form is to be seen on an effigy at Saddell Abbey.[351]

Two components made up the Gaelic mail harness: the *sgabal*[352] and the *lúirech*[353] i.e. the standard – also known as the pissane – which enveloped the neck, shoulders and upper chest, and the mail shirt which protected the body. In Irish archaeology, finds of mail are fairly sparse and in relatively poor condition. From the little evidence we have in museums, the mail itself was generally made in the usual European manner in various ring sizes commonly rivet linked in a 4 to 1 ratio with the necessary alterations for tailoring. Other, denser, ratios may also have been used in more vulnerable locations such as the neck.

The *sgabal* was ubiquitous in contemporary iconography in medieval Ireland and Scotland and is well represented on both Irish and Scottish military monumental tomb art. Various forms of the *sgabal* are seen and on some monumental representations the upper layers of mail links on the neck curve upwards to each side, which is reminiscent of earlier knightly representations suggesting the possibility that the *sgabal* is a full coif, i.e. a closely fitted hood of mail which covers the entire head and shoulders with an aperture for the face. However the late medieval dating of these effigies and the close fitting appearance of the helmets would argue against this and in balance it is more likely that a standing mail collar incorporating a mail cowl for the shoulders is more frequently what is being represented. Another possibility – especially with earlier bascinets – is that a mail aventail was suspended directly from the helmet itself. However, 'vervelles', also known as staples[354], are apparently absent from the few extant Irish helmets, and effigy evidence in this area is inconclusive. From the hewn sepulchral sources, in the late medieval Gaelic world, in most cases, lower edges of the broad *sgabal* appear as a cowl extending across, and slightly overlapping, the shoulders. The *sgabal* dips deeper at the centre of the chest, characteristically terminating in an acute dipped point, at the mid chest level. Some variations show a less severe, more rounded point, at the front. Other forms probably existed too. In Dürer's 1521 illustration, his second figure from the left – and the only one of the five depicted in mail – has a dagged edge to his *sgabal*. A delineation on the edge of the dagging suggests embellishment in a contrasting metal. Presumably representing copper alloy or a similar decorative metal, in the illuminated 'Book of the De Burgos'[355] several of the chieftains represented have yellow rings as edge decoration on the lower edge of their *sgabals* and a few have a similar arrangement on the upper edges of them too. The rear of these mail collars is not represented but it may be surmised that the rear is in a similar profile to the front. As a result of this limitation in the manner of depiction, fastenings are not shown either but it would seem reasonable to assume that the *sgabal* was at least partly secured in position with a buckle and strap system and that the standing neck was achieved with protective reinforcing textile padding and/or leather to the rear.[356]

A small proportion of monumental effigies, such as figures on the MacMahon/Creagh Tomb's east end at Ennis Friary

---

344 Walsh: *Leabhar Chlainne Suibhne*, p. 45.
345 Caldwell, David H.: "Having the right kit: West Highlanders fighting in Ireland", in: Duffy, S. (ed.): *The World of the Galloglass. Kings, Warlords and Warriors in Ireland and Scotland 1200-1600*, Dublin 2007, pp. 144-168, here: p. 155
346 Dunlevy, Mairead: *Dress in Ireland*, Cork 1989, p. 53.
347 Capwell, Tobias: *The Noble Art of the Sword*, London 2012, pp. 128-129.
348 Thordeman, Bengt: *Armour from the Battle of Wisby 1361*, Highland Village TX 2001, pp. 415-418, Figs. 409-412.
349 Steer and Bannerman: *Late medieval monumental sculpture in the West Highlands*, Fig. 5, Pls. 8A, 8B.
350 Steer and Bannerman: *Late medieval monumental sculpture in the West Highlands*, p. 25; and Caldwell: Having the right kit, p. 153.
351 Steer and Bannerman: *Late medieval monumental sculpture in the West Highlands*, p. 26, Fig. 5.
352 Harbison, Peter: "Native Irish arms & armour in medieval Gaelic literature. 1170-1600", in: *Irish sword*, 12(1), 1975, pp. 173-199, here: p. 188.
353 Ibid., p. 185.

354 Capwell: *Armour of the English Knight 1400-1450*, p. 76.
355 Trinity College Dublin (no date): The book of the de Burgos. Available at: https://digitalcollections.tcd.ie/concern/works/rb68xg028?locale=en.
356 Capwell: *Armour of the English Knight 1400-1450*, p. 85.

A galloglas equipped with the typical *sparth* axe.
(© Claíomh – Niamh O'Rourke 2012)

(Co Clare)357 and the Kilninian (Mull)358 effigy suggest the possibility of a somewhat more bulbous version of the *sgabal*, which may depict something more substantial than a mail standard. It is possible – in a minority of cases – that the mail *sgabal* evolved in the manner of the plate collars associated with the 'great bascinet' in early fifteenth century England and France i.e. that the bascinet

was enforced with either an aventail, likely of overlapping lames, riveted to the helmet, or a standing collar made up of metal plates but unattached to the helmet itself. At least in England great bascinets, and therefore their associated aventails/collars, declined in use in England by the mid fifteenth century to be gradually replaced by armets and sallet/bevor combinations359 but perhaps a few emerged and endured for a while in the Gaelic fringe around the end of the fifteenth century and into the

---

357 Hunt: *Irish Medieval Figure Sculpture*, Pls. 241-242.
358 Steer and Bannerman: *Late medieval monumental sculpture in the West Highlands*, Pl. 25C.

359 Capwell: *Armour of the English Knight 1400-1450*, p. 7.

sixteenth century? Arguing against this is that the lower edge of the *sgabals* dipping down to the mid chest in the typical Irish manner on the MacMahon figures and the Kilninian effigy, would suggest we are still looking at mail collars which may simply be elevated by being very well padded, and therefore hewn relatively wider and higher in relief than usual. Also with such a depth it would be difficult to move in them, which would likely rule out plate aventails attached to the helmet, but perhaps the idea of a standing plate collar could be entertained as a rare alternative to the mail *sgabal*. The mid sixteenth century effigy of William MacLeod of Dunvegan's (Rodel, Harris) collar more overtly overlaps the bascinet, but even in this case it is not clear whether the carver's intention is a plate or mail collar as the monument is well worn and much of the finer detail has long since disappeared.[360]

Judging from contemporary sepulchral tomb evidence from Scotland and Ireland, the use of a mail shirt atop the *cotún* appears to have been more common in the latter than the former. Of course, it is always possible that mail may have been worn beneath the *cotún*. A written account of 1303 appears to imply that upon occasion a *lúirech* could be worn sandwiched between two *cotúns* – one above and one underneath the *lúirech*[361] – however it would seem that this was the exception rather than the rule. Conversely Dürer's second figure appears to have no padding under his mail shirt at all and indeed some sources say so. Mail shirts were expensive pieces of equipment – the labour alone often being up to a hundred days worth – not to mention the expensive raw materials in terms of the iron and the fuel the furnace required. For much of the period contemporary written sources, illustrations and effigies, indicate that mail shirts worn by galloglas were generally long of skirted with Spenser confirming the galloglaigh wore a 'long shirt of mayle downe to the calfe of his leg'[362] and appear on monumental tomb art with generally short elbow length sleeves. However, slightly shorter habergeons and longer wrist length sleeves are also represented.[363]

The weight of this protective gear was not for the fainthearted at approximately 8–12 kg for the mail shirt alone. Then add 4.5–5.5kg for the bascinet and pissane combined, plus a further 6–10 kg for the undercloth, fittings and *cotún*. Although only represented on the tombs of Anglo-Irish magnates, iron gauntlets – if present – could add up to another kilogram and a half. All in all this would give a possible total of approximately 20–29 kg in encumbrance. And that is not including any offensive weaponry…

Offensive Weaponry

Sparth Axes

English descriptions of galloglas frequently occur under the Tudor administrations of the sixteenth century. Whereas the English sources can often be disparaging of the Gaelic-Irish – and in particular of the lighter armed kern, galloglas – and their formidable axes – appear to have evoked a sense of dread, but also wonder in the Tudor psyche.

To the denizens of The Pale, the axe of the Irish was referred to as the 'sparth axe', or derivatives e.g. simply the 'sparth'. It is doubtless the weapon most closely associated with the galloglass and was apparently the main tool by which they plied their grim trade.

The origins of the sparth as a weapon of war goes back to the Viking Age in when the old broad axe was evidently adopted by the native Irish due to Norse influence as Giraldus Cambrensis surmised.[364] Axes of iron are documented in contemporary literature, as well as in the archaeological record, albeit, the latter have thus far been yielded from largely unstratified contexts. In Irish sources military axes are named *tuagh catha*[365] – literally 'battle axe' or simply *tuagh*[366]. Side arms could include the sword or the quintessential Irish long single edged knife, the *scian*. But it was for their use of the sparth axe that they are best remembered, so much so that the terms 'galloglass axe' and 'sparth axe' seem virtually interchangeable. The term 'galloglass axe', however, can be a misleading one, and it is probably the wiser course to consider the usage of these axes of Viking broad axe descent as a phenomenon unique to Ireland and the Western Highlands in the late medieval period.[367] That said there is no denying the close affiliation between warrior and weapon: one galloglass constable by the name of Henry MacCabe was famously recorded to have been 'buried at Cavan and there were fourteen score of axes or more in his funeral procession'. Doubtless this was a very impressive display of galloglass power.[368] The close association imprinted by the galloglas at the funeral procession literally being referred to by the arms they bore. The term 'spar(th)' was itself also the name for the unit of the galloglass himself and his two followers. Both of these men had particular

---

360 Steer and Bannerman: *Late medieval monumental sculpture in the West Highlands*, p. 80, Pl, 34B.
361 Caldwell: *Having the right kit*, p. 154.
362 Hadfield and Maley: *Edmund Spenser*, p. 74.
363 Hayes-McCoy, Gerard Anthony: *Irish Battles. A Military History of Ireland*, Belfast 1969, Pl. 10.

364 Cambrensis, Geraldus: *Expugnatio Hibernica. The Conquest of Ireland* (translated by A. B. Scott and F. X. Martin), Dublin 1978, p. 319.
365 Walker, Joseph C.: *Dress of the Ancient and Modern Irish*, Uckfield 1788, p. 123.
366 Harbison: *Native Irish arms & armour in medieval Gaelic literature, 1170-1600*, p. 208.
367 Halpin, Andrew: "The gallóglach axe revisited", in: Condit, T. and Corlett, C. (eds.): *Above and Beyond*, Bray 2005, pp. 361-372, here: p. 370
368 Freeman, A. Martin (ed.): *Annála Connacht: The Annals of Connacht,* Dublin 1944, p. 499.

roles: the senior one was the bearer and maintainer of the galloglass' harness; the more junior boy was the carrier of provisions and cook.[369]

Although the odd galloglass may indeed have utilised a halberd once in a while, it is not surprising that Mountjoy's secretary, Fynnes Moryson, mentions the use of 'halberts'[370] in lieu of anything closer to compare the sparth with. John Dymmok, also during Elizabeth I's time, informs us that the galloglas were armed with 'a batle axe, or halberd, six foote longe, the blade whereof is somewhat like a shomakers knyfe, and without pyke; the stroake whereof is deadly where yt lighteth'.[371] Spoken with the voice of experience, it is a vivid picture presented by Dymmok, and it leaves us in no doubt that the sparth was like no halberd of The Pale.

Irish descriptions not be outdone can also stir the imagination with their sparse but arresting narratives. For example, in describing some of Shane O'Neill's bodyguard while out in the field campaigning in the late 1550s on the frontier between Tyrone and Tyrconnell, the annals provide us with a vivid night-time vignette of two of O'Donnell's spies reconnoitring the O'Neill camp and proceeding 'from one fire to another, until they came to the great central-fire, which was at the entrance of the son of O'Neill's tent; and a huge torch, thicker than a man's body, was constantly flaming at a short distance from the fire, and sixty grim and redoubtable galloglas, with sharp, keen axes, terrible and ready for action …' who were in attendance with the duty of, 'watching and guarding the son of O'Neill'.[372]

One question which arises is why did galloglass military society give such pre-eminence to the long handled sparth axe rather than, say, the two handed sword? After all, in the late medieval period the *bidenhänder* was becoming a feature of *landsknechte* warfare on the continent, and closer to home the slightly smaller, but still formidable and impressive 'twahandit swordis', were becoming more prevalent in the Western Highlands – often fitted with imported German blades. Certainly it would have been the case that the two-handed sword would have been more costly given the larger proportion of iron to forge the long blade and hilt furnishings, not to mention the expertise involved. It is understandable therefore that many historians have speculated that only the wealthiest in Gaelic martial society could afford them.[373] However Ross Mackenzie Crawford has convincingly argued, using the example of the massacre at Ardnaree in Co Mayo, the *claidheamh da láimh* (liter-

Roscommon Abbey.
(Photograph: Maximilian Bunk)

ally two handed sword) may have been more widespread. At that particular 1586 engagement, 1,400 MacDonalds – including some c. 550 West Highland mercenary 'redshanks' (the rest being civilians) – who were driven into the River Moy and slain, the English recovered some 300–400 of 'their long swords' from the riverbed.[374] This strongly suggests that these swords were not exclusive pieces of panoply restricted only for the elite, but were fairly widespread – at least in the hands of seasonal professionals – as were the redshanks.[375] Therefore galloglas must have – generally – preferred axes to two handed swords as their first weapons of choice for reasons other than purely economic.

---

369 Nicholls: *Gaelic and Gaelicised Ireland in the Middle Ages*, p. 89.
370 Kew: *The Irish Sections of Fynes Moryson's Unpublished Itinerary*, p. 70.
371 Dymmok, John: *A Treatise of Ireland*, Dublin 1842, p. 7..
372 Annals of the Four Masters, CELT Project (2016) Annals of the Four Masters https://celt.ucc.ie/published/T100005E.html (Accessed: 27 January 2022).
373 Steer and Bannerman: *Late medieval monumental sculpture in the West Highlands*, pp. 167-9.

374 Crawford, R.M.: *Warfare in the West Highlands and Isles of Scotland c. 1544-1615*, Unpublished PhD thesis. University of Glasgow, Glasgow 2016, p. 96.
375 Although, as with the galloglass kindreds, they originated from the Western Isles and Highlands, Redshanks were fair weathered seasonal mercenaries who entered service in Ireland after the fourteenth century integration of galloglas in Irish society. They came to prominence from the mid sixteenth century onwards.

Glaive and Type C sparth.
(© Claíomh – Dave Swift 2021)

Opposite page:
Galloglass armed with the Derryloughan axe (Type C).
(© Claíomh – John Nicholl 2014)

In terms of axe typology there were three main types of 'native' military axe used in late medieval Ireland. The first of these – and earliest, Halpin's Group A, resembles a rough version of Petersen's Type M of the late Viking Age.[376] Generally the Type M is ascribed an eleventh century date but it is likely many were still in use well into the twelfth century. The Type M is well represented on the Irish record with examples from e.g. Strokestown crannogs (Co Roscommon)[377], Dysart (Co Westmeath), Robe Abbey (Co Mayo) and the relatively recent finds of three axes found together in a boat from Lough Corrib (Co Galway). Dating for the Lough Corrib axes was recorded of c. 1020–1150. The c. twelfth century development of the Group A that develops out the Type M is exemplified in archaeology by a specimen in the National Museum from the River Corrib at Dangan Lower (Galway),[378] and in history by its apparent great use by the Irish, with some effect, during the Cambro-Norman invasion of the late twelfth century.[379] In terms of morphology Group A may be seen as being wider at the neck than their more aesthetically elegant Type M predecessors. Nevertheless the Group A axe does share the old Petersen Type M characteristics of an asymmetrical – if rather broad necked – triangular blade, with a long steep concave curve to the upper horn and a slightly shorter steep concave curve to the lower horn. It is reckoned unlikely that these axes were in common circulation after the twelfth century and that they may have waned out of existence altogether or, at least, to negligible numbers by the time of the introduction of galloglas in Ireland from the mid thirteenth century. A carbon date of likely c. 1040–1290[380] on the timber haft associated with the Dangan Lower Type A axe would appear to confirm this.

In some areas of overlap, Halpin's Group B axes are fairly similar to Group A in so far as they are thin in section, have widely splaying, asymmetric shallowly curved, blades and developed projecting spurs – where they survive – extending from the shaft hole upwards and downwards parallel with the haft. However the necks are comparatively wider than the Group A axes and the upper horns have a more pronounced pointed trajectory. It is possible that unlike either Type A or Type C that this pronounced upper horn could have acted as a thrusting option for the user against lighter armoured opponents while the axe edge itself was still the main component to

---

376 Harrison, Mark and Embleton, Gerry: *Viking Hersir*, Oxford 1993, p. 32.
377 Halpin: "The galloglach axe revisited", Pl. 3.
378 Ibid., p. 365.
379 Cambrensis: *Expugnatio Hibernica*, pp. 37, 115, 137 and 163.
380 Halpin: "The galloglach axe revisited", p. 365.

use against medium and heavier infantry. Based on the few (literally!), still extant, this group of axes tend to have cutting edges which measure some 18–19 cm.[381]

Group B axes are problematic to date as they are thus far either riverine finds without stratification or else they tend to be old finds without any precise context not to mention even a townland in most cases. The National Museum has the couple of examples in its keeping understandably cautiously dated very widely '13th to 16th century', and the axe recorded by Flanagan from the River Callan at Benburb[382] is equally difficult to pin down. There does at least appear to be consensus that these Group B axes do not pre date the thirteenth century but the possibility remains that their advent is considerably later.[383] In monumental art a hooded figure carrying a horn and wielding an axe two-handed on the presumed mid fifteenth century cross[384] of Alexander MacMillan at Kilmory in Knapdale[385] appears to be the closest match to the morphology of Group B which would make the axes chronologically close enough to the centre of the extended period currently advocated by the National Museum. The fourth arcaded figure (out of the eight) from left on the Felim O'Conor tomb frontal at Roscommon Abbey would be another fairly close match to the Group 2 series and is also believed to be of fifteenth century date.[386]

As to whether the Group B series of axes has any traction in the sixteenth century, it may also be a possibility. Sentleger reporting to Henry VIII in 1543 remarked that each galloglass 'having every [one] of them his weapon, callyd a sparre, moche like the axe of the Towre...'.[387] Interestingly, like the Group B axes, and as Halpin has pointed out,[388] the axe of the tower is fairly transparent in advertising its Viking ancestry. Albeit that the Tower of London axe is considerably bigger than our Group 2 series, and assuming that the axe of the Yeoman Gaoler of the Tower has changed little over the years,[389] it certainly would bear some similarity to Group B – especially with regard to the asymmetrical upward splay of its blade terminating in a pronounced upper horn. Group B axe comparisons with contemporary sixteenth century pictorial sources such as John Derricke's 'The image of Ireland' (1581)[390] the City of Dublin charter of January 1583[391] are rather tenuous as the axes presented in these sources are symmetrical, perhaps as a result of relying on second hand information. Likewise, Dürer's 'axes' in the hands of a pair of kern with glibs to the right of his 1521 illustration,[392] are not paralleled in the Irish archaeological record thus far. The pole arms borne are more akin to glaives rather than what we may conventionally define as an axe.

Like Group B, Halpin's Group C axes appear to be another development from the earlier Group A axes. Like the other groups of military axes, the blades were thin in section but the widely splaying blades had an almost straight edge to the blade. The necks were proportionately shorter on the haft than the Group B axes and had well formed spurs extending to each side of the haft socket where present. The haft holes themselves were fairly small and sub oval in shape. The steep concave curve to the lower horn is still similar to the Group A and B axes, perhaps a fraction more acute in the case of Group C. The main feature that differentiates Group C is that the journey from the socket to the upper horn has now become strongly convex as opposed to concave as it had been for all the other types. In one descriptive passage from a late sixteenth century Gaelic poem, the *tuagh* is described as 'broad, narrow-necked, curve-backed (*cúl-croma*)'.[393] It seems likely this last term is an appraisal of the distinctive morphology of the convex top side of the axe.

Unlike the Group B series this latter development in the Group C *cúl-croma* axes would negate any point at the top of the axe head that could potentially have been used for thrusting. To assuage this possible disadvantage, the design of Group C axes could seen to have potentially thrown more weight to the top of the axe – adding to the velocity and force of a downward blow – at the expense of a thrusting dynamic – to the upper horn? Perhaps this was seen as a necessary response as the late medieval period advanced and nuances in the make up of armour, or tactics, changed over the centuries. It could be argued that this would have made the axe more deadly to foes in a similar harness of *cotún*, *luirech* and *sgabal* which galloglas themselves wore. In fact, it would invariably be the nature of the profession, and of the era, that frequently battlefield foes of galloglas could inevitably be other galloglas.

Of the two Group C axes recorded by Adolf Mahr in the 1930s in the National Museum in Dublin the Ballina (Co Mayo) axe has a cutting edge of 14.2 cm[394] and the

---

381 Flanagan, L. N. W.: "A late Sixteenth-Century Battleaxe from Benburb", in: Ulster Journal of Archaeology (vol. 23), 1960, p. 59 f., here: p. 59.

382 Ibid., 59-60.

383 Halpin: "The gallóglach axe revisited", p. 36.

384 Steer and Bannerman: *Late medieval monumental sculpture in the West Highlands*, p. 57.

385 Ibid., Figs. 14, 20; Pl. 24B..

386 O'Conor and Shanahan: *Roscommon Abbey*, p. 44.

387 Hayes-McCoy, Gerard Anthony: *Scots Mercenary Forces in Ireland*, Dublin and London 1937, p. 105.

388 Halpin: "The gallóglach axe revisited", p. 368.

389 Ibid., Pl. 6.

390 University of Edinburgh: *The Image of Irelande by John Derricke*, Edinburgh (no date).

---

391 Dunlevy: *Dress in Ireland*, Ill. 44.

392 Ibid., Ill. 43.

393 Harbison: "Native Irish arms & armour in medieval Gaelic literature, 1170-1600", p. 208.

394 Mahr, Adolf: "The Galloglach Axe", in: Journal of the Galway Archaeological and Historical Society, vol. 18 (1/2), Galway 1938, pp. 66-68, here: p. 66.

Depending on the situation, the galloglass may have chosen to either rely on his spear or his axe.
(© Claíomh – Dave Swift 2016)

Donegal axe's edge is 17.5 cm.[395] The latter, therefore, is of a similar general scale and size to the Group B axes. In scale, and to some small extent profile, the axe born by Raghnall of Islay may represent However a more recent finding of a group of three axes dredged from the River Blackwater (Co Tyrone) – now in the keeping of the Ulster Museum – and noted in Bourke's typology as 'Class 21' have given much pause for thought when it comes to the Group C series.[396] Advocacy for the addition of a 'Blackwater Group' sub category of Group C might be necessary as these three axes yielded in the early 1990's – although similar in general profile to the standard Type C axe – including the distinctive convex 'curve-backed' side leading to the upper horn - are on a very different scale in terms of size and are much longer in their cutting edge – averaging at about 30 cm. Also the cutting edge is near perfectly straight i.e. straighter than the other Group C axes. The lower side of the Blackwater axes is neither convex nor concave but straight and the lower horn therefore terminates in a far more acute point – almost a spike.[397]

The Blackwater variation of Group C axes are apparently well represented in contemporary imagery. Among the iconographic evidence that survives, the tomb of Alasdair MacLeod of Harris at St Clement"s Church in Rodel features a hunting scene with Alasdair (or attendant bodyguard?) in full Gaelic harness, holding a long-handled axe in one hand and a claymore in the other.[398] This axe-head appears to conform exactly to the Blackwater sparth type. Of two sparth axe bearing casqued and harnesses figures appearing on the tomb of Donat O'Suibhne at Sligo Abbey c. 1577, one appears to bear the Blackwater variant of the Group C axe but that the lower horn, as well as the upper, appears convex – perhaps in error by the carver?[399] The axes seen on John Goghe's 1567 map in the grip of three mailed and helmeted figures representing the triad of MacSweeney septs of Tyrconnell, also bear broadly similar characteristics despite the simplicity of their rendering.[400] On another period picture map c. 1600, MacDonnell of Donaghmore is depicted bearing a similar style of curved-back axe at the inauguration of an O'Neill at the site at Tullyhogue.[401]

The Blackwater Group C axes would also, with demonstrably longer cutting edges of one foot long (i.e. 30 cm), better fit the vivid description of contemporary Tudor observer and Dubliner, Richard Stanihurst who informs us that the galloglas wield 'foot-long axes, razor-sharp and attached to spear-shafts'[402] that inflicted dreadful wounds. The long length of the haft of the axe – six foot according to John Dymmok[403], which is borne out by several contemporary images, would have added leverage and velocity, making the wounds inflicted by such sharp axe blades all the more devastating.

One of the surviving Group B axes (unprovenanced), and three of the Group C axes (from Mayo and Donegal[404] Clonteevy, Co Tyrone)[405] are decorated with patterns of silver appliqué and/or silver inlay. This was possibly ceremonial, a sign of military rank, and/or the mark of a specialist gallogláss bodyguard.[406]

While the evidence for the dating of both Groups B and C would appear to be towards the end of our period of study, it is quite possible that both Groups B and C developed more or less contemporaneously and complimented each other as variations of the same tool for different nuances of the profession at hand.

Spears

Spears appear to have been a supplemental weapon for galloglas and there is evidence enough that they were used both as light throwing weapons akin to Gaelic darts and as more substantial stouter thrusting weapons. The latter, used in tandem with other weaponry, would have been particularly useful for a galloglas battle that was engaged with cavalry. Linguistically, the spear has more terms in the Irish Gaelic than any other weapon of war which speaks of its manifold uses and adaptability. Of course the reasons for this could be attributed to regional variances and over time, as much as to any wholly typological differences pertaining to use and form. As with other weapons, references to spears in contemporary Irish sources are characteristically more poetic than scientific. Doubtless they covered a wide range of weaponry ranging from light throwing javelins and darts to long, robust pike-like thrusting spears – although definitive terms are difficult to ascertain in most cases. During the age of the galloglass in Ireland *ga*[407] is – after 1380 – by far the most common form and appears to refer to an adaptable spear which could have been either thrown or retained for hand-to-hand use while a *foga*[408] appears to have been a more dedicated light dart. In the literary evidence the *craoiseac*[409] appears to be an altogether

---

395 National Museum of Ireland (no date) Topographical Files (Accessed: 09 January 2013).

396 Bourke, Cormac: "Antiquities from the River Blackwater III: Iron Axe-Heads", in: The Ulster Journal of Archaeology (vol. 60), Belfast 2001, pp. 63-93, here: pp. 88-89.

397 Ibid., pp. 82-83.

398 Steer and Bannerman: *Late medieval monumental sculpture in the West Highlands*, Pl. 32B.

399 Hunt: *Irish Medieval Figure Sculpture*, p. 219.

400 Swift: *Historical Maps of Ireland*, p. 23, Fig. 7.

401 Bourke: "Antiquities from the River Blackwater III: Iron Axe-Heads", Pl. 1.

402 Lennon, C.: *Richard Stanihurst*, Dublin 1981, p. 152.

403 Dymmok, John: *A Treatise of Ireland*, Dublin 1842, p. 7.

404 Halpin: "The gallóglach axe revisited", Pls. 1, 2.

405 Bourke: "Antiquities from the River Blackwater III: Iron Axe-Heads", pp. 85, 88-89.

406 Mahr: "The Galloglach Axe", p. 68.

407 Harbison: "Native Irish arms & armour in medieval Gaelic literature, 1170-1600", p. 202.

408 Ibid., p. 206.

409 Ibid., p. 203.

heavier weapon more dedicated to mêlée, although there are inferences that, it too, could be thrown as the onset of an fracas.⁴¹⁰

Although common weapons amongst traditional Irish cavalry and kern as well as the rising out in times of war, both in their thrown and hand-held forms, the spear would appear to be a far less frequent weapon among the galloglas with whom the sword and axe were favoured. However the dynamism of spears and the relative cheapness of their manufacture in comparison to more costly weapons would have made them useful tools of the trade if only in a secondary role. One reference, committed to written form in the sixteenth century but referring to the conditions of employment of MacSweeney galloglas in Tir Connel during the reign of Turlough O'Donnell (1380–1422) however denotes that a fine of a groat (or four pence) would apply to a galloglass who failed to bring his spear to a muster which 'groat the constable should get'.⁴¹¹

Swords

Although most prominently famed as axe-men – galloglas must have been adept swordsmen too. As Fergus Cannan points out, there are no records of poor weapon skills concerning galloglas.⁴¹²

Asides foreign imports there were two main types of Gaelic sword in circulation in Ireland during the galloglass era: one group which appears to have been dominant for at least the duration of the fifteenth century, and another group of swords which appear to have reached a zenith in terms of use at some point during the early to mid sixteenth century. These two general sword types fall into Halpin's designated 'Group 2'⁴¹³ and 'Group 3'⁴¹⁴ of Irish medieval swords.⁴¹⁵ Often colloquially known as 'Corrib Swords' in Ireland, as several were found in that particular river in Galway, Group 2 swords had several features in common with swords from the Western Highlands and Isles. These characteristics include relatively wide tapering blades, downward sloped arms to the cross-guard, a high central collar from whence the quillons extend from, and expanded terminals to the quillons. On the other hand, Group 3 swords appear to be a distinctive insular native Irish type. These latter are characterised by having more or less parallel blades until near the point, open ring shaped pommels – the open ring visibly exposing the tang of the blade within. They have either straight or elongated S-shaped guards with flattened triangular

Ledger of Gilbert de Greenlaw (d. 1411).

or fan-shaped terminals to the quillons.⁴¹⁶ Like the Group 2 swords they often do have extended langets of varying lengths extending from the quillon block but do not feature a high collar extending upwards to the grip. The blade marks that survive indicate that a considerable proportion of the blades from both groups of swords may have been commonly imported into Scotland and Ireland from Germany, with the hilt furniture being finished by local cutlers.

Prior to the mid fourteenth to fifteenth century – or what is often referred to in Ireland as the 'Gaelic Resurgence' – swords in Gaelic-Irish hands appear to have diverged little from the then current English and European norms. There would also appear to be little to differentiate the stylistics of highland and lowland hilts in Scotland in the same era. Even the probable continual persistence in the Western Highlands of the distinct lobated pommel of Viking origin was a tradition which had also survived on, for example, some English funerary monuments into the late thirteenth and early fourteenth centuries.⁴¹⁷ Distinctions in the form of the highland hilt became more pronounced

---

410 Ibid., pp. 201-203.

411 Walsh: *Leabhar Chlainne Suibhne*, pp. 44-45.

412 Cannan, Fergus and Ó Brógáin, Sean: *Galloglass 1250-1600, Gaelic Mercenary Warrior*, Oxford 2010, p. 14.

413 Halpin, Andrew: "Irish Medieval Swords c. 1170-1600", in: Proceedings of the Royal Irish Academy (vol. 86 (C) 5), Belfast 1986, pp. 183-230, here: pp. 195-207.

414 Ibid., pp. 207-213.

415 Halpin: "Irish Medieval Swords c. 1170-1600".

---

416 Halpin, Andrew: "Arms and Armour", in: Moss, Rachel (ed.): *Art and Architecture in Ireland*, Dublin 2014, p. 397.

417 Cannan, Fergus: *Scottish Arms and Armour*, Oxford 2009, p. 29; as well as Steer and Bannerman: *Late medieval monumental sculpture in the West Highlands*, p. 25.

The Clonca gravestone.
(Author's collection)

from at least the onset of the fifteenth century, if not a little earlier. It was particularly in the area of hilt furnishings that the swords used by West Highlanders during the latter half of our period of study, became more distinctive in form in comparison with those in service with their lowland and English contemporaries. With the advent of the *claidheamh dá láimh*[418], or two-handed sword, perhaps a decade prior to the turn of the sixteenth century, it was to be a tradition which continued right through to the end of this study's period of interest.

The most representative sword of the late medieval Western Highlands was a single-handed broad fullered blade mounted with a hilt encompassing quillons which sloped – or drooped – sharply downwards towards the blade from the block of the cross-guard. The terminals of the quillons of these swords are depicted both in archaeology and on Hebridean grave slabs with either a rounded, pointed spatula or tear drop shape. On extant examples the block of the quillons is high and continues upwards towards the grip and short tapered langets typically extend downwards from the block in the direction of the blade itself.[419] The greatest evidence for these swords in Scotland is their frequent representation upon the decorated stone grave slabs which mark the resting places of chiefs and warriors in the Western Isles – notably at Argyll, Iona, Colonsay and Islay.[420] More often than not these grave-slabs represent the pommel of the sword to be of lobated form although round pommels with high tang blocks are also represented – one early example of the latter being the grave slab of Robert de Greenlaw who was killed at Harlaw in 1411.[421] Although usually ostensibly single-handed, these swords were often apparently large enough to be wielded two-handed and it was due to this feature that contemporary Lowlanders referred to these swords as 'halflangs' meaning 'hand-and-a-half'.[422] The type, in all probability, emerged in the Western Highlands as early as the mid fourteenth century and was manifestly widespread in that part of the world throughout the fifteenth century.

The fifteenth century West Highland sword as depicted on graveslabs is most often shown worn scabbarded and at the waist. An exception to this in Ireland is a sword depicted on a gravestone in Clonca Graveyard in County Donegal on the Inishowen peninsula. This sword's pommel is of lobated form and is located on the lower right section of the stone grave slab's face and is interestingly depicted with a hurl and *sliotar* in that quarter. As such this is one of the earliest physical depictions of the ancient game of hurling. The name on this slab is identified as Magnas MacMhoireasdain 'of the Isles' – a probable galloglass.[423] In contrast to the appearance of such swords on contemporary stone funerary monuments, the comparatively small number of archaeological survivals of such swords in Scotland tend to have wheel pommels with extended tangs covered with square section mounting blocks above the pommel where the blade would have been peened when fitted. One example of a 'halflang' on the Irish archaeological record was a Halpin Group 2 sword yielded from the River Barrow at Kilberry in Co Kildare and recorded by the National Museum of Ireland in 1931. This sword features a cross-guard with downward sloping quillons and a high collar of octagonal section which makes up part of the grip which appears to have been likely made of alder. The pommel is interesting in that it has eroded to such a state that it can be seen that either side of the pommel originally would have

---

418 Capwell, Tobias: *The Real Fighting Stuff*, Glasgow 2007, p. 84.
419 Capwell: *The Real Fighting Stuff*, p. 30-31.
420 Wallace, John: *Scottish Swords and Dirks*, London 1970, p. 9
421 Oakeshott, Ewart: *Records of the Medieval Sword*, Woodbridge 1991, p. 235.
422 Cannan: *Scottish Arms and Armour*, p. 30.
423 O'Toole, Fintan: A history of Ireland in 100 objects: Galloglass gravestone, 15th or 16th century. Available at: https://www.irishtimes.com/culture/art-and-design/a-history-of-ireland-in-100-objects-1.474794 (Accessed: 13 February 2022).

been mounted as a rather thin convex plate which was brazed to a circular band leaving a seemingly hollow and therefore rather lightweight counter to the weight of the blade itself. The overall profile of the pommel is circular like many West Highland examples of the fifteenth century with a long tang that extends beyond the pommel indicating that a high collared nut has since decayed.[424] Other swords with similar cross-guards and blades on the Irish archaeological record survive but most often their pommels do not.[425] It appears that the type was introduced to Ireland 'presumably by *gallóglaigh* [or agents acting on their behalf], in the fifteenth century'[426] and that they were consequently also used by the Gaelic Irish and possibly even the Anglo-Irish to some extent.

Halpin's 'Group 2' of Irish swords, which he dates to the fifteenth century, is clearly a very close, if not a parallel, relation of the Scottish 'halflangs'. Furthermore, in terms of preserved examples they are more abundant on the archaeological record than their Scottish counterparts which it could be argued could in itself be an indication of the enduring influence of the galloglass phenomenon in Ireland. It could reasonably be speculated that such weaponry would likely have been utilised by the native Irish also, if not indeed, upon occasion, the Anglo-Irish[427]. Indeed the apparent paucity of extant Anglo-Irish swords for this later period could in itself be regarded as considerable negative evidence in this regard. Also, as Halpin pointed out, the 1502 effigy of Malachy MacOwny O'More[428] depicts the incumbent in Anglo-Irish armour yet he clearly bears a Group 2 sword which illustrates that there was clearly a grey interface of indeterminable size between the extremes of the Gaelic and Anglo Irish worlds.[429]

A fine example of one of these Irish fifteenth century swords is a specimen which was yielded up from the River Corrib in 1979. Although the blade was incomplete, enough of it survived to indicate that it was broad and featured a *ricasso* – this latter being that thick blunt part of a sword blade located closest to the hilt furniture which was ostensibly used for blocking. In this case the ricasso was 7.3 cm long. The blade was twin fullered in the centre with decorative lines located to the outside edge of the fullers on both sides. The sword's hilt furniture has some similar characteristics in common to known halflang examples with downward sloping quillons, a high collar (hexagonal in section), long langets and a well preserved short wooden grip of round section. Differences from the West Highland swords included the pommel which was

Quillon of quatrefoil design.
(© Claíomh – Niamh O'Rourke 2011)

an elongated oval shape but which was constructed in a similar manner to Scottish examples – being apparently hollow and brazed together to the tang. The pommel was mounted with a square section cap. This elongated pommel type would appear to be a regional style as several other examples of the type are known exclusively in Ireland but may also represent a slightly later date than the round pommel versions.[430] Another seemingly distinctively Irish feature on the River Corrib example are the evenly expanding conical terminals at the end of each quillon arm – a thistle shaped decorative feature that somewhat ironically, thus far, only appears on the Irish versions of these swords.[431] It could be argued that these idiosyncrasies could suggest that the hilt furniture of such swords was locally produced by Irish cutlers with local flourishes but in the same general West Highland style.

Towards the very end of the fifteenth century or just at the beginning of the sixteenth century the 'twahondit' sword emerged as that most visually arresting of Gaelic

---

424 Halpin: "Irish Medieval Swords c. 1170-1600", pp. 199, 222.
425 OOakeshott, Ewart: *European Weapons and Armour*, Woodbridge 1980, p. 143.
426 Halpin: "Irish Medieval Swords c. 1170-1600", pp. 215-216.
427 Ibid., p. 197.
428 Hunt: *Irish Medieval Figure Sculpture*, Pl. 156.
429 Halpin: "Arms and Armour", p. 396.

430 Halpin: "Irish Medieval Swords c. 1170-1600", p. 196.
431 Ibid., p. 197..

A sword with a ring pommel typical of Irish weapons.
(© Claíomh – Dave Swift 2011)

weapons.[432] A two-handed sword by Oakeshott's[433] and Cannan's[434] reckoning, Wallace regarded the 'claymore' as a hand-and-a-half sword.[435] Wallace's opinion appears to be formulated upon the fact that the claymore was somewhat smaller than its continental relations. The continental hand-and-a-half sword differs from double handed types in so far as it had just the measure on its grip for the user to engage it with two hands – as opposed to a true two handed sword which would have a longer handle which would give the sword greater leverage and power – particularly in terms of cutting attacks.

The advantage of the hand-and-a-half sword was that it could – at least theoretically – be wielded in one hand, especially when mounted – whereas two-handed swords could only be borne effectively in two. The *claidheamh dá láimh* (two-handed Highland sword) differed in several other aspects from their double-handed continental counterparts such as their lack of *parierhaken*, or lugs and although their grips are long they do not tend to have the moulded leather shoulders that are so commonly seen on continental examples.

The cross-guards of the sixteenth century 'twahondit' sword were classically West Highland in style with their downward straight quillons falling from a high central block and their – often relatively long – langets extended from the block downwards and parallel with the blade on either side. Perhaps the most characteristic of all the

---

432 Wallace: *Scottish Swords and Dirks*, p. 10; and Oakeshott: *Records of the Medieval Sword*, p. 147.

433 Oakeshott: *European Weapons and Armour*, p. 147.

434 Cannan: *Scottish Arms and Armour*, pp. 29-30.

435 Wallace: *Scottish Swords and Dirks*, p. 10.

sixteenth century 'twahondit' sword's features were the terminals of the iconic quillons which appear to have evolved from the older spatula type terminal seen earlier in the Highlands, to the form of open quatrefoils i.e. four rings of iron joined together.[436] Finally in terms of size, claymores were typically between 1.3 and 1.4 metres in overall length and weighed some 2.5 kilograms – considerably less than their heavier and longer continental two-handed equivalents.[437]

Very few original examples of the sixteenth century *claidheamh dá láimh* in their common form have been known in collections in Ireland. One case example is a sword which had for much of the twentieth century reposed in Clontarf Castle in Dublin, but which had earlier been kept at Rostellan Castle in Co Cork since at least 1813. This particular sword had a more old fashioned wheel pommel which would indicate a relatively early date for the sword – specimens with expanding globular, or spherical pommels, are generally ascribed a later sixteenth century date. Among other features of interest on the Clontarf sword was that the blade was marked with the running wolf symbol of the renowned blade producing city of Passau in south Germany, a motif which was later copied by the even more famous bladesmiths of Solingen. Traces of copper alloy indicated that the markings were originally inlaid.[438] The likely origin of the blade is unsurprising, as German manufacture was typical of West Highland blades generally.[439] Although growing numbers of 'redshanks' – seasonal mercenaries from the same Western Highlands from which the galloglas themselves had originally hailed – were coming into Ireland bearing such favoured weapons – it is not inconceivable that the longer established galloglas in their waning decades of service may have used these great swords upon occasion.[440]

Contemporary illustrations by artists like Lucas De Heere and Albrecht Dürer backed up by data from the archaeological record indicate that swords of hollow ring-hilted type appear to have been in widespread use in Gaelic-Ireland throughout for much of the sixteenth century. Such swords were classified by Halpin as 'Group 3' swords. Although there may be at least one exception to this general rule,[441] the type is reckoned to be an indigenous Irish style due to the paucity of evidence for these swords in other parts of Europe including even in Scotland. The relatively high frequency of ring-hilted swords on the archaeological record – especially in Gaelic controlled areas of Connacht and Ulster – further strengthens the argument for the type being of native Irish origin. Generally speaking the Group 3 swords are narrower than the Group 2 specimens with more or less parallel blades until near the point. The blades are of oval section and are between 2.8–3.6 cm in breadth[442], although some apparently wider specimens have emerged in more recent times. Group 2 swords – as recorded in 1986 – are at least 3.8 cm in width[443] but are often considerably wider and have a more acute taper to the tip. With very few exceptions to date, Halpin Group 3 swords have no fullers on the blade, although narrow linear grooves are fairly commonplace. Ricassos appear to be near ubiquitous to the type.

At the time of Halpin's 1986 publication six of these single-handed swords Group 3 swords were known. The provenances of these early findings were the River Suck near Ballinasloe (Co Galway), River Suck at Coreen (Co Roscommon), Lough Neagh (Co Antrim/Co Derry), Portglenone (Co Antrim), River Corrib at Townparks in Galway City (Co Galway) and Tullylough (Co Longford).[444] As of November 2001 a total of fifteen swords of the type were known to the museum shortly before the acquisition of the Buckinghamshire sword.[445] This latter, an elegant – and rare – hand-and-a-half ring-pommel sword, is presumably the sixteenth in the series. Since 2001 more Group 3 have been yielded – one as recently as late 2021. In the 1521 Albrecht Dürer illustration, the second figure's sword's ring-pommel would classify it as a Halpin Group 3 sword. The quillons, however, with their thistle shaped terminals are more reminiscent of the Halpin Group 2 class. The treble fullers or flutes do have some parallels with one or two or the more unusual, and larger, Irish swords[446] but the sword illustrated is on an altogether greater scale than what has been found on the Irish archaeological record, or from what can be deduced from contemporary iconography, and so it therefore seems more likely that Dürer was inspired by the *schlacht*, or slaughter, swords of the continental Swiss/German type which he would have been more accustomed to in Nürnberg, where he was from, or indeed Antwerp where the illustration was likely executed, for that matter. However this does not necessarily mean that the Dürer ring sword is not inspired by a real weapon and the combination of components noted above could represent an interesting transitional period from the Group 2 – largely fifteenth century – to the presumably later, Group 3 swords.

Another sword that may be suggested as to represent a type of hybrid would be the Lough Gara sword discovered in 1953 and found resting in a dug out canoe with an axe

---

436 Oakeshott: *European Weapons and Armour*, p. 147; and Capwell: *The Real Fighting Stuff*, p. 84.

437 Cannan: *Scottish Arms and Armour*, p. 30.

438 Hayes-McCoy, Gerard Anthony: *Sixteenth Century Irish Swords in the National Museum of Ireland*, Dublin 1977, p. 37.

439 Halpin: *Irish Medieval Swords*, p. 214.

440 Wallace: *Scottish Swords and Dirks*, p. 11.

441 Lindholm, David and Nicolle, David: *Medieval Scandinavian Armies (2) 1300-1500*, Oxford 2003, p. 14, p. 46.

442 Halpin: *Irish Medieval Swords*, p. 208.

443 Ibid., p. 195.

444 Ibid., pp. 225-227.

445 National Museum of Ireland (no date) Topographical Files, (Accessed: 09 January 2013).

446 Oakeshott: *European Weapons and Armour*, pp. 143-144.

Fringe-decorated scabbards were popular in 16th-century Ireland.
(© Claíomh – Katharina Temirati 2022)

in County Sligo.[447] At a glance, its long slender almost parallel blade is much like the blades seen on the Group 3 ring-pommel swords, but its high collar, elongated hollow wheel-pommel brazed in two parts, and its downward sloping guards of elongated lozenge form sandwiching the grip which retains some of its original ash wood, speaks more of a Group 2 sword in its characteristics.

As warriors of Gaelic ethnicity galloglas would have most likely have favoured swords of Gaelic type – whether they be of Irish or Scottish origin. However it is also probable that galloglas – especially those in English or Anglo-Irish service – would have utilised weapons of a more general contemporary English or European cast, either as a preference or as a pragmatic choice should stocks of traditional Gaelic weaponry become scarce. Evidence from contemporary picture maps[448] indicates towards the end of the period – especially during the Irish Nine Years War that ravaged the country from the 1590's until the early seventeenth century – swords of native Gaelic type had largely fallen out of use in favour of swords with foreign stylistics. It should therefore be seen as a misnomer to use the term 'galloglass sword' for any of the swords that galloglas happened to use, just as for the 'galloglass axes' described above.

Sword scabbards

Many of the scabbards seen for Group 2 swords on West Highland effigies or on monuments such as at Ballinakill Abbey at Glinsk illustrate standard European scabbards suspended at the waist which taper to the form of the blade and are presumably made of a wood core, perhaps lined with fleece, and wrapped in either textile or leather or a combination thereof. Dated twelfth to fourteenth century one surviving scabbard is recorded from the River Bann in Co Derry and is kept at the Ulster Museum in Belfast. The scabbard is made of two lathes of wood, is bound in linen and has the tip mounted with the remains of a protective leather chape. The top of the scabbard is reinforced with decorative linen appliqué and the imprint of a girdle can still be made out on its surface.

In quite a few sources of contemporary imagery from the sixteenth century (e.g. the anonymous Ashmolean woodcut of kern, and the Lucas De Heere illustrations[449]) very distinctive scabbards with parallel sides, and thus

---

447 Oakeshott: *Records of the Medieval Sword*, p. 237.
448 O'Neill, James: *The Nine Years War 1593-1603. O'Neill, Mountjoy and the Military Revolution*, Dublin 2017, Ill. 3.
449 Dunlevy: *Dress in Ireland*, Ill. 37, Pls. 2, 4.

Galloglas weapons (from left to right): Corrib sword, Kilcumber skein, ring pommel sword.
(© Claíomh – Dave Swift 2021)

terminating in a distinct square tip, are often depicted in context with Group 3 swords in particular. Normally these – undoubtedly Gaelic – scabbards are heavily fringed at the base and are seemingly carried by their users – usually depicted as kern – until discarded when the sword springs into use. In the Lucas De Heere paintings – c. 1575 but likely copied after 1540's originals – and on the 1583 charter to the City of Dublin depicting a galloglass guardsman, the impression being conveyed is that the scabbards are thickly fringed down the sides as well as the base. Incidentally the sword donned by the charter galloglass itself looks to be of decidedly antique (recycled?) and non-Gaelic medieval – but perhaps of Pale/Dublin – origin? As no scabbard of this type has thus far survived in archaeology, we can only guess as to whether this scabbard type customarily had a wood core, was fleece lined, leather covered and what exactly the thick fringes were made of and other questions pertaining to construction. In a recent find of a ring-pommel sword in the west of Ireland some wood was attached to the blade so it seems likely that it must be the case that at least some of this class of scabbards had a wood core. Contemporary pictorial evidence from the end of the sixteenth century during the Nine Years War also appears to indicate that although native styles of Gaelic swords were falling out of use, that the old style square profiled scabbards were still enduring until at least c. 1600.[450]

Skeins

A common side arm used in Gaelic Ireland was the *scian* anglicised to skein.[451] The skein appears to be a weapon of great longevity in use and its form appears relatively recognisable with evidence from Scotland and Ireland from the start and unto the finish of the age of the galloglass and beyond.

The skein was a characteristically long iron knife which Froissart – writing in the fifteenth century – described as a 'pointed, broad-bladed, two edged weapon to cut throats'.[452] The archaeological evidence however provides that skeins had long narrow blades, typically with one sharp edge and a blunt heavy back making a triangular blade in section. The best known surviving skein yielded from the River Shannon at Corbally (Co Limerick) was 66.5 cm in length, the blade being 56.2 cm long and 5.2 cm wide and 1.2 cm thick at its widest point

---

450 O'Neill: *The Nine Years War*, Ills. 3, 16.

451 Cannan: *Galloglass 1250-1600*, p. 14.

452 Heath: *Armies of the Middle Ages*, p. 104.

where the shoulder meets the hilt. At the tip the point is acute and often double edged near the tip. Other Irish finds related to skeins also indicate long slender lengths including an exceptionally well preserved sheath from Kilcumber (Co Offaly) – likely dated fifteenth to sixteenth century – which measured 56.4 cm long. Two other well preserved skein blades in the national collections, one from a crannog at Lagore (Co Meath) and another of no known locality, had blades measuring 48.7 cm and 63.2 cm respectively. By far the longest skein found in Ireland was a near pristine crannog find from Corcreey (Co Tyrone) and was 91.2 cm long, of which 80 cm comprises the blade which was itself only 1.5 cm wide at the hilt but almost as thick. As with various other extant skeins, the tang was roughly round in section. Shorter – and intact – blades have also being yielded including specimens from Ballycolliton (Co Tipperary) and the River Corrib (near Galway City).[453] These two Irish examples have comparatively stouter blades and blade lengths of no more than 30 cms. Another skein from Argyll[454] with perhaps a slightly longer blade has likely similar proportions to these two.

Unlike swords, and some daggers of the period, the hilts of skeins are bereft of quillons, or guards of any sort, or pommels *per se*. With the possible exceptions of, perhaps, ring mounts or washers at top and bottom, the remainder of the grip – where preserved – is made of timber. The evidence would imply that these wooden grips are often ornate whether decorated in winding barley twist in relief – such as with examples from the River Shannon in Corbally – carved 4mm deep – or the stylistically similar River Corrib find. The Corbally barley twist is lightly scored along its course in the centre and the top and bottom of the grip are retained with sub circular iron bands averaging 1.6 cm in length. There is a small sub circular iron washer at the top where the tang of the blade is peened. The sub circular peened end of the Corbally grip measures approximately 2.9 cm in diameter.[455] Two other known skein grips are incised with a saltire as with finds from Tonybaun (Co Mayo) and from the River Shannon (near Athlone).[456]

Judging from evidence from the well preserved bog find from Kilcumber kept in the National Museum of Ireland, for example, the leather sheaths of these skeins appear to have been quite elaborate and artistically decorative as well as functional. In the case of the Kilcumber example the sheath was stitched vertically down the centre of the rear and was heavily tooled on the front with knotwork tapering within a panel down the length of the blade. The tip of the Corbally skein, when originally found, was also originally bound with a wire chape of 7.4 cm length – this length being deduced from the length of the tip of the blade which had not been subject to corrosion. Lockets, i.e. metal scabbard mouths, may also have been occasional features of skein sheaths too as the Corbally skein originally had traces of an approximately 1 cm wide band associated on one face of the blade. These remains appear to have been copper alloy and were located on the blade 2.8 cm down from the hilt but are no longer extant. It appears that the Kilcumber sheath may have had similar binding as its tip was marked with the spiralling scars of what appears may have once been a wire bound reinforcing chape. The top of the sheath expands in such a way as to envelope the lower half of the skein's grip. The front of this expanded part of the sheath was incised with decoration in the form of an asymmetric saltire – much like the wooden grips of the Tonybaun and Athlone examples mentioned above. The implication of the latter being of course that perhaps it was customary that the pattern of the grip was duplicated on the sheath itself. The top edge of the Kilcumber sheath was scalloped in a pleasing finish. Pairs of slit perforations at the top of the Kilcumber sheath provided purchase for leather cording which may have facilitated carriage on a belt or similar.[457]

Not all daggers borne by galloglas need have been skeins of course. In his 1521 illustration of Irish warriors, a couple of Dürer's subjects bear daggers. The second figure from the left is presented with a dagger of apparently more or less standard European proportions suspended from his right hip, with a continental influenced crescent shaped pommel. Such daggers, when and where available, could have represented an alternative to native side arms. One such crescent dagger pommel was yielded in Glen Lyon at Fortingall in Perthshire Scotland. Traces of red enamel were present indicating a fairly high status piece. Such pommels have a fairly wide date range in terms of manufacture ranging from the thirteenth to the fifteenth centuries which would not preclude their continued use into the early sixteenth century – although this latter may be Dürer's attempt to provide a suitably archaic sidearm to fit with an exotic context from the contemporary continental view.[458]

---

453 National Museum of Ireland (no date) Topographical Files, (Accessed: 09 January 2013).

454 Ancient Monuments (2013) *Dun Mac Sniachan, forts and dun, Benderloch*. Available at: https://ancientmonuments.uk/127201-dun-mac-sniachan-forts-and-dun-benderloch-oban-north-and-lorn-ward?fbclid=IwAR0gu_mguY0gxrzeagm8cEvv4gxzWxemx-sECTa5huWH4JPzSqu5srJmsms8#.YghmL9_P3IW (Accessed: 13 February 2022).

455 Rynne, Etienne: "A 16th or 17th century skean from the River Shannon at Corbally, Co. Limerick", in: North Munster Antiquarian Journal (vol. 28/5), Limerick 1986, pp. 40-45, here: p. 44.

456 Ibid., pp. 41-43.

457 Ibid., p. 44.

458 Caldwell: Caldwell, David H.: "A medieval crescent-shaped dagger-pommel from Fortingall, Perthshire", in: Proceedings of the Society of Antiquaries of Scotland, Edinburgh 1976 (vol. 107), p. 322 f, here: pp. 322-332.

Carrickfergus Castle. (Photograph: Marko Tjemmes)

ing any attempt at foreign settlement in the area.[464] Sir Richard subsequently had four chieftains of the Burkes of Mayo brutally executed on the scene of the massacre. During the Nine Years War, the MacDonnells of Antrim ostentatiously remained neutral despite many of the clansmen choosing to fight as redshanks in the ranks of the rebels, especially the troops of Red Hugh O'Donnell. Many Scottish mercenaries joined the rebels via Antrim. The Macdonnells purchased muskets and black powder in Glasgow, selling it to the Earl of Tyrone's rebels. The only stronghold of the English crown of any military value in Antrim at the time was Carrickfergus Castle, which could be supplied by sea.

In 1597, the new governor of Carrickfergus Castle, John Chichester, was able to score a number of military successes against the O'Neills of Clandeboye. His troops had also come to blows with the son of Sorley Boy MacDonnell, James MacSorley MacDonnell, who had been engaged in a series of local attacks. The Scottish clan was angered by a number of cavalry raids which had occurred in the absence of the governor. Negotiations resulted in a truce and the MacDonnells of Antrim were permitted to forward claims at recompensation for the damage. A meeting was fixed for 4th November 1597. Without Chichester's knowledge however, James MacSorley MacDonnell met the Earl of Tyrone on 1st November. Tyrone promised him his daughter in marriage, and dispatched 500 arquebusiers to reinforce MacDonnell's troops.[465]

On 4th November 1597, MacDonnell was spotted marching in the direction of Carrickfergus at the head of a considerable force. Although he had not turned out his entire fighting force, the sheer number of men under arms was deemed unusual for the occasion. Chichester decided to act and marched out to meet him with five companies of foot and one of horse. At Aldfracken Glen some miles

---

464 Falls: *Elizabeth's Irish Wars*, p. 158-161.

465 O'Neill, James: *The Nine Years War 1593-1603. O'Neill, Mountjoy and the Military Revolution*, Dublin 2017, p. 69.

THE REDSHANKS

The mercenaries hired by Naill Garbh O'Donnell in Scotland in 1428 were the first to be called Redshanks by contemporary sources, and indeed they constituted a completely new type of warrior[459]. At a time when the galloglas were only beginning to establish themselves as the new warrior élite in many regions of Ireland, other Scottish mercenaries were making an appearance while representing a completely different way of fighting.

The redshanks were recruited from the clans of the West Highlands: the MacLeans, the MacLeods, the seafaring MacNeils, and especially the MacDonalds and a handful of smaller clans. Large numbers of redshanks hailed from the Donald South clan whose chiefs were closely related to the MacDonnells of Antrim. Many sources do not even bother to differentiate between the mercenaries who came across the sea as seasonal fighters[460] and MacDonnells of Antrim proper, indiscriminately calling them redshanks regardless of their respective origins. Regarding employment, pay, commander's status etc. the redshanks were treated similarly to the galloglas. There were, however, significant differences in outward appearance.

In the 16th century the redshanks mostly woe long coats of mail and were armed with two-handed claymores, or one-and-a-half-handed swords. A common and popular weapon was the bow. Mail coats vanished almost completely in the 17th century, and the basket-hilted broadswords became the redshanks' most important weapon. Protection was provided by a small round buckler known as a targe. Like the bow, claymores and long-handled lochaber axes remained in use, but firearms were swiftly adopted as soon as they became available.

The redshanks acquired their name by their habit of wearing the traditional belted plaid, which did not cover the knees and calves. Footwear (if worn) consisted of half-boots of coarse leather called *cuarans*.[461]

For the English crown, the redshanks were undoubtedly the more dangerous opponents – they tended to adopt military novelties at a faster pace than the more conservative galloglas, and their part was not as firmly ingrained in Irish political culture as the galloglas. Armed quarrels between Irish chieftains and between their potential successors were an integral part of this culture. Often enough, one of the opponents would ally himself with the Dublin government if such a move suited his political ends. From an English or Anglo-Irish point of view, redshanks were nothing else but rebels. In 1566 Sir Francis Knollys wrote to Queen Elizabeth that three hundred of these Scots were more difficult to defeat than six hundred Irish.[462]

Heavy woollen cloaks of D-shaped cut are in archaeological evidence throughout the entire period under examination.
(© Claíomh – Dave Senior 2010)

In a battle fought at Glenshesk on 2nd May 1565, redshanks were found in both opposing armies, while galloglas only fought on one side. On this day, Shane O'Neill defeated the MacDonnells of Antrim. Among O'Neill's 2,000 warriors were 40 redshanks armed with swords, and 120 Scottish archers. Interestingly, these 160 Scots were commanded by Brian Carrach MacDonnell, a brother of James MacDonald of Dunyveg, who fought for the enemy.

Many redshanks also fought on the side of the MacDonalds of Antrim, among them many MacLeods and

---

459 Duffy, Séan: *Medieval ireland. An Encyclopedia*, New York et al., 2005, p. 554.
460 Also referred to a „New Scots" in English sources.
461 Seehase: *MacDonald*, p. 137.
462 Heath and Sque: *Irish Wars*, p. 11.

The redshanks, who at first only appeared occasionally on Irish battlefields, were to influence Irish political and military affairs considerably.
(© Claíomh – Will O'Shea 2018)

Opposite page:
The longbow formed an integral part of the redshanks' equipment.
(Illustration by Sascha Lunyakov)

MacNeills. The O'Neills won the battle, the enemy losing 700 dead. Among the prisoners taken was James MacDonald of Dunyveg, who subsequently died in captivity.

In the year 1584 around 4,000 Redshanks were operating in Ulster, in the following year Sorley Boy MacDonnell alone commanded 2,000 of them.[463]

The year 1586 was to form a grisly highpoint in the redshanks' fighting record: there is reason to believe that this time they intended to stay on Irish soil and settle there, which was considered a novelty since until now the redshanks had returned to their homes in the Scottish Highlands as soon as their seasonal contracts expired. Some individuals and a handful of small groups had found new homes with their Irish relatives, the MacDonnells of Antrim. However, the events of 1586 were to acquire a completely new quality.

In early September 1586, several ships with redshanks mainly from the Donald South clan landed in Killala Bay in Mayo. At this time, the Burkes of Mayo and the MacPhilbins were in rebellion against the English rule. Donnell Gorm MacDonnell of Carey and Alexander Carragh MacDonnell of Glenarm, both sons of the James MacDonald of Dunyveg mortally wounded at Glenshesk and nephews of Sorley Boy MacDonald of Antrim, had brought with him a party of 2,000 Scots, among them women and children, to the coast of Ireland. Obvioulsy, the Scots intended to stay.

For two weeks, the redshanks fought the troops of Sir Richard Bingham, Lord President of Connacht, around Sligo. On the night of the 23rd September 1586, the English troops attacked the redshank camp at Ardnaree on the bank of the River Moy. In the ensuing hand-to-hand fighting, nearly all of the remaining Scots were killed. The non-combatants were either slaughtered on the spot or drowned in the river. Any stragglers that had managed to make their escape were hunted down and killed by the local population of Tirawley, who was set on prevent-

---
463 Ibid., p. 10.

from Carrickfergus, Chichester had his advance guard halt in order to permit his remaining force to catch up. During a brief council of war, he asked one of his officers, a certain Captain Marmion: "Now, Captain, yonder be your old friends. What say you? Shall we charge them?" Marmion[466] favoured this move, as did Chichester's commander of horse Moyses Hill, who was related to James MacSorley MacDonnell by marriage. Chichester ordered the attack, and the MacDonnells promptly gave ground. Seven hundred sword fighters from MacDonnell's force were visible on the nearby rise, MacDonnell having posted a further eight hundred – three hundred archers and Tyrone's arquebusiers – behind the crest and out of sight. The English soldiers advanced straight into a massed Irish volley and were then attacked by the Irish swordsmen. Chichester was shot in the head. Several other English officers also perished along with a number of cavalry and foot soldiers. News of the reverse reached Carrickfergus Castle, and the remaining garrison, among them the sick and wounded, set out to rescue their beleaguered comrades. English losses amounted to altogether 180 dead and around 30 wounded. The so-called "Battle of Pin Well" was over.

Chichester's body was decapitated and the head delivered to Tyrone by four horsemen. Many years later, James MacSorley MacDonald's brother and heir Randal MacSorley MacDonald visited Carrickfergus and stood in contemplation at Chichester's tomb, Chichester's effigy prompting the baffled remark: "How the de'il he cam to get his head again? For he was sure he had anes ta'en it frae him."[467]

After 1560, redshanks from the Campbells and other associated clans had begun to settle in the Laggan region (County Donegal). All of these were of Presbyterian denomination. After the collapse of the Tyrone Rebellion and the subsequent Flight of the Earls these people had no trouble adapting to the newly-arrived Scottish settlers adhering to the same faith, and gradually became absorbed.[468] Many redshanks of MacDonald stock were stout Roman Catholics however. One of these Catholic Scots was Gillespie Fiacall MacDonald, who died on Rathlin Island around 1570 leaving a pregnant widow. His son Coll Ciotach (later anglicized as "Colkitto") was to become one of the most notorious troublemakers and ne'er-do-wells at large on the Hebrides. In his youth he fought as a redshank in Ireland under his uncle Randal's patronage. Colkitto's son Alastair MacColla, born in 1610, was the last of the great redshanks. When the Irish rebellion broke out in 1641, a regiment was formed from the Earl of Antrim's[469] vassals and landholders in order to protect the Earl's estates. The regiment consisted of Catholic and Protestant companies. One of the Catholic companies was commanded by MacColla, while Tirlough Óg O'Cahan commanded the other. Before dawn on 2nd January 1642, these two Catholic companies fell upon the Protestant companies at Portnaw, inflicting severe losses. On 11th February MacColla ambushed his former superior officer Stewart of Ballintoy at Bendooragh. For the first time in military history MacColla's men applied tactics which were to become known as the "Highland Charge", firing a full volley before closing in at a run with swords drawn.

The following months saw MacColla's redshanks together with Irish troops under Sir Phelim O'Neill pitted against a Protestant force of Anglo-Scottish settlers commanded by Robert Stewart (the "Army of the Laggan") in Donegal. After a brief skirmish on 15th June 1642, Robert Stewart was forced to withdraw, only to resume his advance on the enemy in the following night. At a distance of about one kilometre from the Irish camp, Stewart took up a fortified position on a rise not far from the hamlet of Glenmaquin, which itself was not far from Raphoe. According to Stewart's own words, his command comprised no more than 2,000 foot soldiers and 300 horse, while the enemy force numbered at least 4,000. At sunrise, the opposing forces could clearly make each other out. Both held high positions separated only by a stretch of low ground. Stewart was hoping for the enemy to attack, while MacColla began to form his force into two battle lines. The Highlanders and Antrim troops, led by himself and his brother Ranald, formed the first line, with the remaining troops under Phelim O'Neill forming the second. Stewart dispatched a mixed body of crack musketeers and cavalry to harass the enemy. These troops proceeded to take the Irish force under sustained fire. This move proved successful, prompting MacColla's men to abandon their positions and attack. Stewart's men beat a hasty but orderly retreat. MacColla nevertheless believed the enemy were on the run and pressed his attack without providing for his own safety. According to Scottish and Irish sources which soon enough were to make a highly romanticized legend of MacColla, his lone figure was to be seen running well ahead of his own men, making for the enemy breastworks. Suddenly he was hit in the thigh by a musket ball, while many more of his men were struck down by the Army of the Laggan's withering fire.[470] MacColla's men wavered and eventually turned and ran, spreading confusion in the approaching second line under Phelim O'Neill. Seeing their comrades' predicament, these men also took to their heels, with their commander looking on helplessly. MacColla himself was fortunate enough

---

466 Nearly all sources on the incident give the name of Merriman, yet Marmion appears correct.

467 Quoted after Hall, Samuel C.: *Ireland. Its Scenery, Character and c.*, London 1843, p. 119.

468 A closer examination of the topic is provided in McCain, Barry: *The Laggan Redshanks. The Highland Scots in West Ulster 1569-1630*, Oxford 2014.

469 Ranald MacDonnell of Antrim, 2nd Earl of Antrim, later 1st Marquis of Antrim (1609-1683).

470 Among the rebels which the Army of the Laggan had to face in Donegal were also the MacSweeneys, an ancient gallogas clan.

The equipment and clothing of these Irish warriors combine typical Celtic elements with military equipment common to most European armies of the day.
(© Claíomh – Niamh O'Rourke 2012)

to have been rescued by a soldier of the O'Cahans, who managed to evacuate him to safety on a horse-drawn stretcher. MacColla lived to fight another day, taking part in the Marquis of Montrose's ill-fated Scottish campaign and returning to Ireland after its collapse.

In the Battle of Dungan's Hill in August 1647 between the Irish Confederates under Thomas Preston and an English army commanded by Michael Jones, the 900 Confederate redshanks were able to penetrate the English encirclement with another Highland Charge. The redshank commander, Angus MacDonnell of Glengarry, was killed.[471]

At the battle of Knocknanuss on 13th November 1647, a bloody close-quarter combat developed between the Irish Confederate troops under Taaffe and Lord Inchiquin's Protestant forces. Murrough O'Brien, Lord Inchiquin, was a skilled and ruthless commander – and a direct descendant of High King Brian Boru himself. Mac-Colla's men advanced and fired two volleys before drawing their swords. The sloping ground favoured the attack, the men charging the enemy head-on downhill. A credible account of events composed a few years after the battle relates how MacColla himself at the head of a group of assorted swordsmen hacked himself into the enemy formation. Although Inchiquin had placed his most experienced fighters on that wing, they were unable to resist the force of the Highland Charge. One of Inchiquin's officers observed that MacColla's men came "*routing downe like a Torrent impetuously on our foot*." It must be taken into account that MacColla's men were veterans of Montrose's famous Highland campaign. MacColla's attack carried Inchiquin's two cannon, his men immediately turning one around against its former owners. Between forty and fifty men of Inchiquin's force were killed outright, the rest fled. Among the dead were several high-ranking officers, e. g. Colonel Gray and Sir William Bridges. Completely ignorant of what was happening on the other side

---

[471] Seehase, Hagen and Oprotkowitz, Axel: *Montrose. Der Feldzug in den Highlands*. Greiz 2002, p. 183.

This galloglass carries a broadaxe of Group B type.
(© Claíomh – Will O´Shea 2022)

of the field, MacColla's men set about plundering the enemy baggage. In fact, Inchiquin's men had beaten the Irish Confederates on the other wing. MacColla had only just begun to regroup his men when they were hit by an attack by Inchiquin's cavalry. Only half-formed up and with only few musketeers at their disposal to keep the enemy cavalry at bay, MacColla's men stood no chance. In the ensuing rout, MacColla was killed along with his second-in-command Archibald Óg MacDonald of Sanda, nine captains, and most of his men.

The exact circumstances surrounding MacColla's death remain obscure and thus a matter of debate. Apparently, he had originally received quarter but was killed shortly after. Having surrendered to a certain Cornet O'Grady, MacColla was recognized by O'Grady's superior officer and shot in the head.

A few weeks later, Donald MacDonald of Moidart sailed to Ireland with 300 Highlanders. Little did he know that this was to be the final expedition of Scots redshanks from the Hebrides to Ireland. Together with 1,200 Scottish survivors of the battles of Knocknanuss and Dungan's Hill, these men formed a regiment commanded by Alexander MacDonnell of Antrim, a brother of the Earl of Antrim. Alexander had become embroiled in the quarrels which had arisen among the leaders of the Irish Catholic Confederation. Fearing a putsch by radical elements within (among whom Antrim was numbered), the Confederate Supreme Council sought to neutralize the redshank force. At Athy in Kildare, the regiment was destroyed, Donald MacDonald of Moidart was captured but later ransomed.[472] He and those of his men that had survived the last battle then sailed back to the Hebrides, whence nearly 400 years previously the first warriors of Somerled's tribe had sailed to offer their swords to the Irish kings.

---

472 Ibid., p. 184.

Evidence for the use of gauntlets among galloglass is scanty.
(© Claiomh-Katharina Temirati 2022)

This galloglass is armed with a sword with a Corrib-type pommel. (© Claiomh – Judith Schoen 2014)

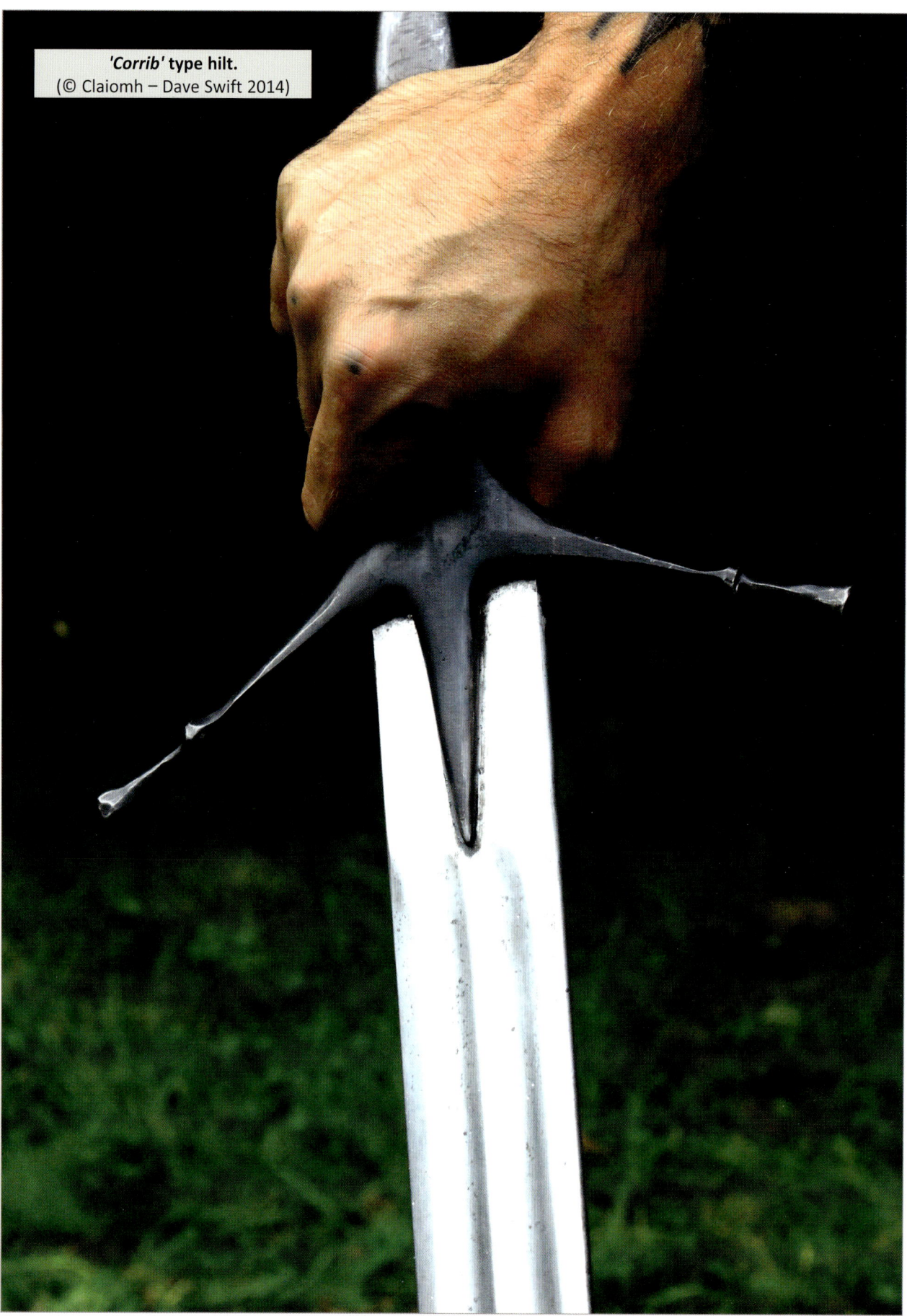

'Corrib' type hilt.
(© Claiomh – Dave Swift 2014)

Left to right:
Derryloughan axe, Portglenone Co Antrim, Buckinghamshire, Lough Gara swords and Derricke type skein.
(© Claiomh – Will O'Shea 2022)

BIBLIOGRAPHY

Ancient Monuments (2013) *Dun Mac Sniachan, forts and dun, Benderloch*. Available at: https://ancientmonuments.uk/127201-dun-mac-sniachan-forts-and-dun-benderloch-oban-north-and-lorn-ward?fbclid=IwAR0gu_mguY0gxrzeagm8cEvv4gxzWxemxsECTa5huWH4JP-zSqu5srJmsms8#.YghmL9_P3IW (Accessed: 13 February 2022)

Anders, Sabine and Seehase, Hagen: „Die Schlacht bei Clontarf. Geburt einer Nation", in: *Geschichte* 7/2015 (2015), p. 36 f.

Annals of the Four Masters CELT Project (2016) *Annals of the Four Masters* https://celt.ucc.ie/published/T100005E.html (Accessed: 27 January 2022).

Bardon, Jonathan: *The Plantation of Ulster*, Dublin 2012.

Beckett, James Camlin: *Geschichte Irlands*, Stuttgart 1977.

Berleth, Richard: *The twilight Lords. Elizabeth I and the plunder of Ireland*, Lanham 2002.

Borrowes, Sir Erasmus D.: *Tenekille, Portarlington, and Glimpses of the MacDonnells*, Belfast 1854.

Bourke, Cormac: "Antiquities from the River Blackwater III: Iron Axe-Heads", in: *The Ulster Journal of Archaeology* (vol. 60), Belfast 2001, pp. 63-93.

Bourke, Cormac: "A Medieval Helmet from Lough Henney, Co. Down", Lecale and Downe historical society, Dundrum (ed.): *Lecale Miscellany* 1990.

Bourke, Cormac: 'Beauties of the Bann and Blackwater: reflections on riverine archaeology in Northern Ireland', in Murray, E. & Logue, P. (eds.) *Battles. Boats and Bones.* Belfast: TSO Ireland 2010.

Bradley, John: "Anglo-Norman Towns", in: Ryan Michael (ed.): *The Illustrated Archaeology of Ireland*, Dublin 1991, p. 177-183.

Bugge, Alexander: *Die Wikinger*, Halle 1906.

Burke, John: *A General and Heraldic Dictionary of the Peerage and Baronetage of the British Empire*, London 1832.

Caldwell, David H.: "A medieval crescent-shaped dagger-pommel from Fortingall, Perthshire", in: *Proceedings of the Society of Antiquaries of Scotland*, Edinburgh 1976 (vol. 107), p. 322 f.

Caldwell, David H.: "Having the right kit: West Highlanders fighting in Ireland", in: Duffy, S. (ed.): *The World of the Galloglass. Kings, Warlords and Warriors in Ireland and Scotland 1200-1600*, Dublin 2007, pp. 144-168.

Cambrensis, Geraldus: *Expugnatio Hibernica. The Conquest of Ireland* (translated by A. B. Scott and F. X. Martin), Dublin 1978.

Campbell, Kenneth L.: *Ireland's History, Prehistory to the Present*, London et al. 2014.

Cannan, Fergus and Ó Brógáin, Sean: *Galloglass 1250–1600. Gaelic Mercenary Warrior*, Oxford 2010.

Cannan, Fergus: *Scottish Arms and Armour*. Oxford: Shire 2009.

Cambrensis, Giraldus: *Expugnatio Hibernica The Conquest of Ireland*. Translated from the Latin by A.B. Scott and F.X. Martin. Dublin: Royal Irish Academy 1978.

Capwell, Tobias: *The Real Fighting Stuff*, Glasgow 2007.

Capwell, Tobias: *The Noble Art of the Sword*, London 2012.

Capwell, Tobias: *Armour of the English Knight 1400–1450*. London 2015

Capwell, Tobias: *Armour of the English Knight 1450–1500*, London 2021.

Cathcart, Alison: "James V, King of Scotland – and Ireland?", in: Duffy, Séan (ed.): *The World of the Galloglass. Kings, Warlords and Warriors in Ireland and Scotland 1200-1600*, Dublin 2007, pp. 124-143.

Cole, George S.: *A Complete Dictionary of Dry Goods and History of Silk, Linen, Wool & other Fibrous Substances*, Wichita 1890.

Colum, Padraic: *A Treasury of Irish Folklore*, New York 1982.

Connellan, Owen (ed.): *Annals of the Four Masters*, Dublin 1846.

Connolly, S. J.: *Contested Island. Ireland 1460-1630*, Oxford and New York 2007.

Crawford, Henry S.: "The Burke Effigy at Glinsk, Co. Galway", in: Royal Society of Antiquaries of Ireland (ed.): *The Journal of the Royal Society of Antiquaries of Ireland* (vol. 37/3), Dublin 1907, p. 307 f.

Crawford, Ross Mackenzie: *Warfare in the West Highlands and Isles of Scotland c. 1544-1615*. Unpublished PhD thesis, University of Glasgow, Glasgow 2016.

Curtis, Edmund: *Richard II in Ireland 1394–5, and Submissions of the Irish Chiefs*, Oxford 1927.

D'Alton, Edward Alfred: *History of Ireland*, vol. III, London 2012 (reprint).

Duffy, Christopher: *The Fortress in the Early Modern World 1494–1660*, London and New York 1996.

Duffy, Séan (ed.): *Medieval Ireland. An Encyclopedia*, New York et al., 2005.

Dunlevy, Mairead: *Dress in Ireland*, Cork 1989.

Dymmok, John: *A Treatise of Ireland*, Dublin 1842.

Edwards, Ruth Dudley: *An Atlas of Irish History*; New York 1981.

Egan, Geoff and Pritchard, Frances: *Dress Accessories 1150-1450*, London 2002.

Ellis, Steven G.: "The Tudor Borderlands 1485–1603" in: Morrill, John: *The Oxford Illustrated History of Tudor and Stuart Britain*, London et al. 1996.

Evans, Martin Marix: *The Military Heritage of Britain and Ireland. The Comprehensive Guide to Sites of Military Interest*, London 1998.

Falls, Cyril: *Elizabeth's Irish Wars*, Syracuse 1997.

Fissel, Mark Charles: *English Warfare 1511–1642*, London and New York 2001.

Flanagan, L. N. W.: "A late Sixteenth-Century Battleaxe from Benburb", in: *Ulster Journal of Archaeology* (vol. 23), 1960, p. 59 f.

Foster, Robert F.: *The Oxford History of Ireland*, Oxford 2001.

Freeman, A. Martin (ed.): *Annála Connacht: The Annals of Connacht*, Dublin 1944.

Fry, Plantagenet Somerset: *Castles of Britain and Ireland*, London et al., 1996.

Gilbert, John T.: *Facsimiles of the National Manuscripts of Ireland* (vol. 3), Public Record Office of Ireland, Dublin 1879.

Graham-Campbell, James (ed.): *Die Wikinger*, Munich 1994.

Grant, I. F.: *Angus Og of the Isles*, Edinburgh 1969.

Hadfield, Andrew and Maley, Willy (eds.): *Edmund Spenser: A View of the State of Ireland*, Oxford 1997.

Hall, Samuel C.: *Ireland. Its Scenery, Character and c.*, London 1843.

Halpin, Andrew: "Irish Medieval Swords c. 1170–1600", in: *Proceedings of the Royal Irish Academy* (vol. 86 (C) 5), Belfast 1986, p. 183-230.

Halpin, Andrew: "The gallóglach axe revisited", in: Condit, T. and Corlett, C. (eds.): *Above and Beyond*, Bray 2005, pp. 361-372.

Halpin, Andrew: "Irish Medieval Swords c. 1170–1600", in: Proceedings of the Royal Irish Academy (vol. 86 (C) 5), Belfast 1986, pp. 183-230.

Halpin, Andrew: "Arms and Armour", in: Moss, Rachel (ed.): *Art and Architecture in Ireland*, Dublin 2014.

Harbison, Peter: "Native Irish arms & armour in medieval Gaelic literature. 1170–1600", *Irish sword*, 12(1), 1975, pp. 173-199.

Harlaut, Mathieu: *The Company of Saynte George Clothing Guide – Men version 1.1*. Available at: https://companie-of-st-george.ch/publications/costume-guide/ (Accessed: 10 February 2022). http://creativecommons.org/licenses/by-nc-nd/3.0/ for CC BY-NC-ND 3.0.

Harrison, Mark and Embleton, Gerry: *Viking Hersir*, Oxford 1993.

Hayes-McCoy, Gerard Anthony: *Scots Mercenary Forces in Ireland*, Dublin and London 1937.

Hayes-McCoy, Gerard Anthony: *Irish Battles. A Military History of Ireland*, Belfast 1969.

Hayes-McCoy, Gerard Anthony: *Sixteenth Century Irish Swords in the National Museum of Ireland*, Dublin 1977.

Hayes-McCoy, Gerard Anthony: 'The Gallóglach Axe' *Journal of the Galway Archaeological and Historical Society*, 17(3/4), pp. 101-121. 1937

Heath, Ian: *Armies of the Sixteenth Century*, St. Peter Port 1997.

Heath, Ian: *Armies of the Middle Ages, Volume 1: The Hundred Years' War, the Wars of the Roses and the Burgundian Wars, 1300–1487*. Cambridge: Wargames Research Group 1982.

Heath, Ian and Sque, David: *The Irish Wars 1485–1603*, London 1993.

Higgins, Jim: "Medieval Sculptures from Carran Church Co Clare and their significance", in: Shannon Archaeological and Historical Society (ed.): *The Other Clare* 16 (April), Shannon 1992, pp. 21-26.

Hill, George: *The Fall of Irish Chiefs and Clans and the Plantation of Ulster*, Dublin 2004.

Hill, J. M.: *Fire and Sword. Sorley Boy MacDonnell and the Rise of Clan Iain Mor*, London 1993.

Hudson, Benjamin: *Viking Pirates and Christian Princes. Dynasty, Religion, and Empires in the North Atlantic*, Oxford 2005.

Hunt, John: *Irish Medieval Figure Sculpture 1200–1600*, 2 vols., Dublin 1974.

James, Jeffrey: *Ireland. The Struggle for Power. From the Dark Ages to the Jacobites*, Stroud 2017.

Janin, Hunt and Carlson, Ursula: *Mercenaries in Medieval and Renaissance Europe*, Jefferson and London 2013.

Johnson, D. Newman: "Later Medieval Castles", in: Ryan, Michael (ed.): The Illustrated Archaeology of Ireland, Dublin 1991, pp. 188-193.

Johnson, Samuel and Oldys, William: *The Harleian Miscellany*, London 1809.

Jordan, Donald E.: *Land and Popular Politics in Ireland. County Mayo from the Plantation to the Land War*, Cambridge 1994.

Joyce, Patrick Weston: *A Concise History of Ireland*, New York 1903.

Kelly, Matthew (ed.): *Cambrensis eversus seu potius historica fides in rebus hibernicis Giraldo Cambrensi abrogata*, Dublin 1848.

Kew, Graham (ed.): *The Irish Sections of Fynes Moryson's Unpublished Itinerary*, Dublin 1998.

Kluxen, Kurt: *Geschichte Englands. Von den Anfängen bis zur Gegenwart*, Stuttgart 1985.

Lee, Wayne, E.: *Barbarians and Brothers. Anglo-American Warfare 1500-1865*, Oxford 2011.

Lenihan, Padraig: *Consolidating Conquest. Ireland 1603–1727*, Abingdon 2014.

Lennon, Colm: *Richard Stanihurst*, Dublin 1981.

Lindholm, David and Nicolle, David: *Medieval Scandinavian Armies (2) 1300-1500*, Oxford 2003.

Logan, Donald F.: *The Vikings in History*, New York and London 1983.

Lydon, James: "The Scottish soldier in medieval Ireland", in: Simpson, Grant G.: *The Scottish Soldier Abroad 1297–1967*, Edinburgh and Maryland 1992, pp. 1-15.

MacDonald, Micheil: *The Clans of Scotland. The History and Landscape of the Scottish Clans*, London 1991.

Macdonald of Castleton, Donald J.: *Clan Donald*, Gretna 2008.

Mahr, Adolf: "The Galloglach Axe", in. *Journal of the Galway Archaeological and Historical Society*, vol. 18 (1/2), Galway 1938, pp. 66-68.

Marsden, John: *Galloglas. Hebridean and West Highland Mercenary Warrior Kindreds in Medieval Ireland*, Edinburgh 2002.

Martyn, Adrian: *The Tribes of Galway 1124–1642*, Galway 2016.

McCain, Barry: *The Laggan Redshanks. The Highland Scots in West Ulster 1569-1630*, Oxford 2014.

McClintock, H. F.: *Old Highland Dress and Tartans*. Dundalk: Dundalgan Press 1949.

McCormack, Anthony M.: *The Earldom of Desmond 1463-1583. The Decline and Crisis of a Feudal Lordship*, Dublin 2005.

McCullough, David Willis: *Wars of the Irish Kings. A Thousand Years of Struggle from the Age of Myth through the Reign of Queen Elizabeth I*, New York 2002.

McDonald, Russell: *The Kingdom of the Isles. Scotland's Western Seaboard c. 1100-c. 1336*, East Linton 1997.

McGurk, John: *Sir Henry Docwra 1564-1631. Derry's Second Founder*, Dublin 2006.

McInerney, Luke: "The Galloglass of Thomond", in: *North Munster Antiquarian Journal*, vol. 55 (2015), p. 21-45.

McNeill, Tom E.: *Castles in Ireland. Feudal Power in a Gaelic World*, London 1997.

Metzger, Franz: "Irland unter den Tudors. Von der Kolonie zum Königreich", in: *Geschichte* 7/2015, pp. 40-42.

Moran, Gerard P.: *Galway. History and Society*, Dublin 1996.

Morgan, Hiram: *Tyrone's Rebellion. The Outbreak of the Nine Years War in Tudor Ireland*, London 1993.

Morton, Klaas: 'Iconography and Dating of the Wall Paintings', in Manning C., Gosling. P and Waddell, J. (eds.) *New Survey of Clare Island*, 4, pp. 97–121. 2005

Moore, Thomas Sturge: *History of Ireland*, vol. 2, Paris 1840.

Mulvany, William Thomas et al: Appendix No. V: Notices of Antiquities Presented to the Royal Irish Academyby W. T. Mulvany, Esq., M. R. I. A., on the Part of the Commissioners of Public Works' Proceedings of the Royal Irish Academy 1836–1869, 1850–1853(5), pp. xxxi-lxvi 1853, here: p. xxxix.

National Museum of Ireland (no date) *Topographical Files*. (Accessed: 09 January 2013).

Newark, Tim: *Warlord Armies*, Hong Kong 2004.

Newark, Tim and McBride, Angus: *Warlords*, London 1996.

Newman, Roger Chatterton: *Brian Boru, King of Ireland*, Cork 2011.

Nicolle, David: *Medieval Warfare Sourcebook. Warfare in Western Christendom*, London 1995.

Nicholls, Kenneth W.: *Gaelic and Gaelicised Ireland in the Middle Ages*, Dublin 1972.

Nicholls, Kenneth W.: "Scottish Mercenary Kindreds in Ireland 1250-1600", in: Duffy, Séan (ed.): *The World of the Galloglass. Kings, Warlords and Warriors in Ireland and Scotland 1200-1600*, Dublin 2007, pp. 86-110.

Nicholls, Kenneth W.: *Gaelic and Gaelicised Ireland in the Middle Ages*, Dublin 1972.

Oakeshott, Ewart: *European Weapons and Armour*, Woodbridge 1980.

Oakeshott, Ewart: *Records of the Medieval Sword*, Woodbridge 1991.

Ó Cléirigh, Cormac: "Irish frontier warfare – a fifteenth century case study", in: *ACTA 22. Kongress der Internationalen Kommission für Militärgeschichte XXII. Herausgegeben vom Heeresgeschichtlichen Museum/Militärhistorischen Institut*, Vienna 1997, pp. 179-194.

Ó Corráin, Donnchadh: „Ireland, Wales, Man, and the Hebrides", in: Sawyer, Peter (ed.): *The Oxford Illustrated History of the Vikings*, Oxford 1997.

O'Connor, Kieran and Shanahan, Brian: *Roscommon Abbey. A Visitor's Guide*, Boyle 2013.

O'Domnhaill, Rónán Gearóid: *Fadó. Tales of lesser known Irish history*, Kibworth Beauchamps 2013.

O'Laughlin, Michael C.: *The Families of Galway, Ireland*, Kansas City 2002.

O'Laughlin, Michael C.: *The Book of Irish Families Great and Small*, Kansas City 2002.

O'Neill, James: "Tyrone's Proxy War 1593–4", in: *History Ireland* March/April 2015, p. 14-17.

O'Neill, James: *The Nine Years War 1593-1603. O'Neill, Mountjoy and the Military Revolution*, Dublin 2017.

O'Sullivan Beare, Philip: *Ireland under Elizabeth*, Dublin 1903.

O'Toole, Fintan: *A history of Ireland in 100 objects: Galloglass gravestone, 15th or 16th century*. Available at: https://www.irishtimes.com/culture/art-and-design/a-history-of-ireland-in-100-objects-1.474794 (Accessed: 13 February 2022).

Oakeshott, Ewart: *European Weapons and Armour*, Woodbridge 1980.

Oakeshott, Ewart: *Records of the Medieval Sword*, Woodbridge 1991.

Palmer, Patricia: *The Severed Head and the Grafted Tongue. Literature, Translation and Violence in Early Modern Ireland*, Cambridge 2014.

Palmer, William: *The Problem of Ireland in Tudor Foreign Policy 1485-1603*, Woodbridge 1994.

Paterson, James: *History of the County of Ayr* (vol. 1), Ayr 1847.

Patterson, Raymond Campbell: *The Lords of the Isles. A History of Clan Donald*, Edinburgh 2008.

Penman, Michael: *The Scottish Civil War. The Bruces & the Balliols & the War for Control of Scotland*, Stroud 2008.

Penman, Michael A.: "The MacDonald Lordship and the Bruce Dynasty", in: Oran, Richard D. (ed.): *The Lordship of the Isles*, Leyden and Boston 2014.

Perret, Bryan: *The Battle Book. Crucial Conflicts from 1469 BC to the Present*, London 1992.

Pierse, John H.: *The Pierse Family*, London 1950.

Prendergast, Muriósa: "Scots mercenary Forces in Sixteenth century Ireland", in: France, John: *Mercenaries and Paid Men. The Mercenary Identity in the Middle Ages*, Leyden and Boston 2008, pp. 363-381.

Rae, Edwin C.: "Irish Sepulchral Monuments of the Later Middle Ages", in: Royal Society of Antiquaries of Ireland (ed.): *The Journal of the Royal Society of Antiquaries of Ireland (100/I)*, Dublin 1970, pp. 1-38.

Reilly, Gavan: 'Stolen medieval carvings to return to Clare after 150 years', *The Journal*, 20 June. Available at: https://www.thejournal.ie/stolen-medieval-carvings-scattery-island-958260-Jun2013/ (Accessed: 30 November 2021)

Ronayne, Liam: *Donegal Highlands. Paintings and Stories from Northwest Donegal*, Donaghadee 2004.

Rynne, Etienne: "A 16th or 17th century skean from the River Shannon at Corbally, Co. Limerick", in: *North Munster Antiquarian Journal* (vol. 28/5), Limerick 1986, pp. 40-45.

Sadler, John: *Clan Donald's Greatest Defeat. The Battle of Harlaw 1411*, Stroud 2005.

Schlegel, Donald M.: "The MacDonnells of Tyrone and Armagh. A Genealogical Study", in: *Seanchas Ardmhacha*, vol. 10, No. 1 (1980-81), Armagh 1980, pp. 193-219.

Schreiber, Hermann: *Irland. Seine Geschichte – Seine Menschen*, Augsburg 1997.

Seehase, Hagen: „Galloglas – irische Krieger des 13.–16. Jahrhunderts", in: *Zeitschrift für Heereskunde* Nr. 402 (2001), pp. 135-143.

Seehase, Hagen: *Der schottische Clan MacDonald. Aufstieg und Fall der Herren der Inseln*, Greiz 2008.

Seehase, Hagen: und Krekeler, Ralf: *Der gefiederte Tod. Der englische Langbogen in den Kriegen des Mittelalters*, Ludwigshafen 2001.

Seehase, Hagen und Oprotkowitz, Axel: *Die Highlander. Die Geschichte der schottischen Clans* (Band 1), Greiz 1999.

Seehase, Hagen und Oprotkowitz, Axel: *Die Highlander. Die Geschichte der schottischen Clans* (Band 2), Greiz 2012.

Seehase, Hagen und Oprotkowitz, Axel: *Bannockburn. Schottlands Kampf um die Freiheit*, Greiz 1999.

Seehase, Hagen und Oprotkowitz, Axel: *Montrose. Der Feldzug in den Highlands*, Greiz 2002.

Simek, Rudolf: *Die Wikinger*, München 1998.

Simms, Katherine: „The Battle of Dysert O'Dea and the Gaelic Resurgence in Thomond", in: *Dal gCais*, vol. 5 (1979), pp. 59-66.

Simms, Katherine: *From Kings to Warlords. The changing political structure of Gaelic Ireland in the latter Middle Ages*, Woodbridge 2000.

Smith, Charles: *The Ancient and Present State of the County and City of Cork*, vol. 1, Cork 1815.

Smith, Brendan: *Crisis and Survival in Late Medieval Ireland. The English of Louth and their Neighbours 1330–1450*, Oxford 2013.

Smith, Brendan (ed.): *The Cambridge History of Ireland*, vol. 1 (600-1500); Cambridge et al. 2018.

Smith, Brendan and Frame, Robin: *Ireland and the English World in the Late Middle Ages*, Basingstoke 2009.

Steer, K. A. and Bannerman, J. W. M.: *Late medieval monumental sculpture in the West Highlands* (The Royal Commission on the Ancient and Historical Monuments of Scotland), Edinburgh 1977.

Stevenson, David: *Alasdair MacColla and the Highland Problem in the Seventeenth Century*, Edinburgh 1980.

Swift, Michael: *Historical Maps of Ireland,* New Jersey 1999.

Traquair, Peter: *Freedom's Sword. Scotland's Wars of Independence*, London 1998.

Thordeman, Bengt: *Armour from the Battle of Wisby 1361*, Highland Village TX 2001.

Trinity College Dublin (no date) *The book of the de Burgos*. Available at: https://digitalcollections.tcd.ie/concern/works/rb68xg028?locale=en (Accessed: 30 November 2021).

University of Edinburgh (no date) *The Image of Irelande by John Derricke*. Available at: http://www.docs.is.ed.ac.uk/docs/lib-archive/bgallery/Gallery/researchcoll/pages/bg0061_jpg.htm (Accessed: 30 November 2021).

Wakeman, William F.: "Observations on the Principal Crannogs of Fermanagh", in: Royal Historical and Archaeological Association of Ireland (ed.): *The Journal of the Royal Historical and Archaeological Association of Ireland*, vol. 4 (2) 2, Dublin 1873, p. 218 f.

Walker, Joseph C.: *Dress of the Ancient and Modern Irish*, Uckfield 1788.

Wallace, John: *Scottish Swords and Dirks*, London 1970.

Walsh, Paul (ed.): *Leabhar Chlainne Suibhne. An Account of the MacSweeney Families in Ireland*, Dublin 1920.

Williams, Perry: *The Later Tudors. England 1487–1603*, Oxford et al. 1995.

Woolf, Alex: "A dead man at Ballyshannon", in: Duffy, Séan (ed.): *The World of the Galloglas. Kings, Warlords and Warriors in Ireland and Scotland 1200-1600*, Dublin 2007, pp. 77-85.

Wright, Rev. George Newenham: *A Guide to the Giants Causeway and the North-East Coast of the County of Antrim*, London 1823.

Such helmets, a variant of the Morion, were imported from the Continent.
(© Claiomh – Dave Swift 2011)

Hagen Seehase / Detlef Ollesch

The Burgundian Wars

The "Burgundian Wars" are generally considered the campaigns of Charles the Bold, the last Duke of Burgundy, against the Swiss, but they were actually far more extensive. This book presents the European politics leading to the conflicts, then the Dukes campaigns against Liège starting in 1467, his siege of Neuss on the Rhine, the fighting in the Sundgau and Lorraine. It moves on to the battles against the Swiss staring in 1474, and finally addresses the conflict with the Duke of Lorraine in 1477.
Charles the Bold created an impressive army but lost many battles. His defeat and death at the Battle of Nancy in early 1477 and the resulting conflicts over the succession are of tremendous historical significance because they mark the beginning of the German-French relationship as "hereditary enemies".
The book recognizes the often-overlooked role of the allies of the Swiss and it also addresses the significance of the French and English kings fueling in this conflict, as well as the role of the Holy Roman Emperor. The authors present the driving forces behind the war against Charles the Bold and which factors led to his downfall. At the same time, they present some heretofore little-known details about the Burgundian Dukes military innovations and his death.
Paperback, 52 mostly color illustrations, two maps, english text. 104 pages.
ISBN 978-3-96360-014-2

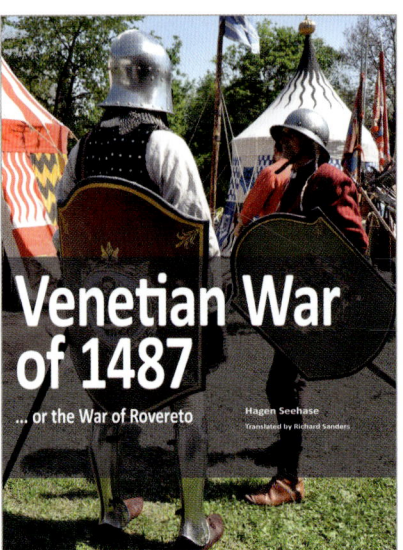

Florian Messner / Hagen Seehase

Venetian War of 1487
... or the War of Rovereto

The 1487 Venetian War between the maritime, major power Venice and the alpine Archduchy of Tirol began from insignificant events and led to considerable political disruptions - especially in Tirol. The conflict is closely tied to Archduke Sigismund of Tirol's partially tragic, partially odd biography. The Venetian War occurred on the threshold between the ending Middle Ages and the beginning of modern times: on one side the knightly duel between Johann von Waldburg-Sonnenberg und Antonia Maria da Sanseverino, and on the other the drawn-out battle with heavy artillery for the city and castle of Rovereto. The Battle of Calliano was decisive: on one side, a veteran of the Burgundian Wars, on the other a highly respected condottiere, with the breathtaking mountains of the Adige Valley as the backdrop. For the first time, the new type of soldier, the Landsknecht was decisive in battle. The material remains of the Venetian War are partially still visible today and a scientific treasure trove for archaeologists and historians. This book came about in close cooperation with reenactment groups from Italy, Austria and Germany. It contains, along with detailed depictions of weapons, color illustrations and some excellent reconstruction drawings by Wolfgang Braun.
Paperback, one map, 41 photos, partly of re-enactment events, nine contemporary images, two b / w drawings, two double-page color drawings by Sascha Lunyakov. 100 pages
ISBN 978-3-96360-027-2

Alexander Querengässer / Sascha Lunyakov

Hussite Warfare
The Armies, Equipment, Tactics and Campaigns 1419-1437

With the outbreak of the Hussite Revolution in 1419, Bohemia found itself opposed by a superior force of European crusader armies. German knighthood was experiencing its last heyday. But the Bohemian heretics' army, under the leadership of energetic commanders like Jan Ziska, developed tactics with which they won one battle after another. The employment of the defensive Wagenburg ("wagon castle") and intensive use of the first cannon as field artillery brought them many successes. The Hussites were the first soldiers since Roman times to employ all the available branches in coordination on the battlefield. This book highlights not just the history of the conflicts, but also the weapons and military branches, organization and tactics of the Hussite armies.
Paperback, 64 moustly colour illustrations, 10 maps, 18 color plates by Sascha Lunyakov. 144 pages.
ISBN 978-3-96360-017-3

**Ask your bookseller or
have a look at the well-known online retailers.**